DEDICATED TO:
KAMALA AND AMALA
(THE WOLF GIRLS OF SINGAPORE)

AND BLIND WILLIE JOHNSON

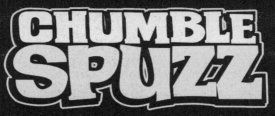

CHUMBLE SPUZZ

Cartoon Stories presents

PIGEON MAN

& DEATH SINGS THE BLUES

WRITTEN AND ILLUSTRATED BY
ETHAN NICOLLE

ADDITIONAL WRITING BY
ISAIAH NICOLLE

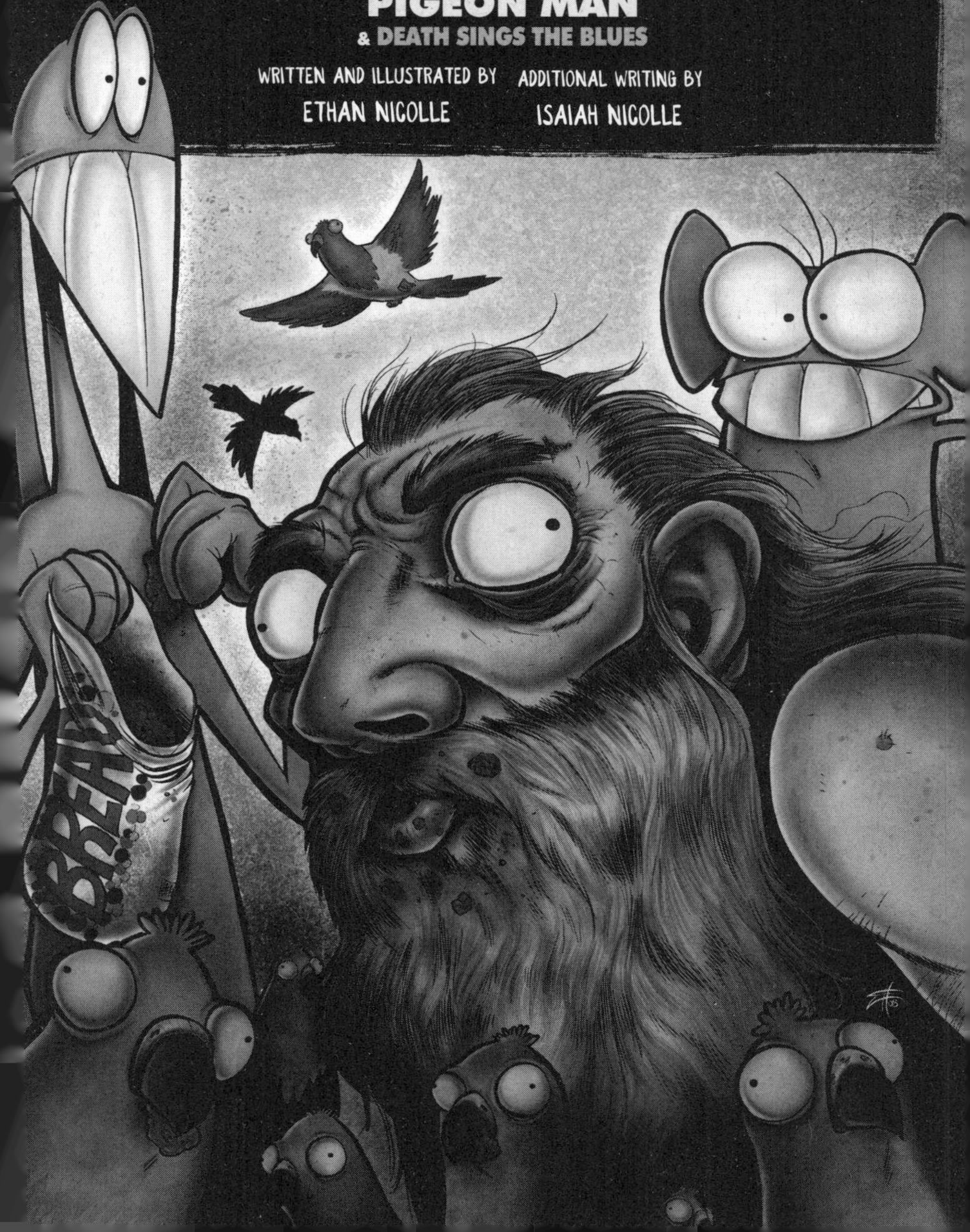
BREAD

A Man Raised by Pigeons

A few years ago I was drawing "Far Side style" single-panel gag strips. Before Chumble Spuzz, these were the only humor comics I could get myself to make. Going onto a second panel scared me -going onto an entire book was out of the question- I liked the safety of just one confined panel to tell the joke in. I did these in high school for the school paper, then later I was "syndicated" if you can call it that- to one weekly paper in New Orleans. Later I made more for a blog, which didn't last long. The story of the Pigeon Man evolved off of one of these gags.

I was brainstorming jokes about an old lady feeding the birds. I came up with one where the pigeons suddenly desire flesh instead of bread. One of my favorites was this idea of a man living in the park, who had been raised by the pigeons from birth. In my cartoon, the old lady looks on in bewilderment as a scraggly naked old hairy man hops out of the bushes and joins his pigeon brethren in the moldy feast.

When I started brainstorming Chumble Spuzz episode ideas, I became fascinated with looking deeper into this "Pigeon Man" story. My first Chumble Spuzz project was a never-to-be-finished flash cartoon about this pigeon man. After finishing Chumble Spuzz book one, I was ready to dust off the Pigeon Man idea and give him another go. The book you hold in your hands is the rebirth of the pigeon man, last seen in 2005 in a gag strip.

While writing this story I did some research on feral humans, and it's actually a really fascinating subject. Most of them never grow into adulthood (at least the ones who have been found), and usually once they are taken back into humanity, they die, because they simply have become the animals they were raised by. Their bodies even developed differently... for instance, the famous story of Kamala and Amala, the Wolf Girls of Singapore, says that "They had spent so long on all fours that their tendons and joints had shortened to the point where it was impossible for them to straighten their legs and even attempt to walk upright. (feralchildren.com)".

The second story in this book, *Death Sings the Blues*, started with the simple idea of Death committing suicide, and what might happen. Everything else just fell into place during brainstorming. My room mate Rich commented that a ton more happens

Becky couldn't believe her eyes. The legend of the man in the park raised by pigeons was true, and he was eating her bread crumbs.

in this 27 page story than in the 109 page *Pigeon Man* story. It's true. Originally meant to be written out at full length, this story could have easily filled 150 pages. But due to time and page restrictions (we'd already solicited the book before I'd started drawing this story), I had to make it all work in 27 pages or less. This ended up being a lot of fun and a great exercise for me. I'm happy with how it turned out, and I think it works well in it's more epic, storybook format.

I had a lot of fun getting my brother Isaiah to join in with me in some of the creating of this book. He's my younger brother, and our minds just think on the same weird level. Thanks for giving it a try, and feel free to let us know what you thought of it.

-Ethan Nicolle
March 31st, 2008
www.myspace.com/cspuzz
the.eef@gmail.com

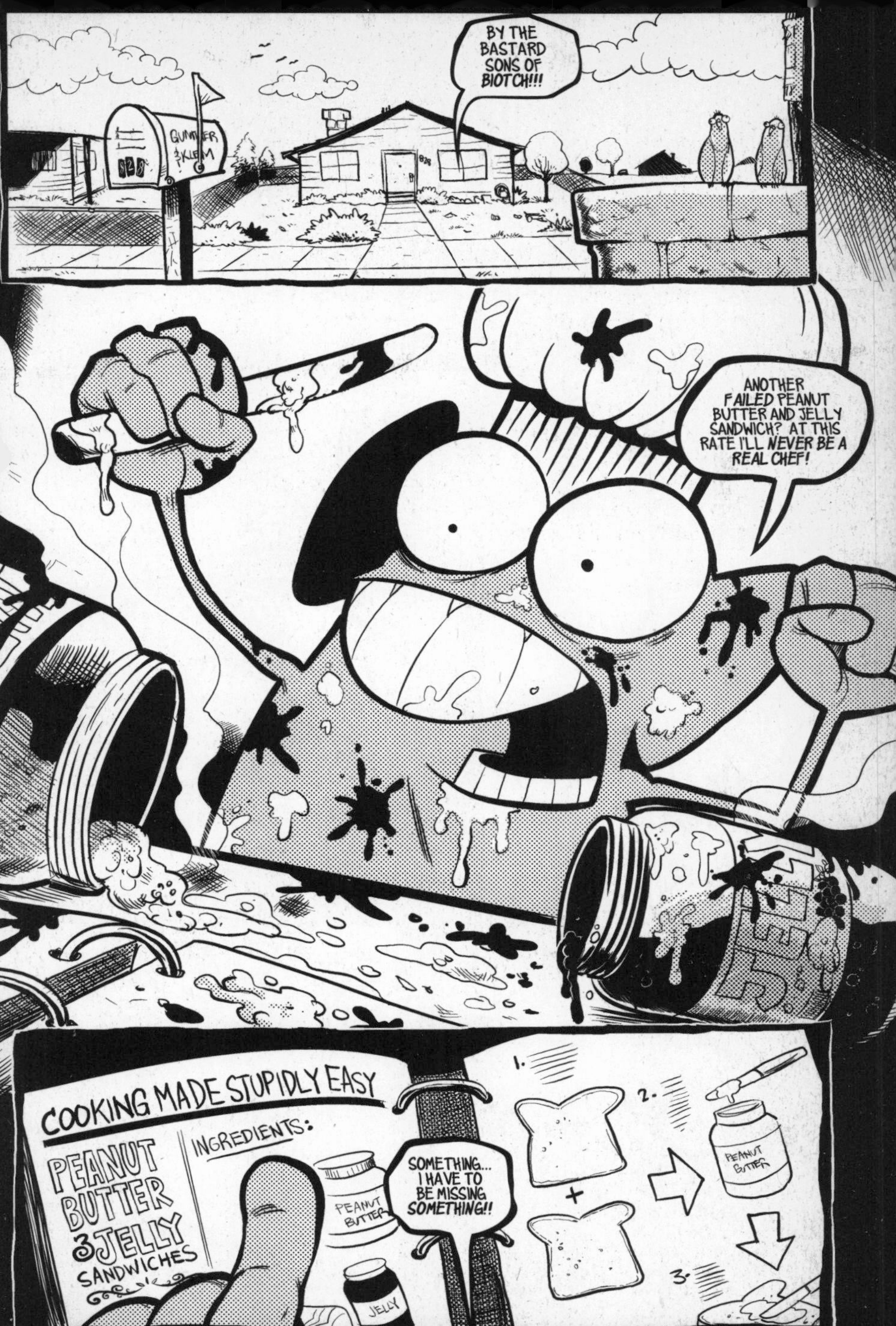
GUMMER & KLEM
828
BY THE BASTARD SONS OF BIOTCH!!!
ANOTHER FAILED PEANUT BUTTER AND JELLY SANDWICH? AT THIS RATE I'LL NEVER BE A REAL CHEF!
COOKING MADE STUPIDLY EASY
PEANUT BUTTER & JELLY SANDWICHES
INGREDIENTS:
PEANUT BUTTER
JELLY
SOMETHING... I HAVE TO BE MISSING SOMETHING!!
1.
2.
PEANUT BUTTER
3.

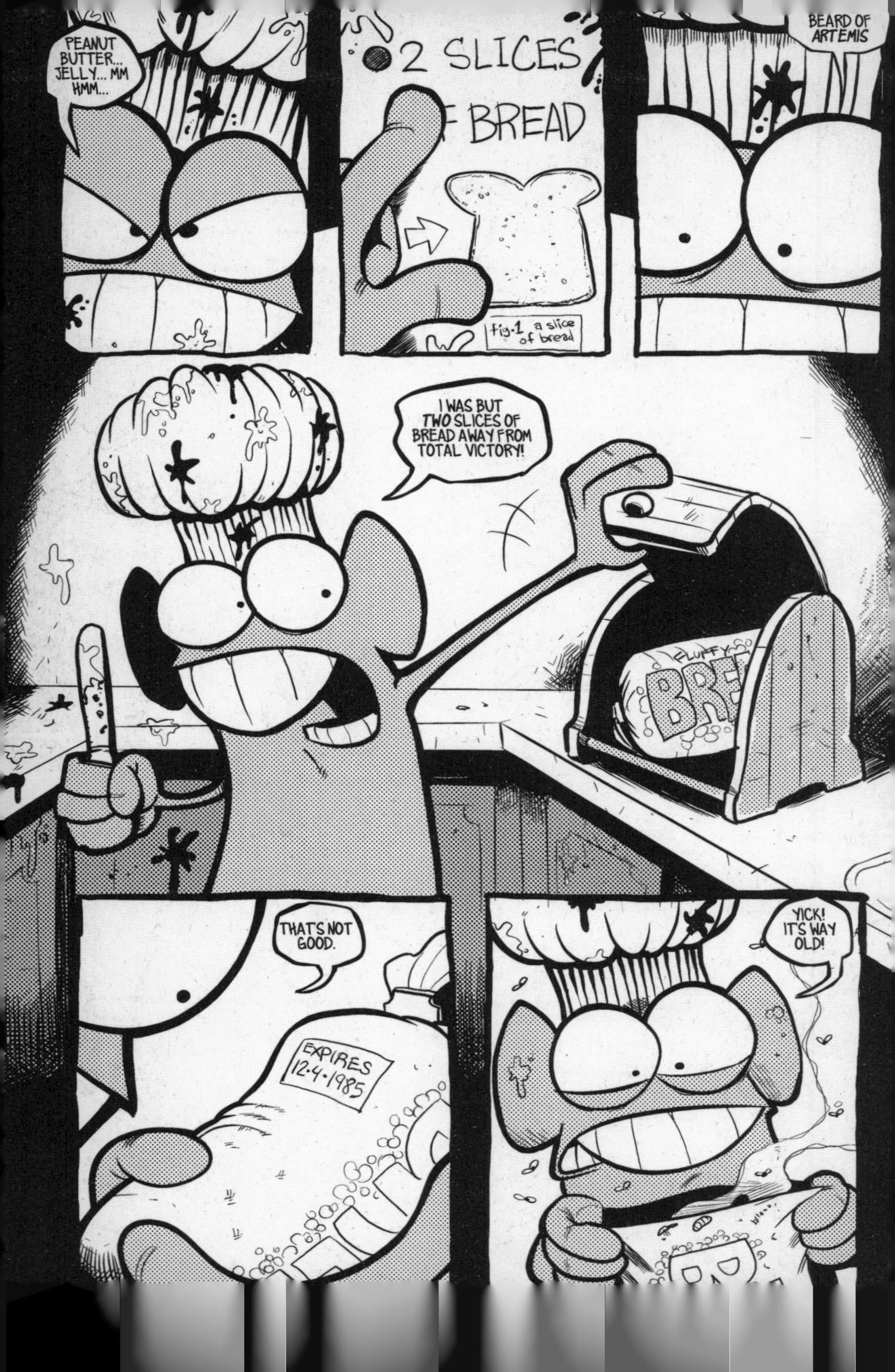
PEANUT BUTTER... JELLY... MM HMM...
2 SLICES OF BREAD
fig.1 a slice of bread
BEARD OF ARTEMIS
I WAS BUT TWO SLICES OF BREAD AWAY FROM TOTAL VICTORY!
FLUFFY BRE
THAT'S NOT GOOD.
EXPIRES 12-4-1985
YICK! IT'S WAY OLD!

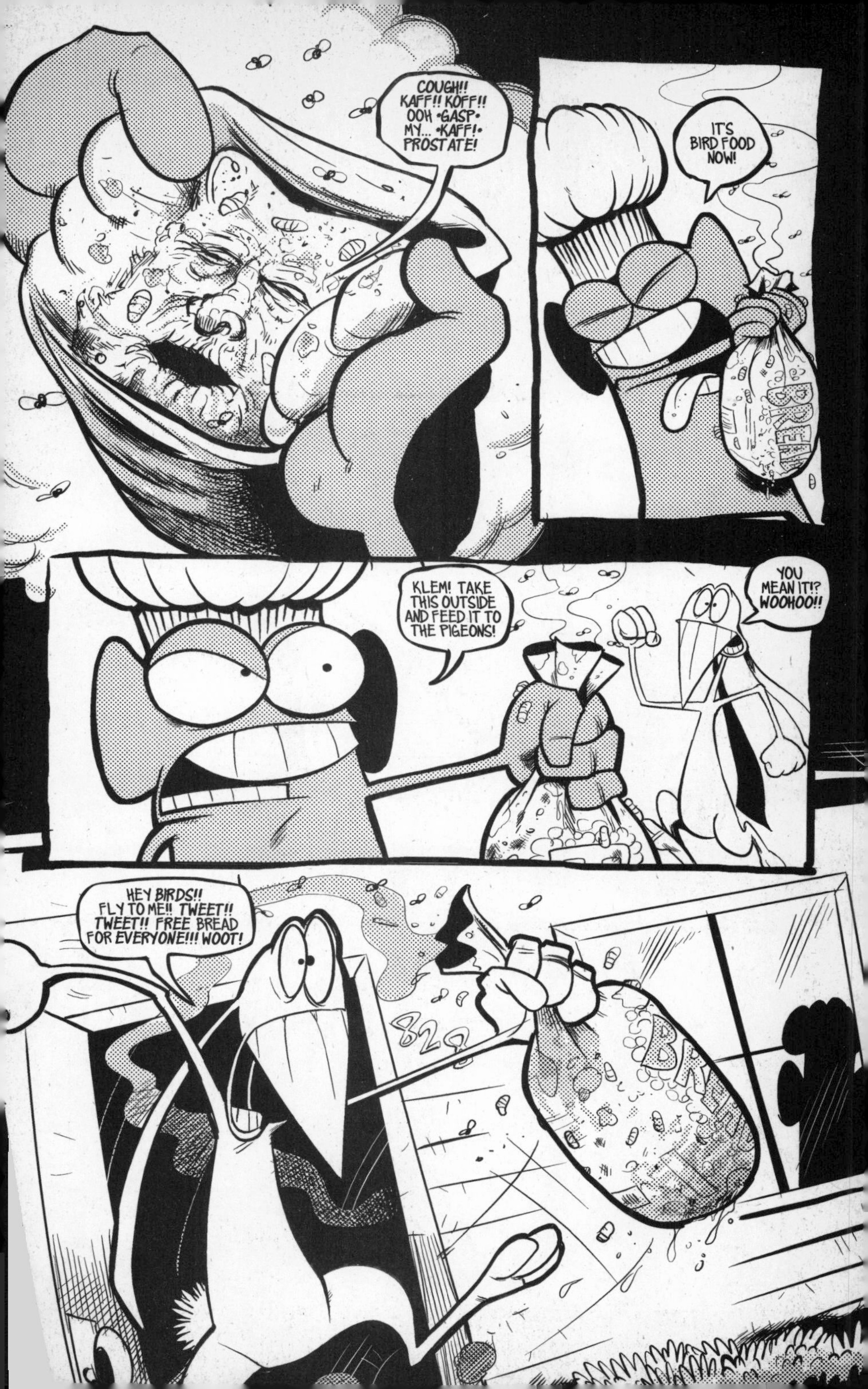
COUGH!! KAFF!! KOFF!! OOH •GASP• MY... •KAFF!• PROSTATE!
IT'S BIRD FOOD NOW!
KLEM! TAKE THIS OUTSIDE AND FEED IT TO THE PIGEONS!
YOU MEAN IT!? WOOHOO!!
HEY BIRDS!! FLY TO ME!! TWEET!! TWEET!! FREE BREAD FOR EVERYONE!!! WOOT!

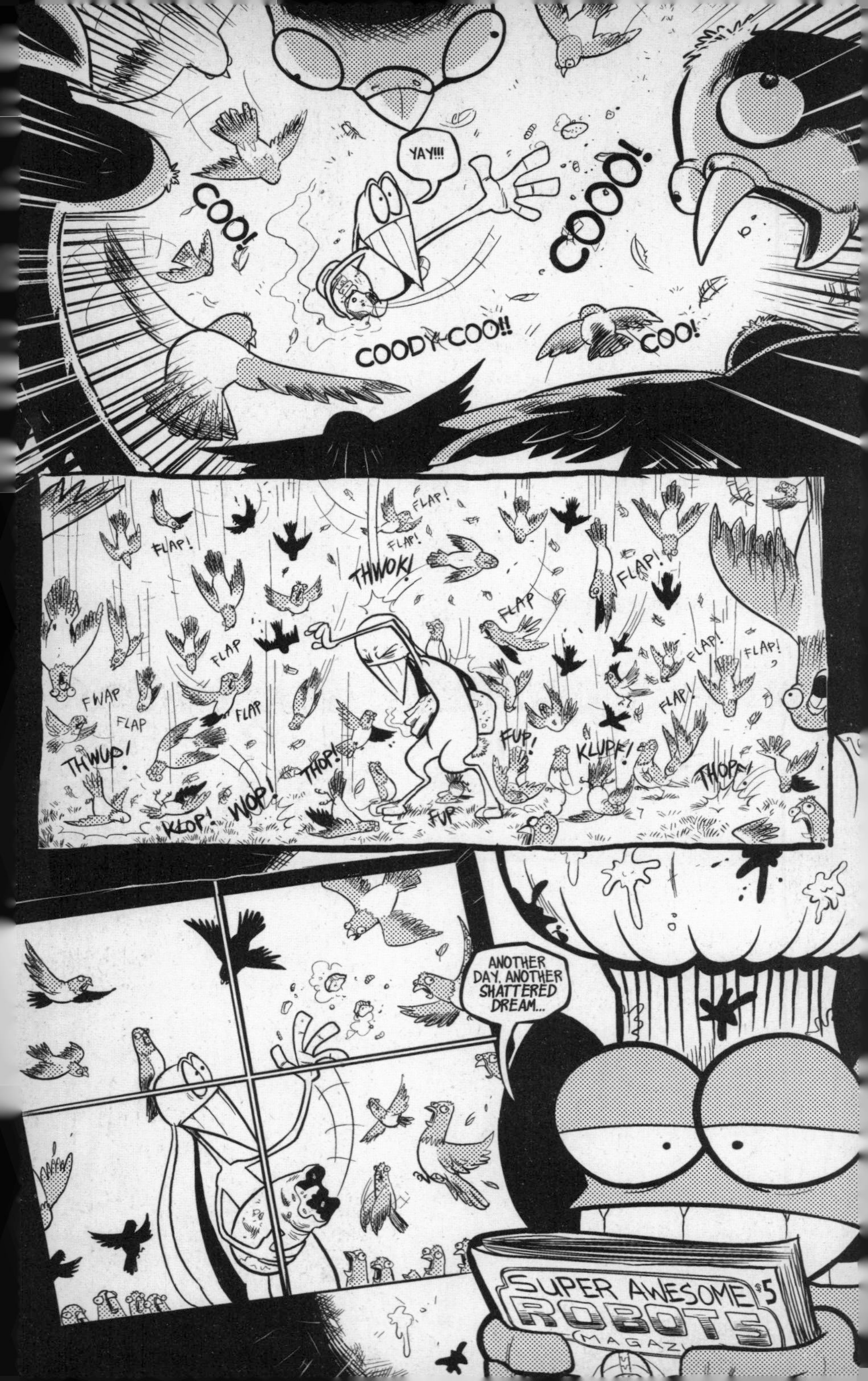

YAY!!!
COO!
COOO!
COODY-COO!!
COO!
FLAP!
FLAP!
FLAP!
THWOK!
FLAP!
FLAP
FLAP
FLAP!
FLAP!
FWAP
FLAP
FLAP
FLAP!
THWUP!
THOP!
FUP!
KLUPF!
THOPF!
KLOP!
WOP!
FUP
ANOTHER DAY, ANOTHER SHATTERED DREAM...
SUPER AWESOME ROBOTS MAGAZ $5

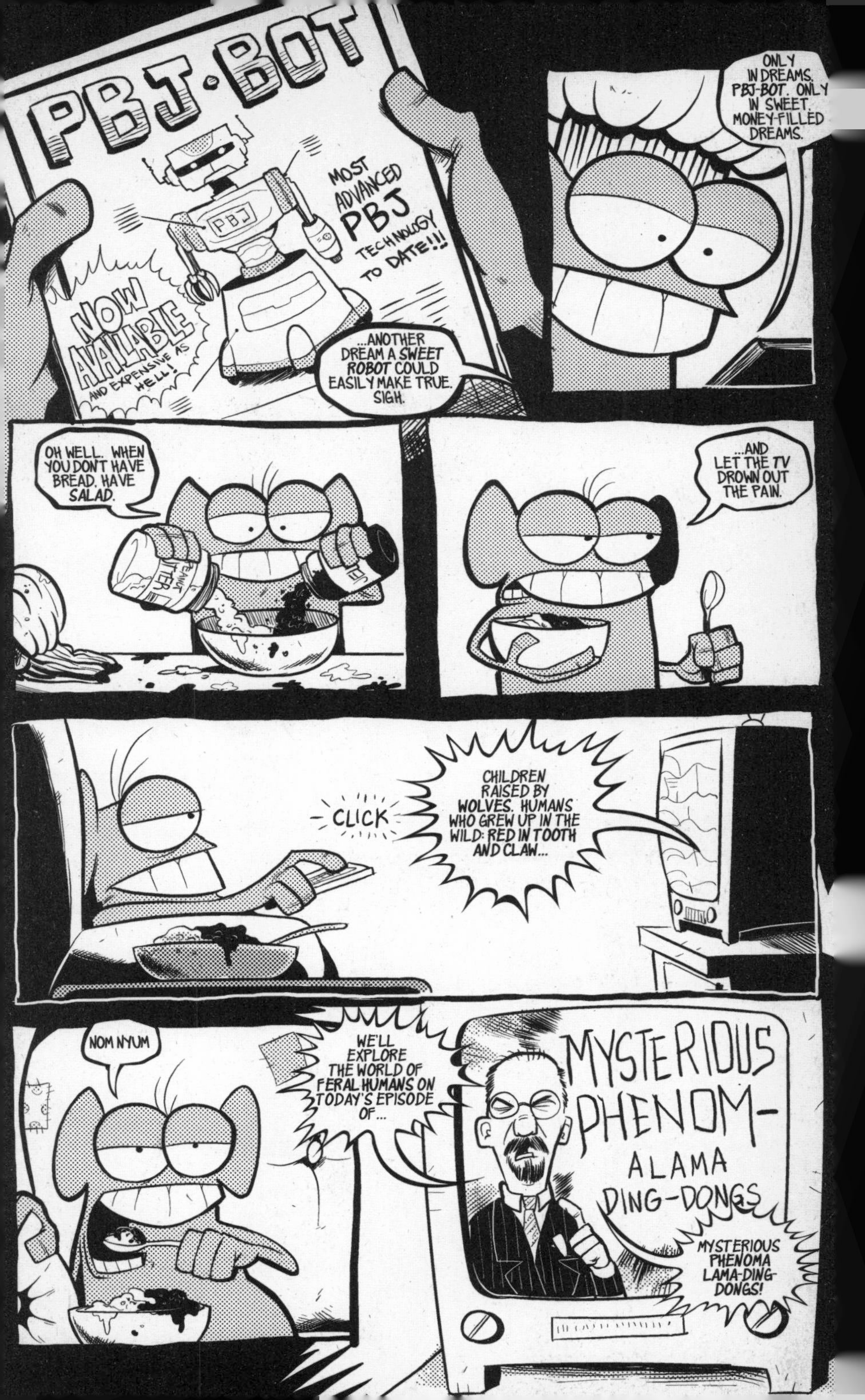
PBJ-BOT
MOST ADVANCED PBJ TECHNOLOGY TO DATE!!!
NOW AVAILABLE
AND EXPENSIVE AS HELL!
...ANOTHER DREAM A SWEET ROBOT COULD EASILY MAKE TRUE. SIGH.
ONLY IN DREAMS, PBJ-BOT. ONLY IN SWEET, MONEY-FILLED DREAMS.
OH WELL. WHEN YOU DON'T HAVE BREAD, HAVE SALAD.
...AND LET THE TV DROWN OUT THE PAIN.
CLICK
CHILDREN RAISED BY WOLVES. HUMANS WHO GREW UP IN THE WILD: RED IN TOOTH AND CLAW...
NOM NYUM
WE'LL EXPLORE THE WORLD OF FERAL HUMANS ON TODAY'S EPISODE OF...
MYSTERIOUS PHENOM-ALAMA DING-DONGS
MYSTERIOUS PHENOMA LAMA-DING-DONGS!

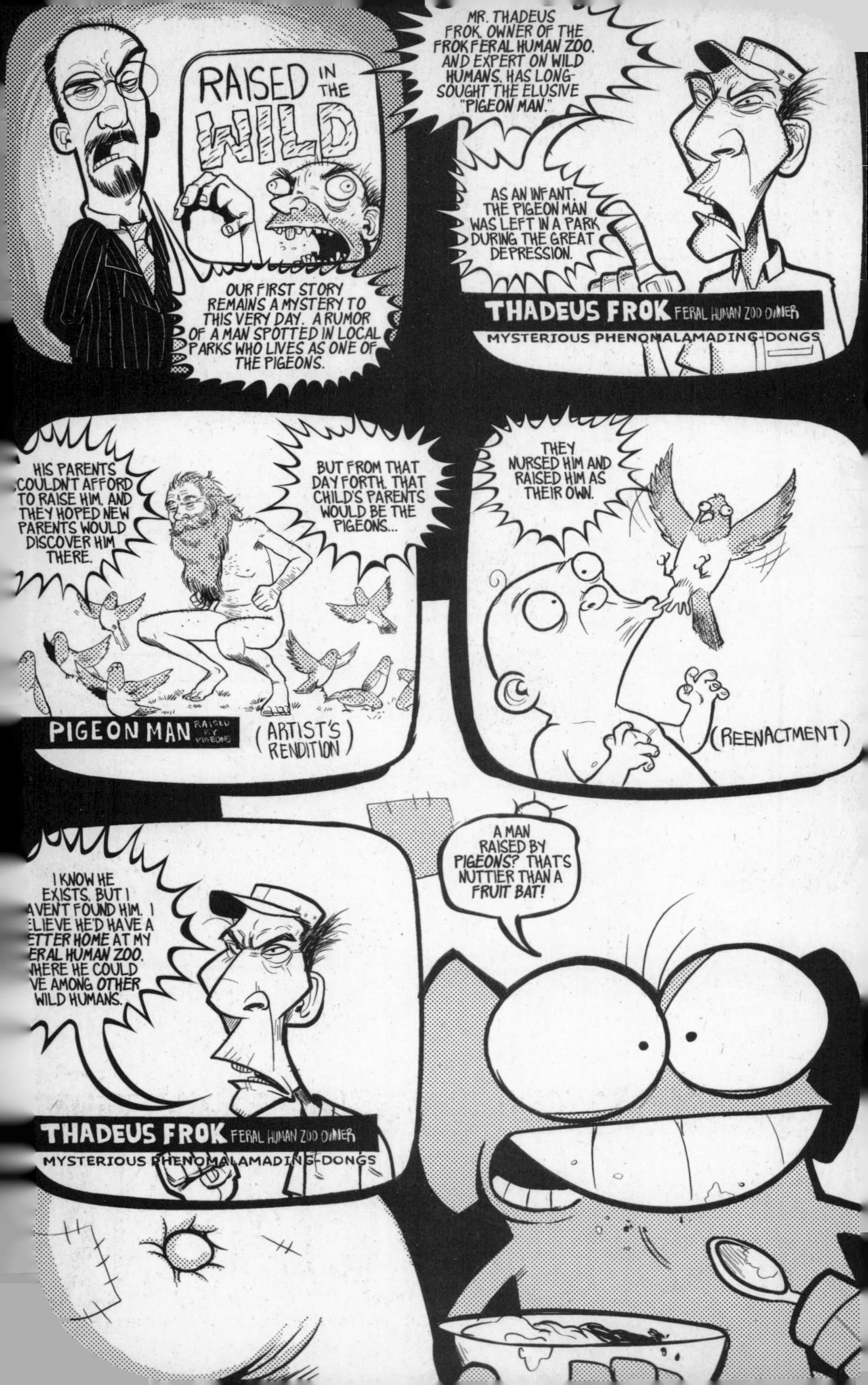
RAISED IN THE WILD
OUR FIRST STORY REMAINS A MYSTERY TO THIS VERY DAY. A RUMOR OF A MAN SPOTTED IN LOCAL PARKS WHO LIVES AS ONE OF THE PIGEONS.
MR. THADEUS FROK, OWNER OF THE FROK FERAL HUMAN ZOO, AND EXPERT ON WILD HUMANS, HAS LONG-SOUGHT THE ELUSIVE "PIGEON MAN."
AS AN INFANT, THE PIGEON MAN WAS LEFT IN A PARK DURING THE GREAT DEPRESSION.
THADEUS FROK FERAL HUMAN ZOO OWNER
MYSTERIOUS PHENOMALAMADING-DONGS
HIS PARENTS COULDN'T AFFORD TO RAISE HIM, AND THEY HOPED NEW PARENTS WOULD DISCOVER HIM THERE.
BUT FROM THAT DAY FORTH, THAT CHILD'S PARENTS WOULD BE THE PIGEONS...
PIGEON MAN RAISED BY PIGEONS
(ARTIST'S RENDITION)
THEY NURSED HIM AND RAISED HIM AS THEIR OWN.
(REENACTMENT)
I KNOW HE EXISTS, BUT I HAVEN'T FOUND HIM. I BELIEVE HE'D HAVE A BETTER HOME AT MY FERAL HUMAN ZOO, WHERE HE COULD LIVE AMONG OTHER WILD HUMANS.
THADEUS FROK FERAL HUMAN ZOO OWNER
MYSTERIOUS PHENOMALAMADING-DONGS
A MAN RAISED BY PIGEONS? THAT'S NUTTIER THAN A FRUIT BAT!

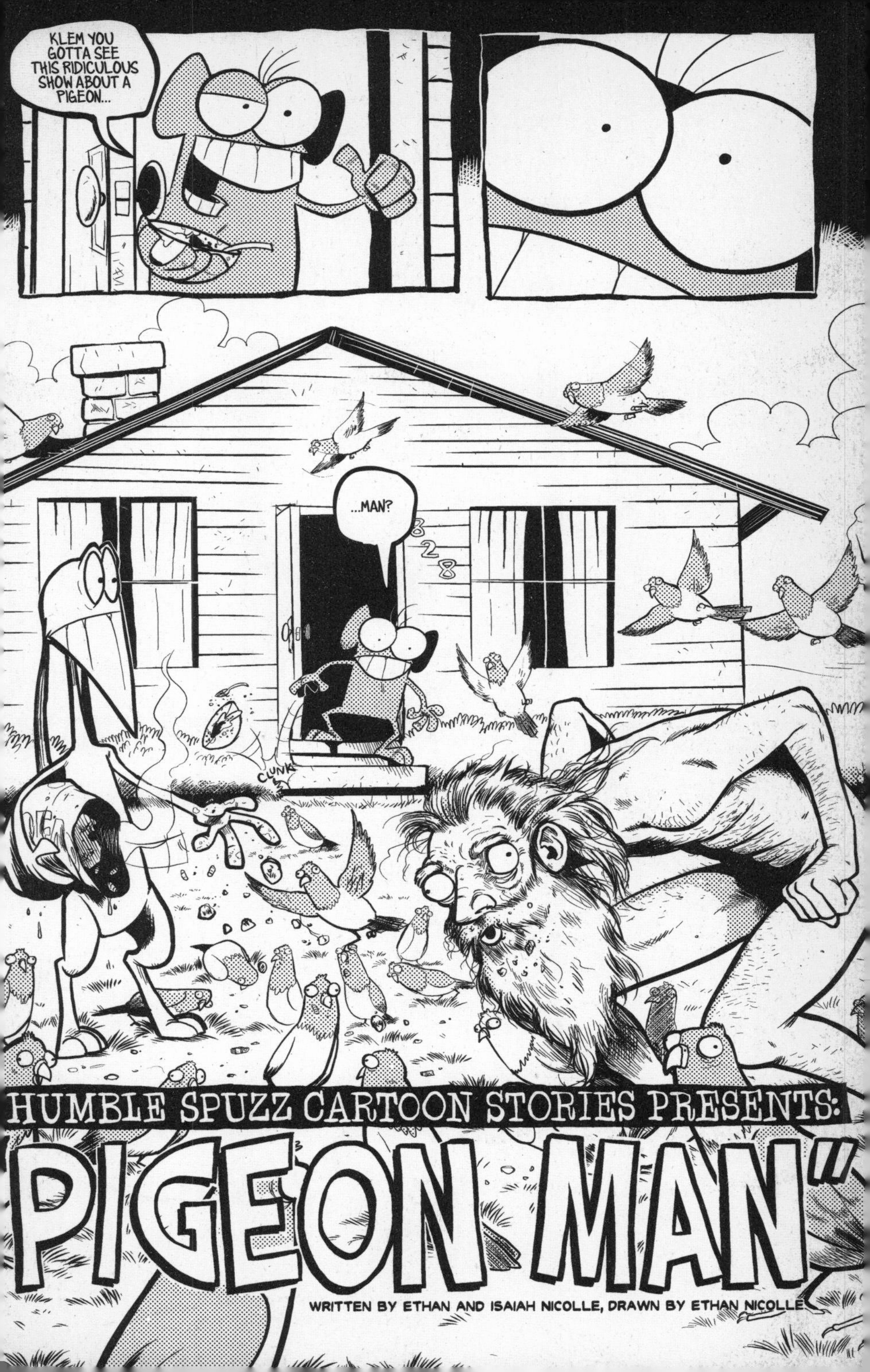
KLEM YOU GOTTA SEE THIS RIDICULOUS SHOW ABOUT A PIGEON...
...MAN?
328
CLUNK
HUMBLE SPUZZ CARTOON STORIES PRESENTS:
"PIGEON MAN"
WRITTEN BY ETHAN AND ISAIAH NICOLLE, DRAWN BY ETHAN NICOLLE

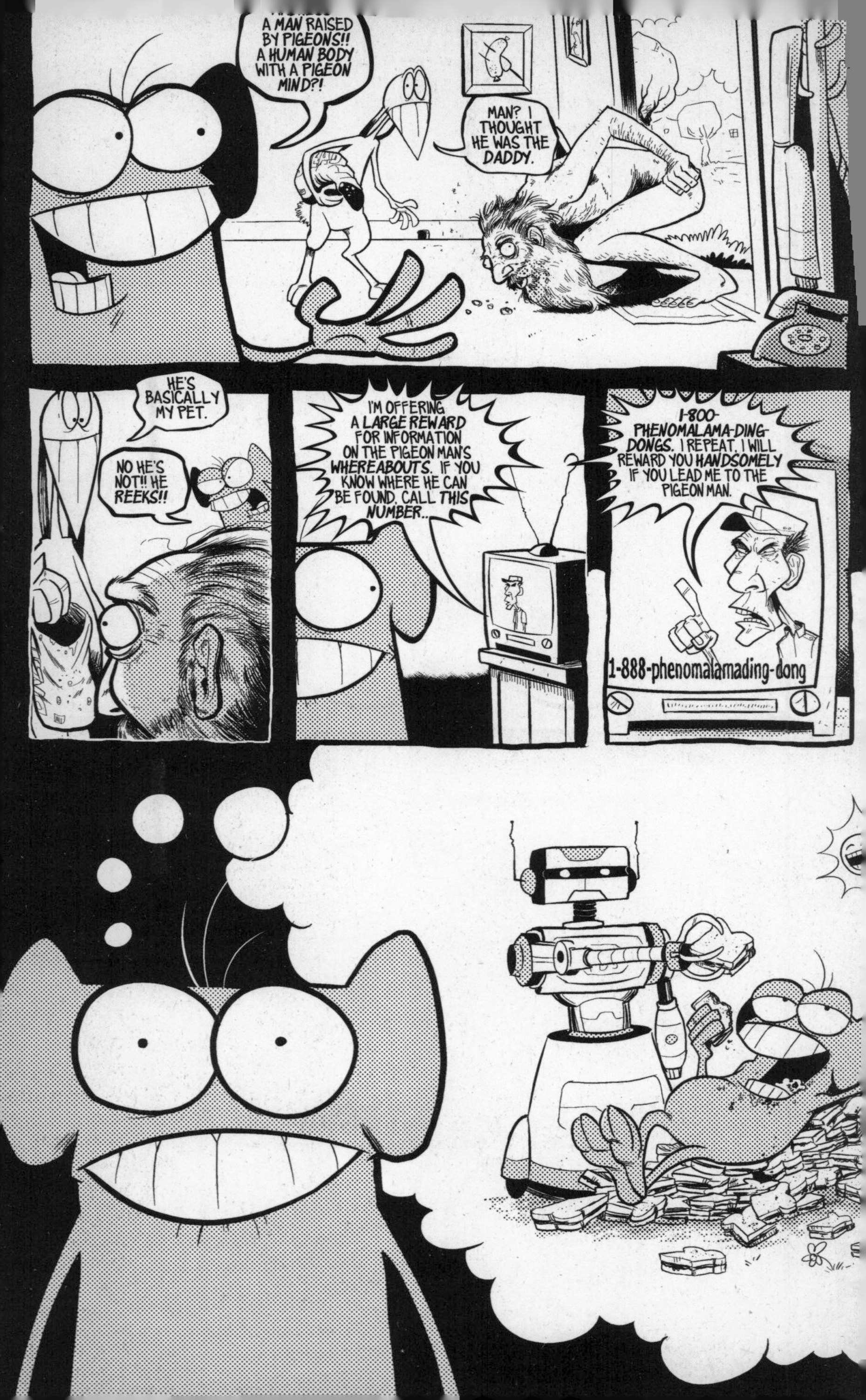
A MAN RAISED BY PIGEONS!! A HUMAN BODY WITH A PIGEON MIND?!
MAN? I THOUGHT HE WAS THE DADDY.
HE'S BASICALLY MY PET.
NO HE'S NOT!! HE REEKS!!
I'M OFFERING A LARGE REWARD FOR INFORMATION ON THE PIGEON MAN'S WHEREABOUTS. IF YOU KNOW WHERE HE CAN BE FOUND, CALL THIS NUMBER...
1-800-PHENOMALAMA-DING-DONGS. I REPEAT, I WILL REWARD YOU HANDSOMELY IF YOU LEAD ME TO THE PIGEON MAN.
1-888-phenomalamading-dong

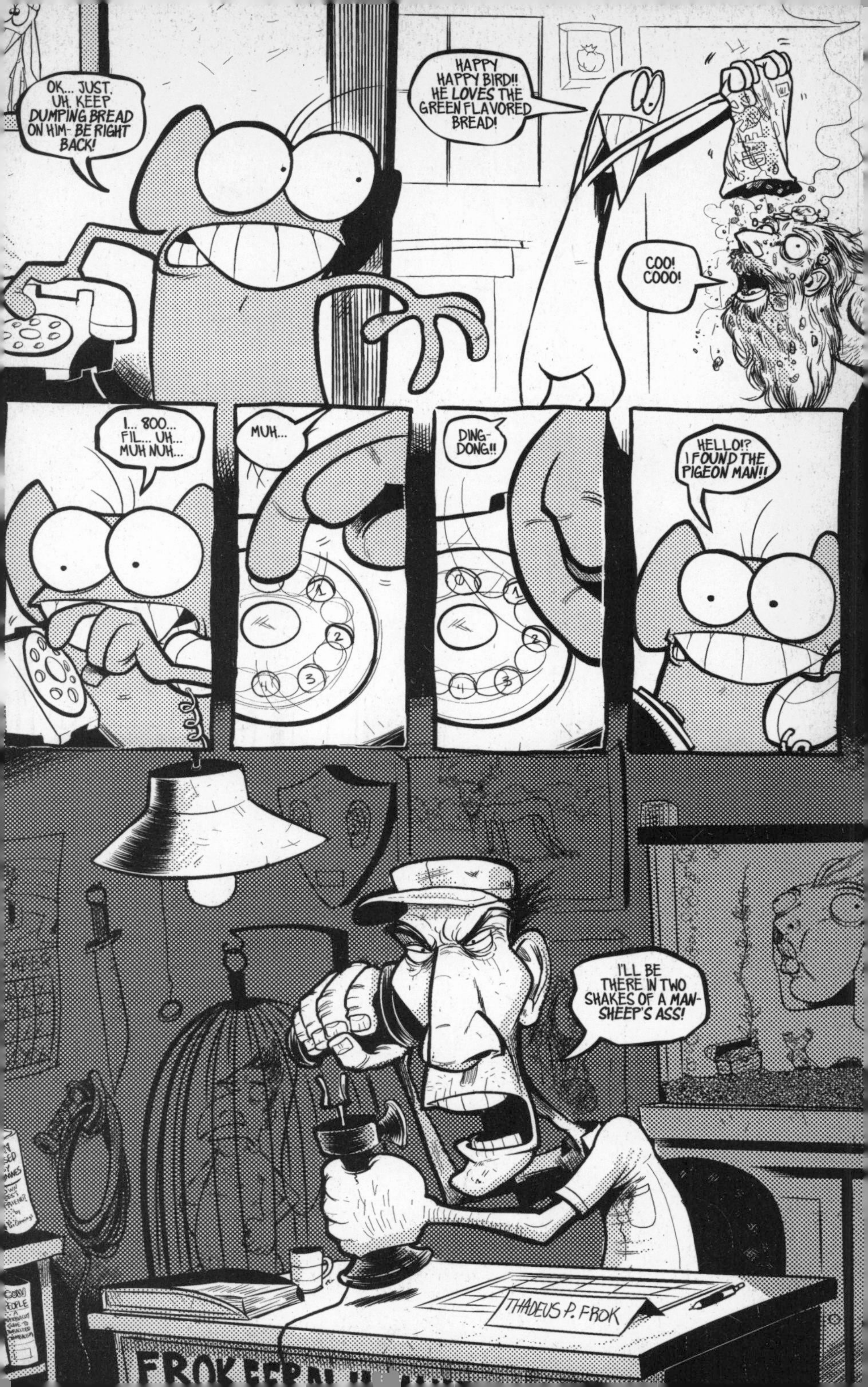
OK... JUST, UH, KEEP DUMPING BREAD ON HIM- BE RIGHT BACK!
HAPPY HAPPY BIRD!! HE LOVES THE GREEN FLAVORED BREAD!
COO! COOO!
I... 800... FIL... UH... MUH NUH...
MUH...
DING-DONG!!
HELLO!? I FOUND THE PIGEON MAN!!
I'LL BE THERE IN TWO SHAKES OF A MAN-SHEEP'S ASS!
THADEUS P. FROK

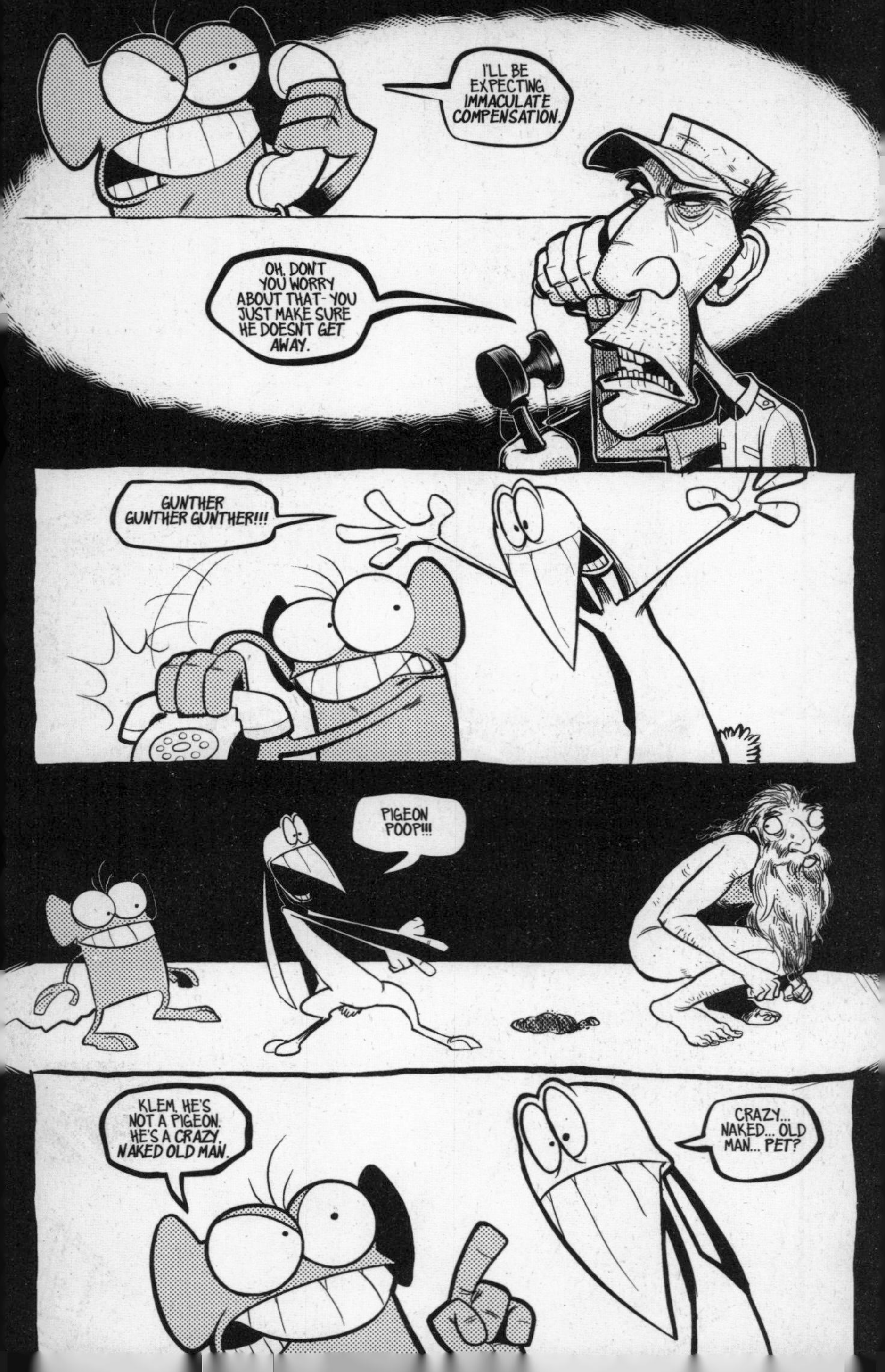

I'LL BE EXPECTING IMMACULATE COMPENSATION.
OH, DON'T YOU WORRY ABOUT THAT- YOU JUST MAKE SURE HE DOESN'T GET AWAY.
GUNTHER GUNTHER GUNTHER!!!
PIGEON POOP!!!
KLEM, HE'S NOT A PIGEON. HE'S A CRAZY, NAKED OLD MAN.
CRAZY... NAKED... OLD MAN... PET?

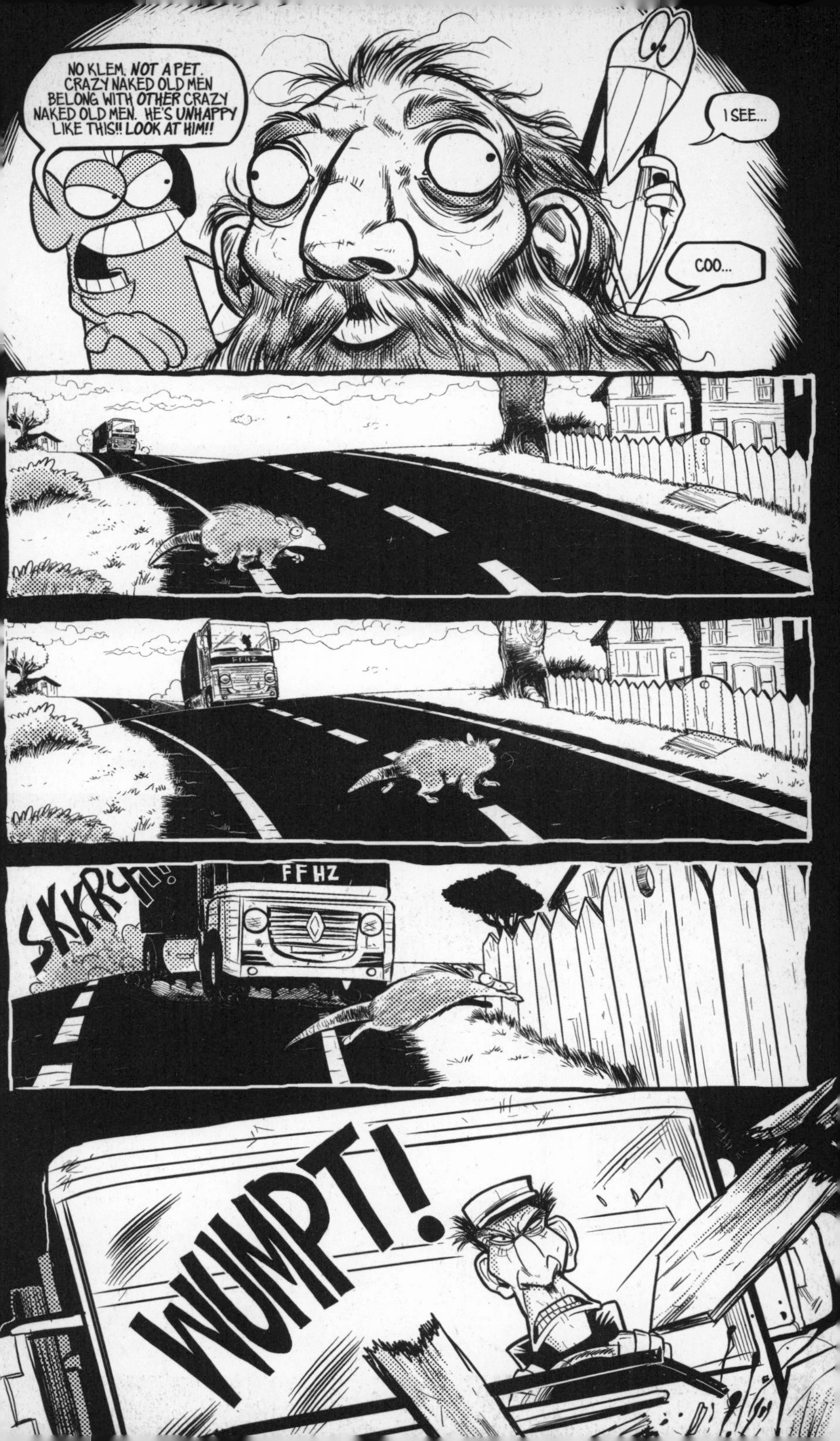
NO KLEM. NOT A PET. CRAZY NAKED OLD MEN BELONG WITH OTHER CRAZY NAKED OLD MEN. HE'S UNHAPPY LIKE THIS!! LOOK AT HIM!!
I SEE...
COO...
FFHZ
SKKRCH!!
FFHZ
WUMPT!

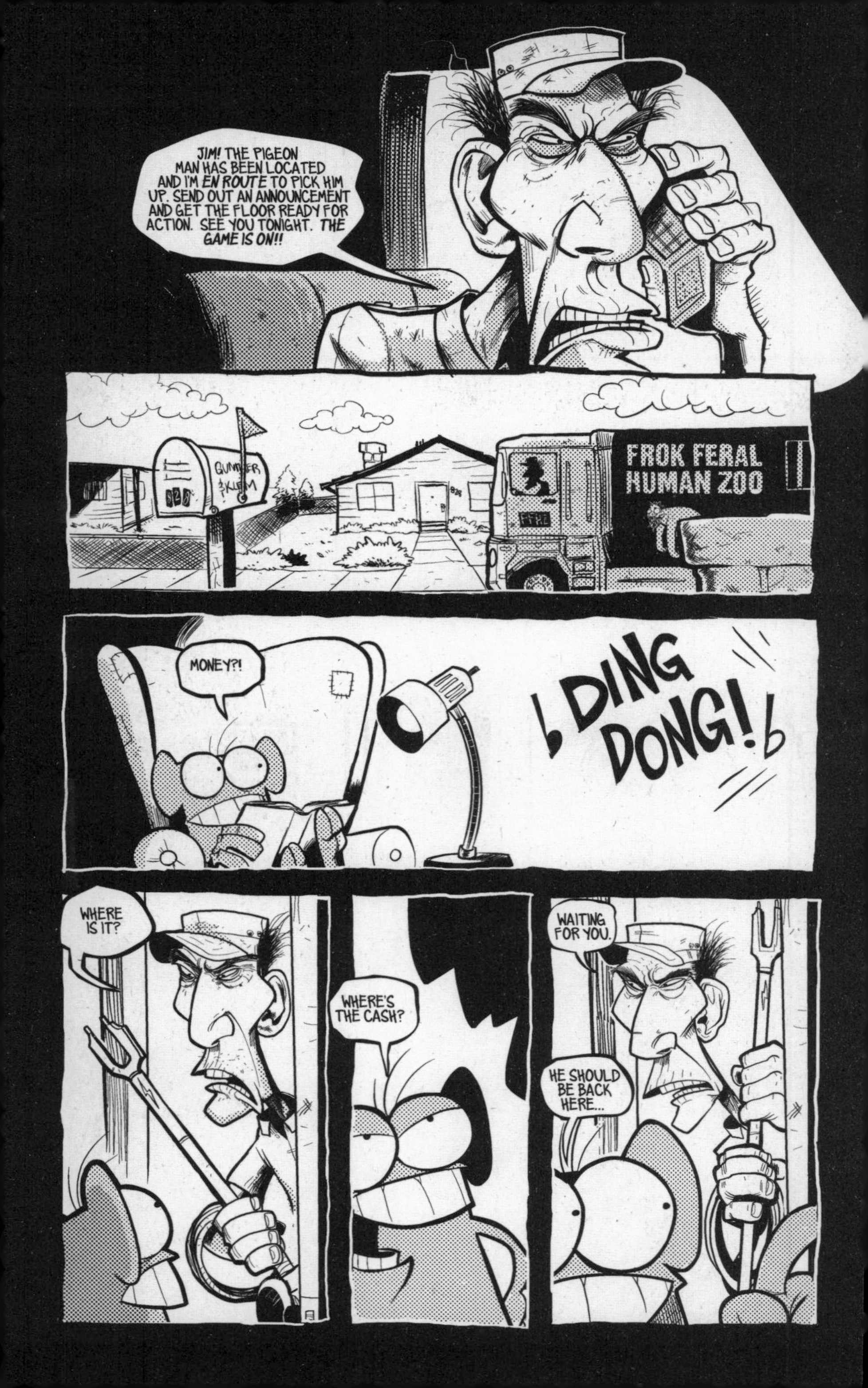
JIM! THE PIGEON MAN HAS BEEN LOCATED AND I'M *EN ROUTE* TO PICK HIM UP. SEND OUT AN ANNOUNCEMENT AND GET THE FLOOR READY FOR ACTION. SEE YOU TONIGHT. *THE GAME IS ON!!*
FROK FERAL HUMAN ZOO
MONEY?!
DING DONG!
WHERE IS IT?
WHERE'S THE CASH?
WAITING FOR YOU.
HE SHOULD BE BACK HERE...

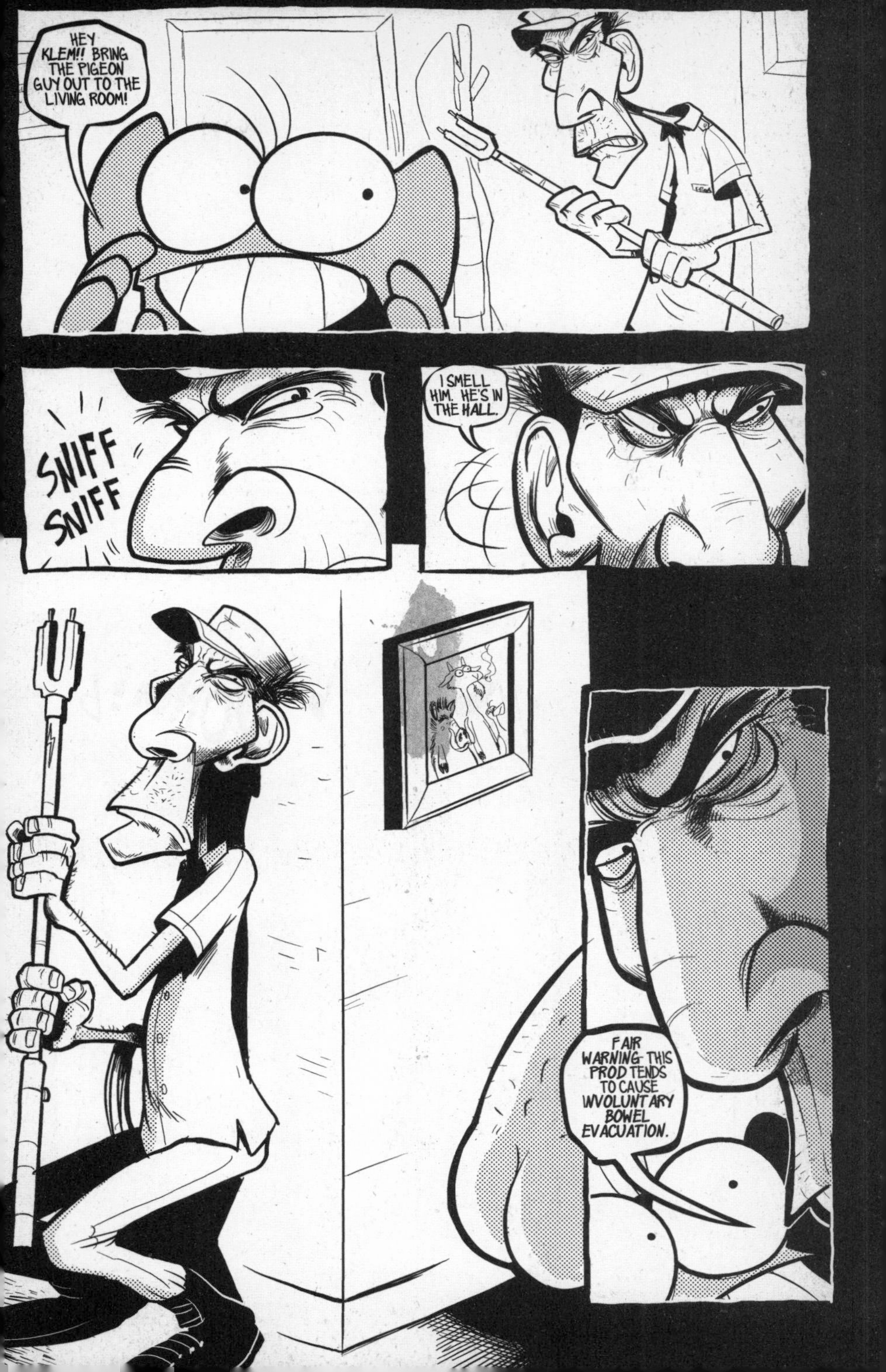
HEY KLEM!! BRING THE PIGEON GUY OUT TO THE LIVING ROOM!
SNIFF SNIFF
I SMELL HIM. HE'S IN THE HALL.
FAIR WARNING- THIS PROD TENDS TO CAUSE INVOLUNTARY BOWEL EVACUATION.

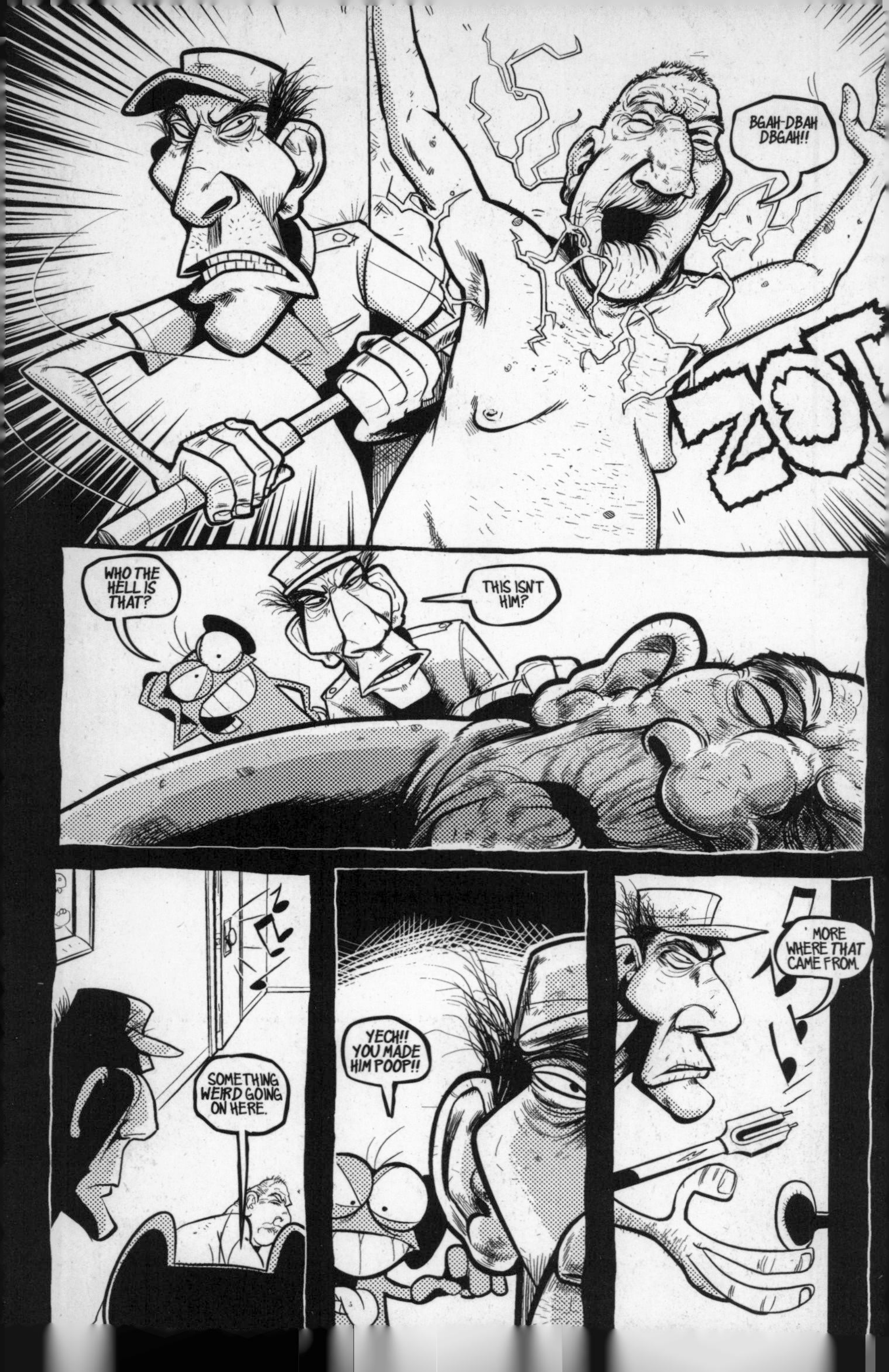
BGAH-DBAH DBGAH!!
ZOT
WHO THE HELL IS THAT?
THIS ISN'T HIM?
SOMETHING WEIRD GOING ON HERE.
YECH!! YOU MADE HIM POOP!!
MORE WHERE THAT CAME FROM.

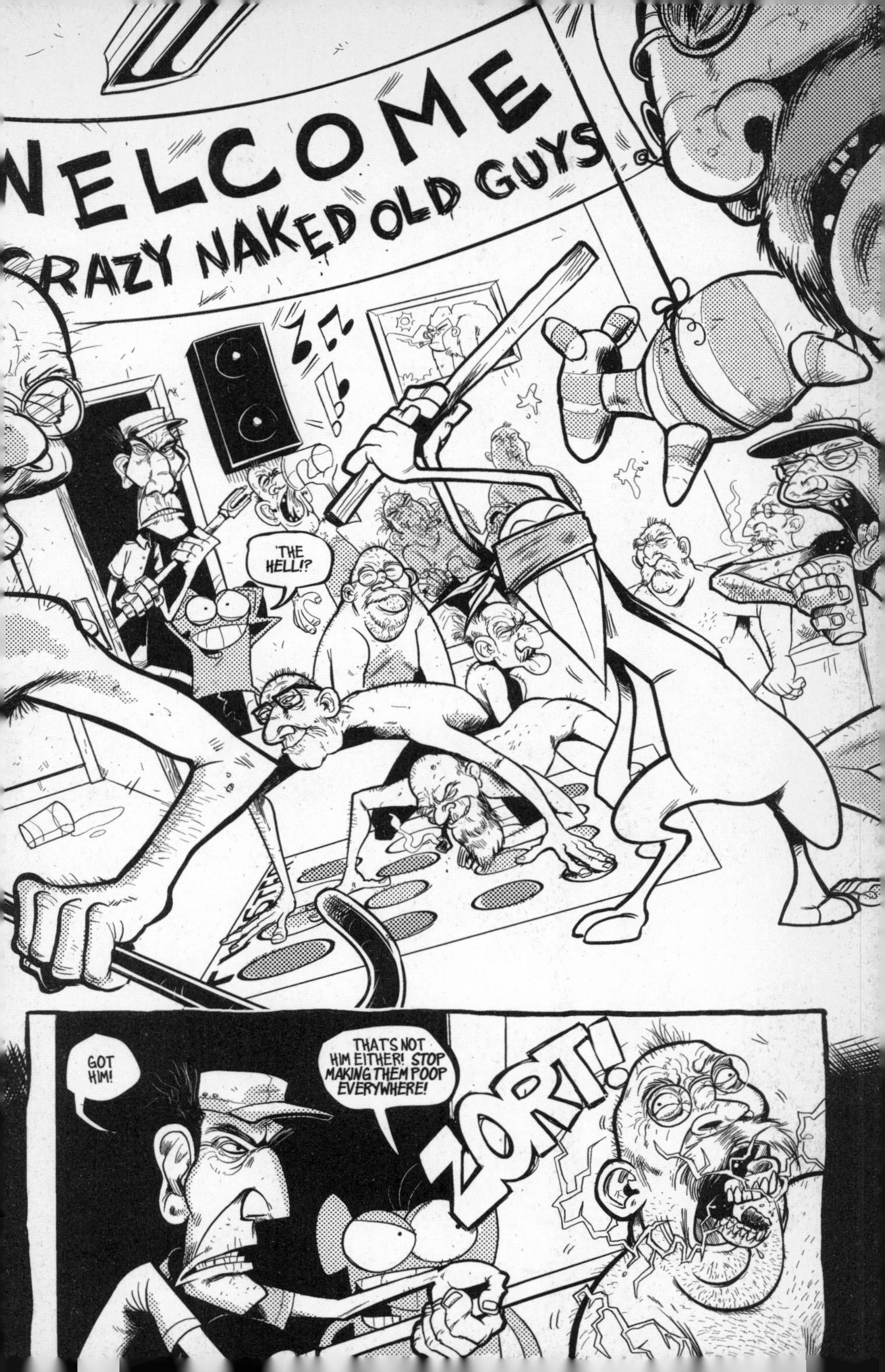
WELCOME
CRAZY NAKED OLD GUYS
'THE HELL!?
GOT HIM!
THAT'S NOT HIM EITHER! STOP MAKING THEM POOP EVERYWHERE!
ZORT!

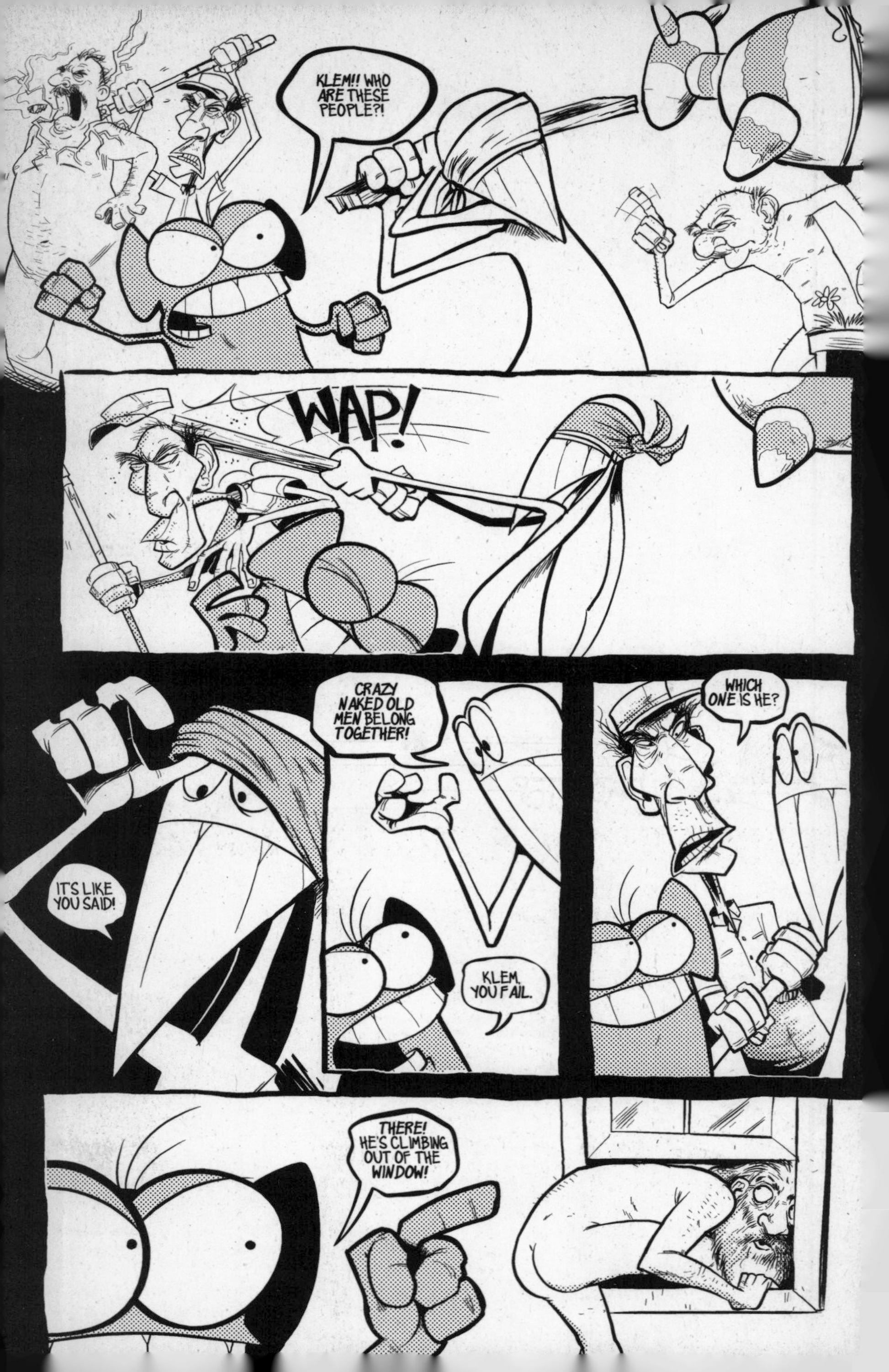
KLEM!! WHO ARE THESE PEOPLE?!
WAP!
IT'S LIKE YOU SAID!
CRAZY NAKED OLD MEN BELONG TOGETHER!
KLEM. YOU FAIL.
WHICH ONE IS HE?
THERE! HE'S CLIMBING OUT OF THE WINDOW!

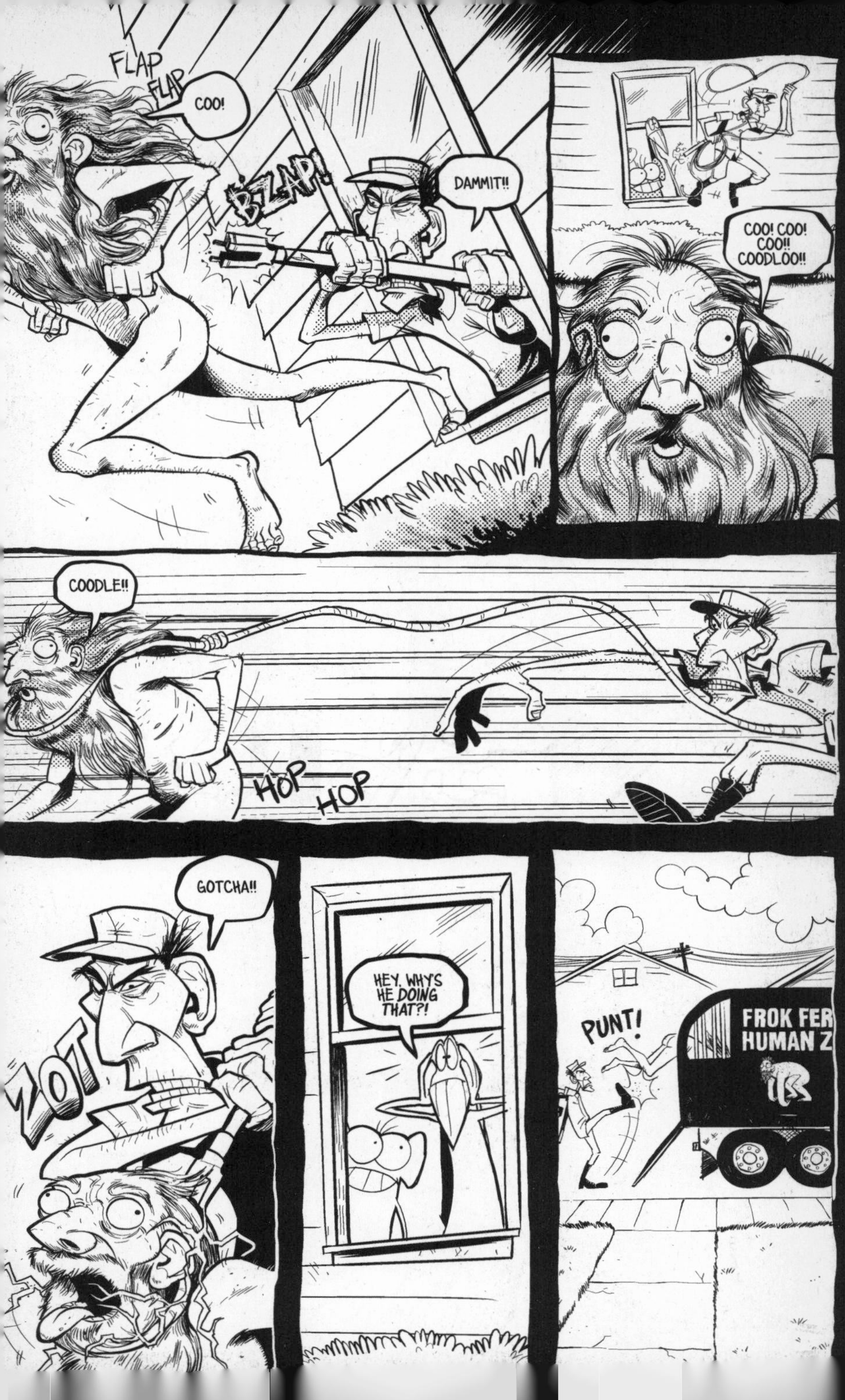
FLAP
FLAP
COO!
BZZAP!
DAMMIT!!
COO! COO! COO!! COODLOO!!
COODLE!!
HOP
HOP
GOTCHA!!
ZOT
HEY, WHY'S HE DOING THAT?!
PUNT!
FROK FER
HUMAN Z

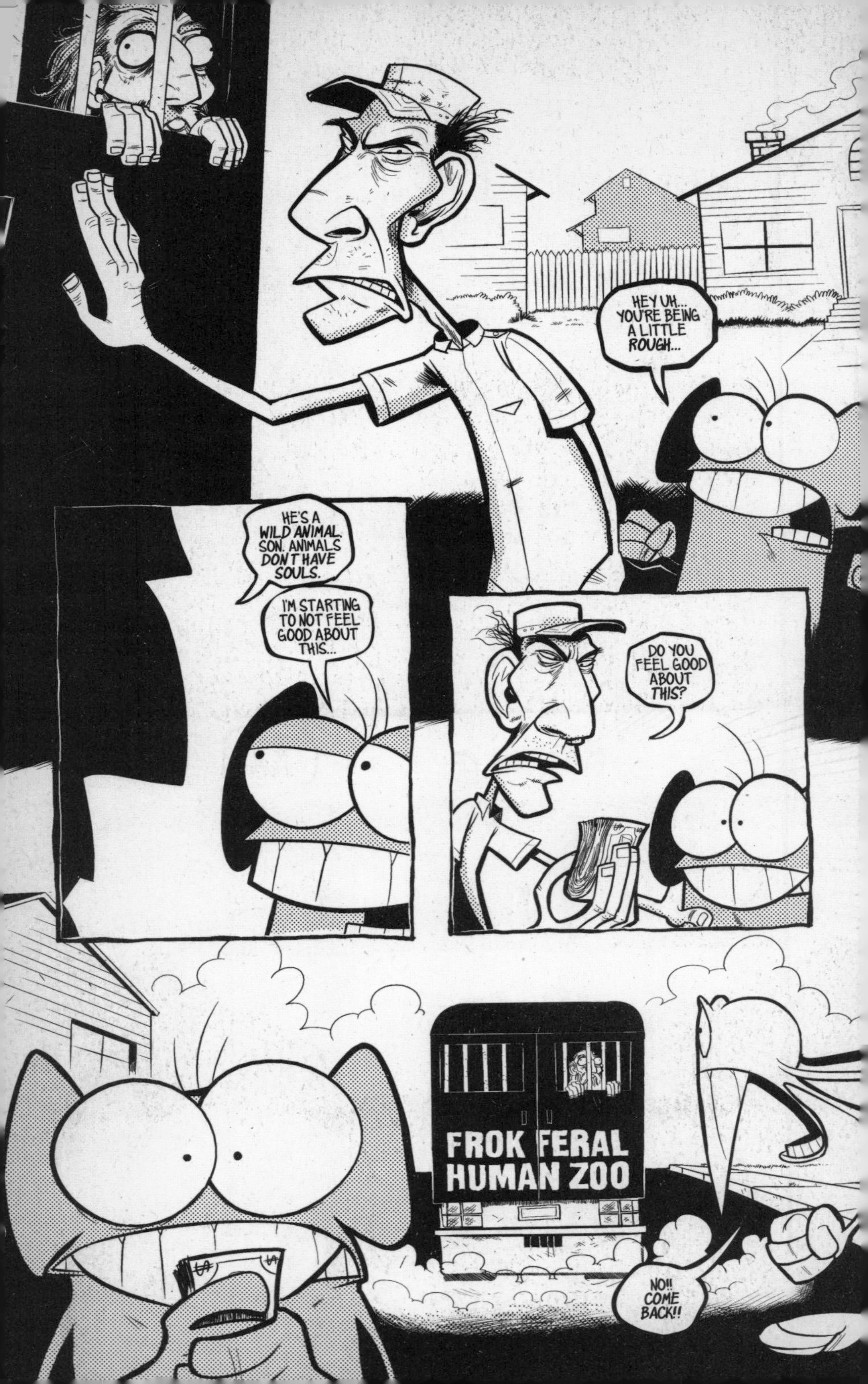
HEY UH... YOU'RE BEING A LITTLE ROUGH...
HE'S A WILD ANIMAL, SON. ANIMALS DON'T HAVE SOULS.
I'M STARTING TO NOT FEEL GOOD ABOUT THIS...
DO YOU FEEL GOOD ABOUT THIS?
FROK FERAL HUMAN ZOO
NO!! COME BACK!!

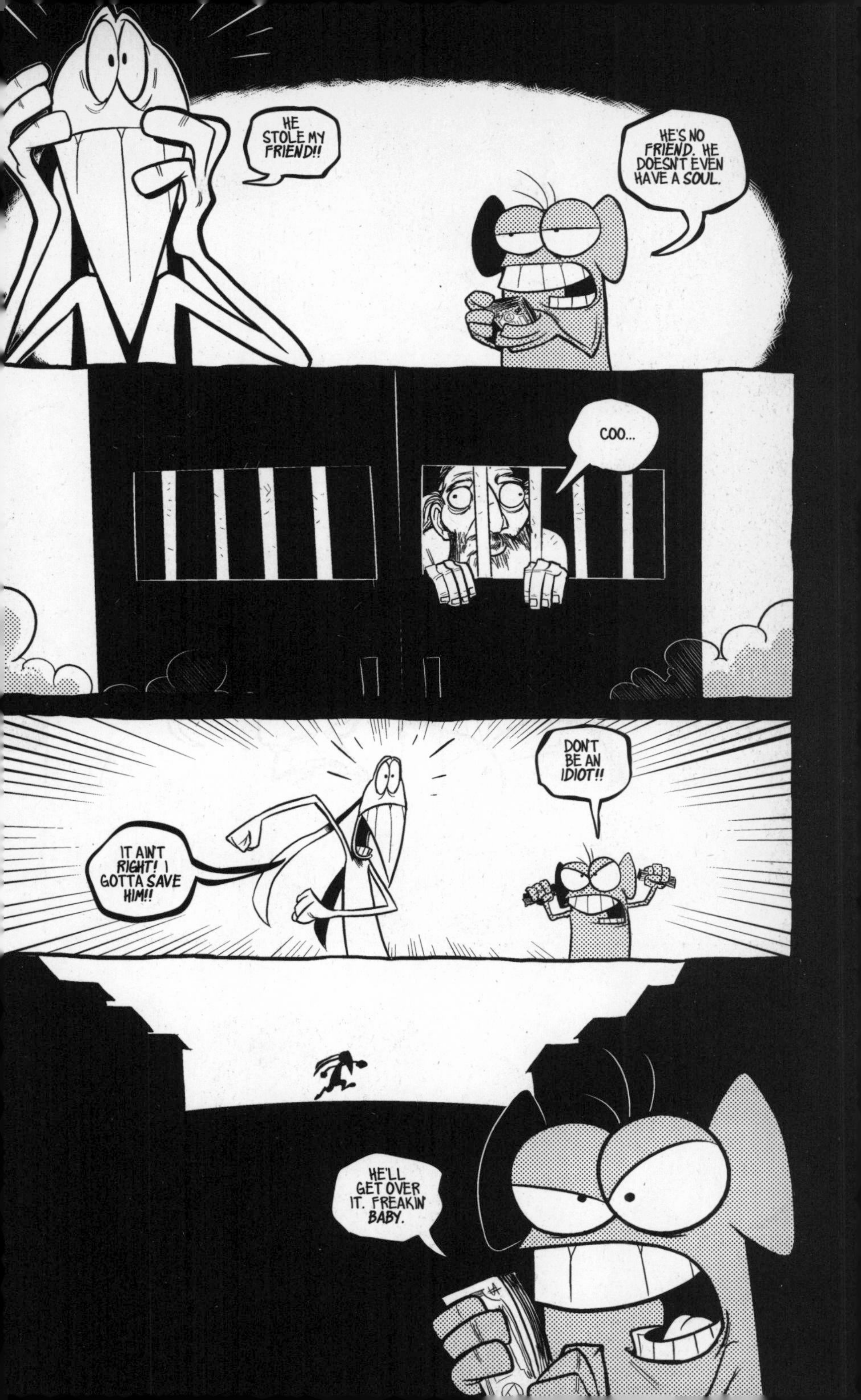
HE STOLE MY FRIEND!!
HE'S NO FRIEND. HE DOESN'T EVEN HAVE A SOUL.
COO...
DON'T BE AN IDIOT!!
IT AIN'T RIGHT! I GOTTA SAVE HIM!!
HE'LL GET OVER IT. FREAKIN' BABY.

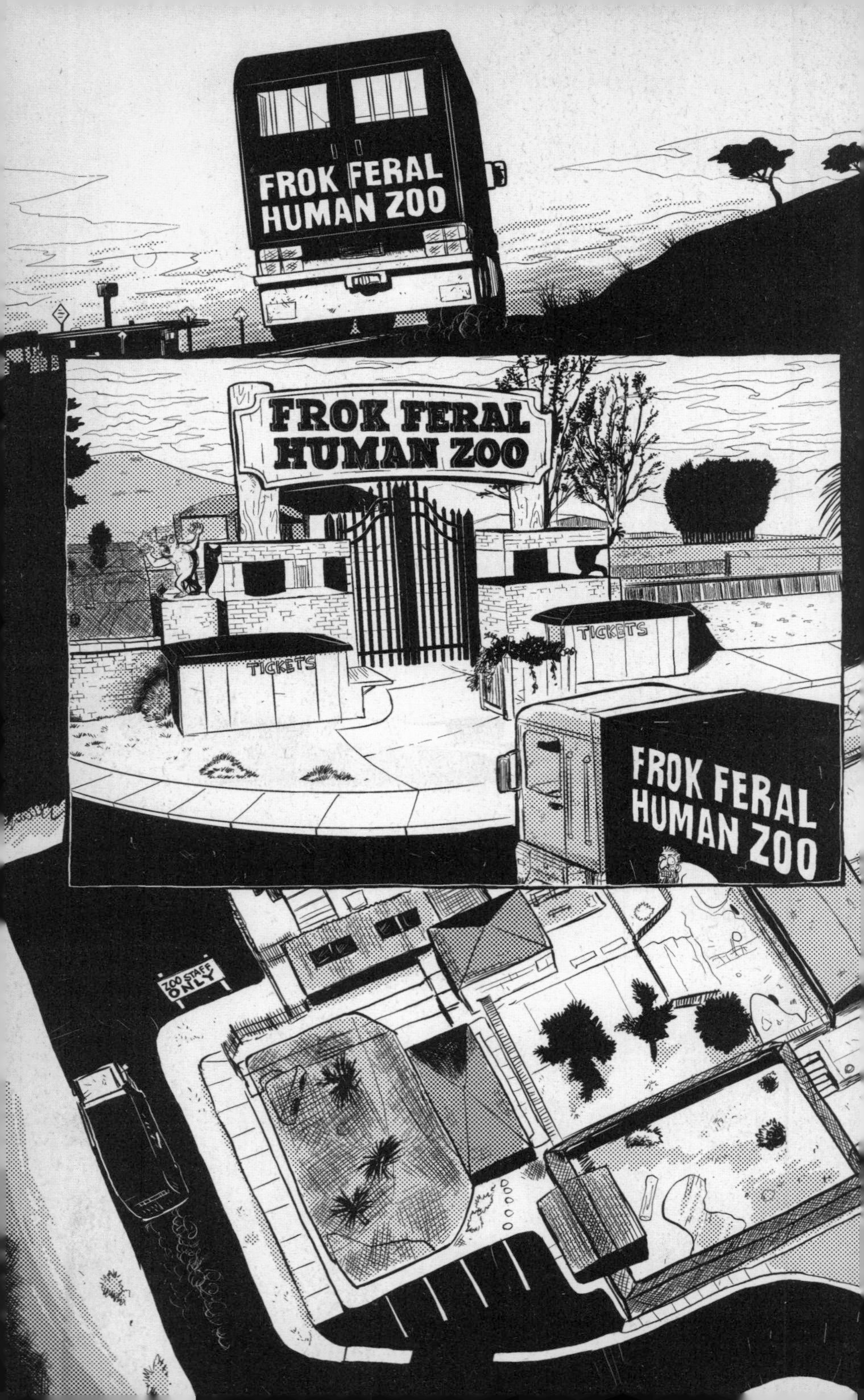
FROK FERAL
HUMAN ZOO
FROK FERAL
HUMAN ZOO
TICKETS
TICKETS
FROK FERAL
HUMAN ZOO
ZOO STAFF
ONLY

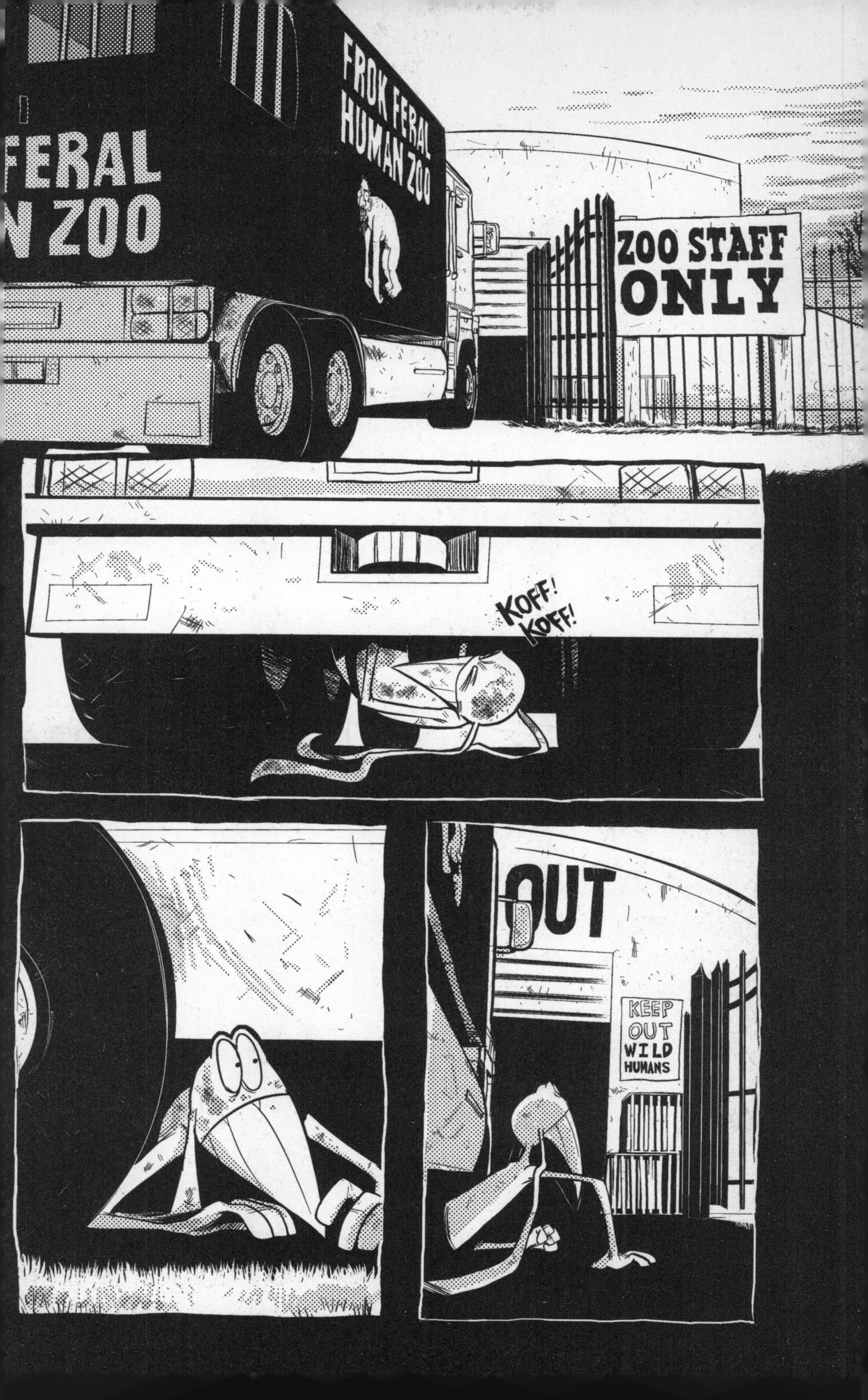
FROK FERAL HUMAN ZOO
FERAL
N ZOO
ZOO STAFF ONLY
KOFF! KOFF!
OUT
KEEP OUT WILD HUMANS

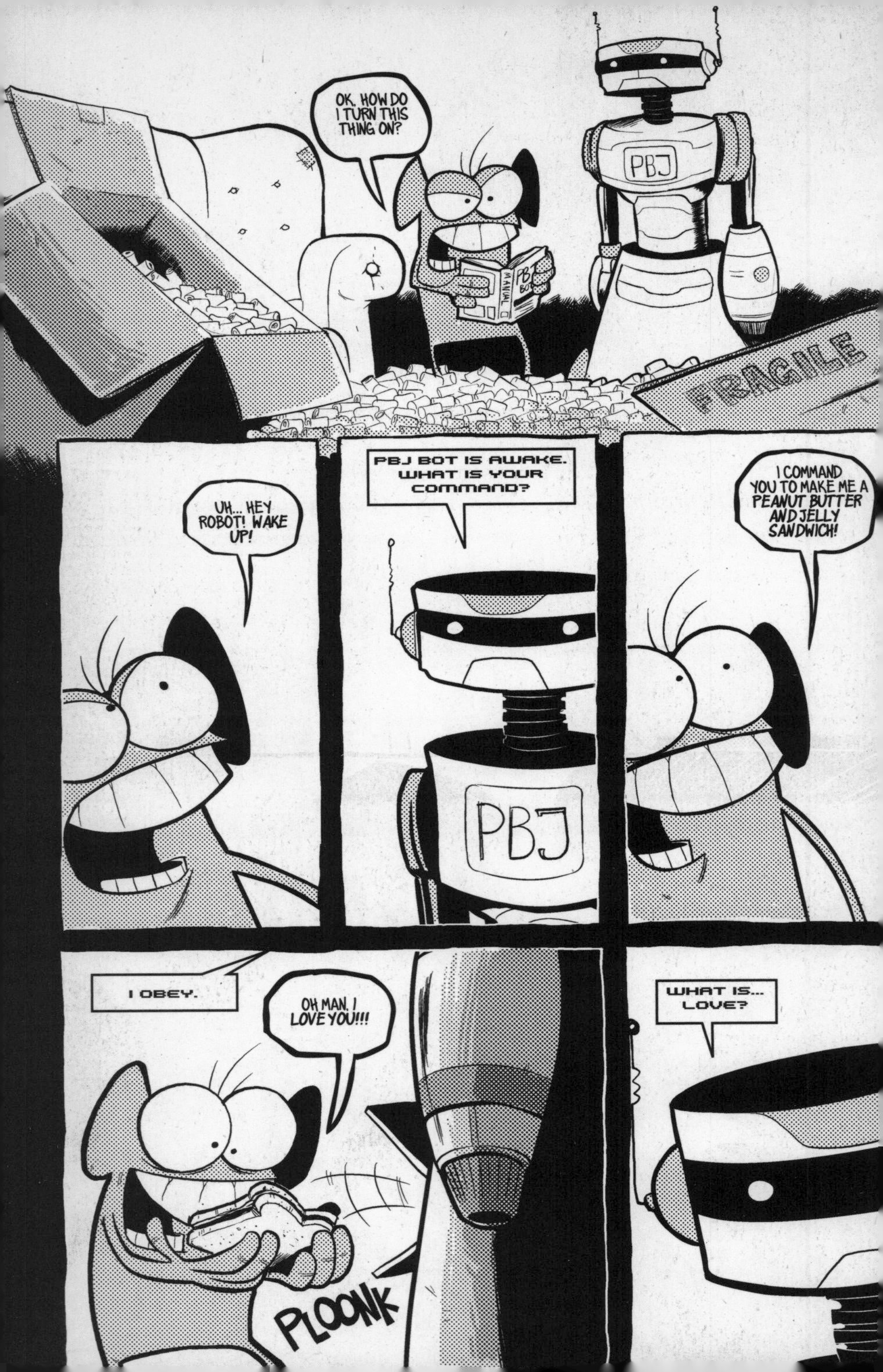
OK, HOW DO I TURN THIS THING ON?
PBJ
MANUAL PBJ BOT
FRAGILE
UH... HEY ROBOT! WAKE UP!
PBJ BOT IS AWAKE. WHAT IS YOUR COMMAND?
PBJ
I COMMAND YOU TO MAKE ME A PEANUT BUTTER AND JELLY SANDWICH!
I OBEY.
OH MAN, I LOVE YOU!!!
PLOONK
WHAT IS... LOVE?

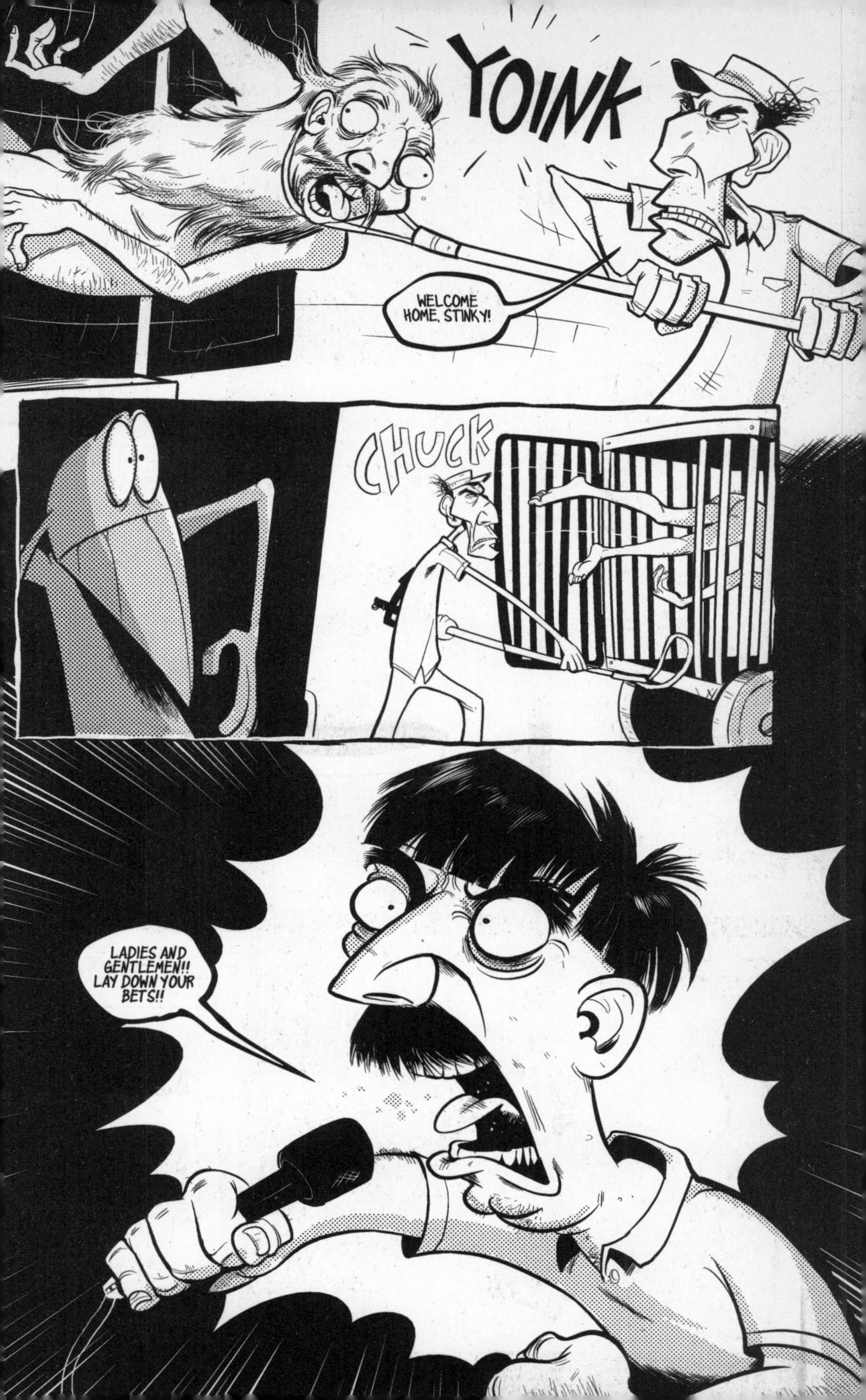
YOINK
WELCOME HOME, STINKY!
CHUCK
LADIES AND GENTLEMEN!! LAY DOWN YOUR BETS!!

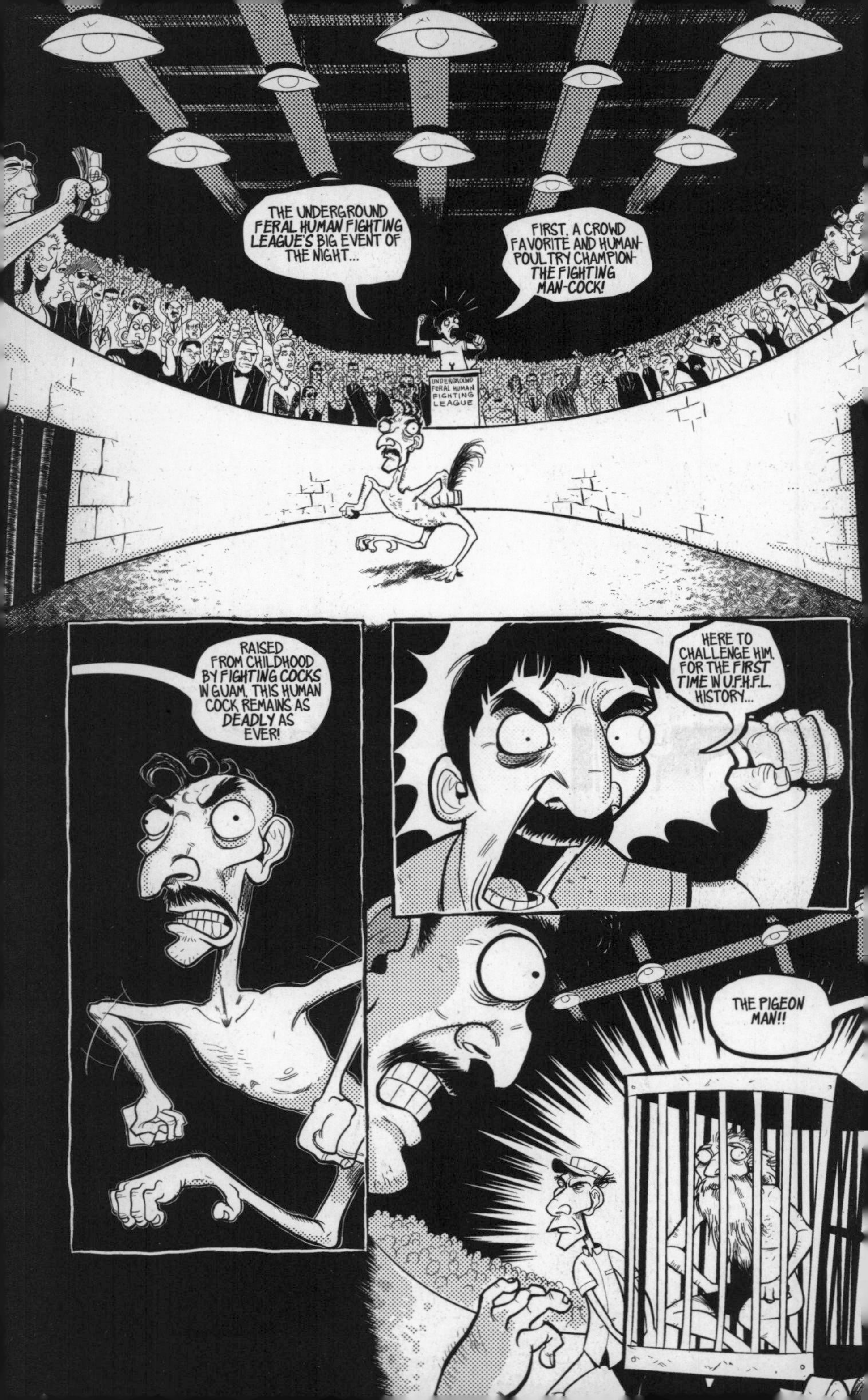
THE UNDERGROUND FERAL HUMAN FIGHTING LEAGUE'S BIG EVENT OF THE NIGHT...
FIRST, A CROWD FAVORITE AND HUMAN-POULTRY CHAMPION- THE FIGHTING MAN-COCK!
UNDERGROUND FERAL HUMAN FIGHTING LEAGUE
RAISED FROM CHILDHOOD BY FIGHTING COCKS IN GUAM, THIS HUMAN COCK REMAINS AS DEADLY AS EVER!
HERE TO CHALLENGE HIM, FOR THE FIRST TIME IN U.F.H.F.L. HISTORY...
THE PIGEON MAN!!

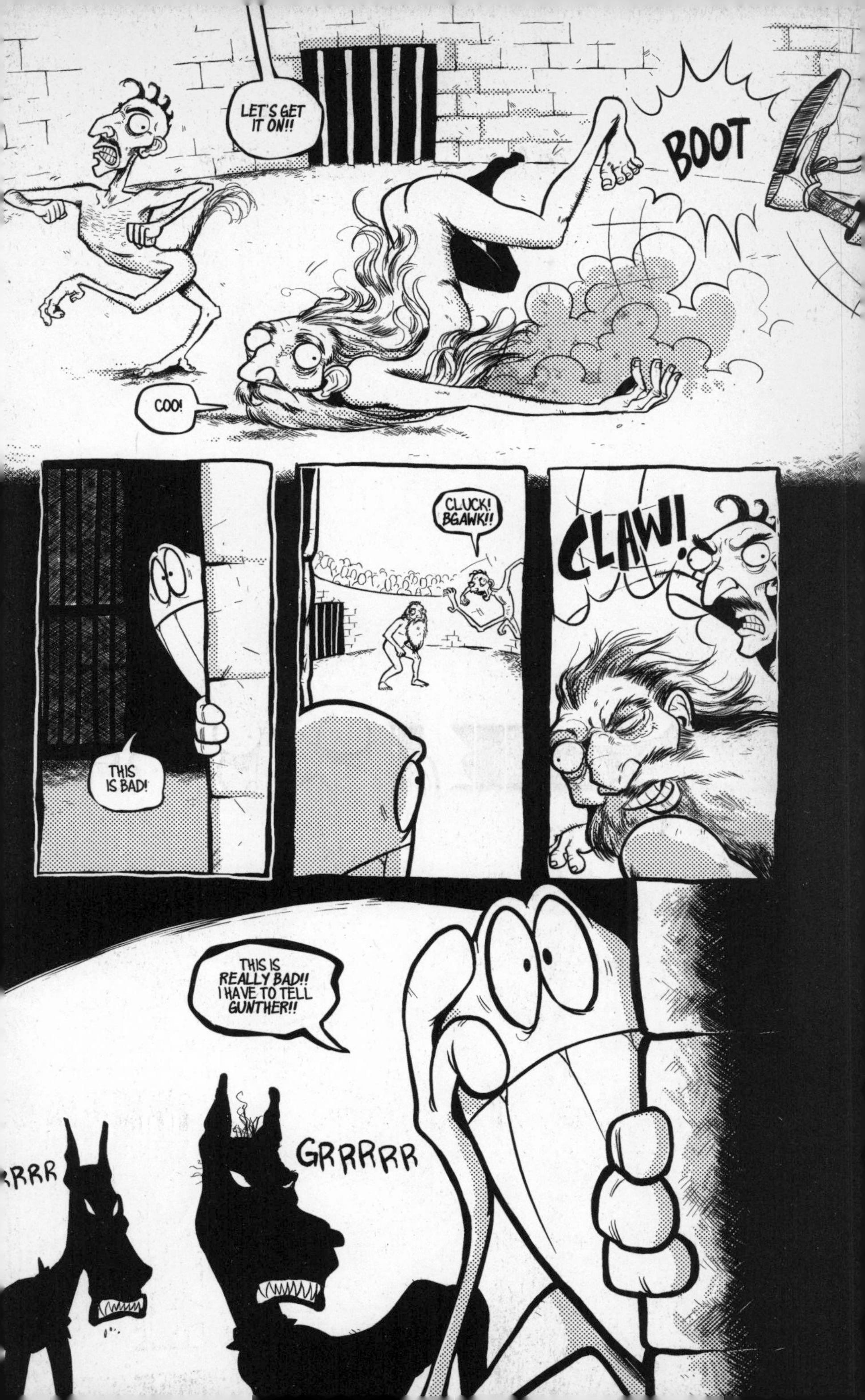
LET'S GET IT ON!!
BOOT
COO!
THIS IS BAD!
CLUCK! BGAWK!!
CLAW!
THIS IS REALLY BAD!! I HAVE TO TELL GUNTHER!!
RRRR
GRRRRR

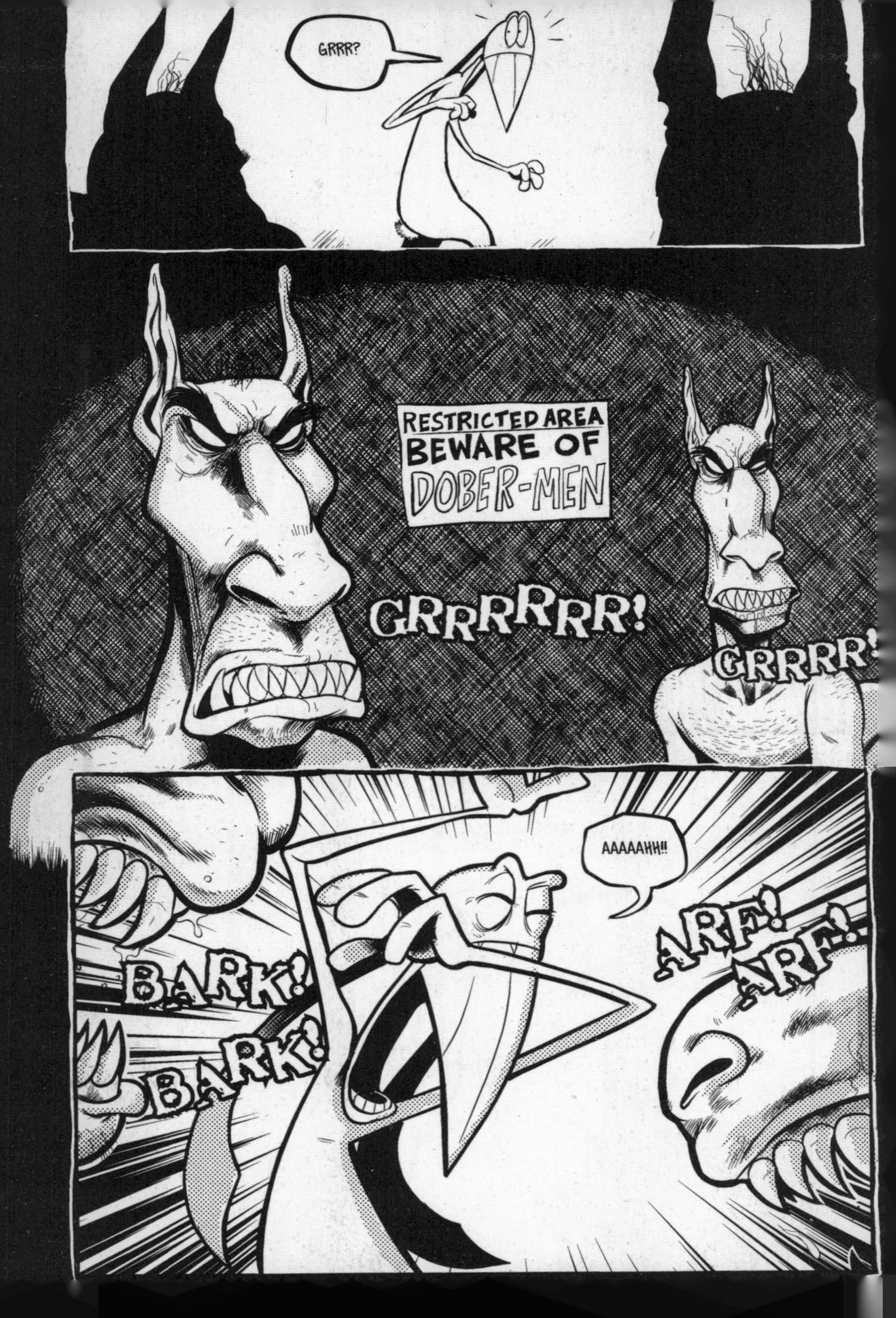
GRRR?
RESTRICTED AREA
BEWARE OF
DOBER-MEN
GRRRRRRR!
GRRRR
AAAAAHH!!
BARK!
BARK!
ARF!
ARF!

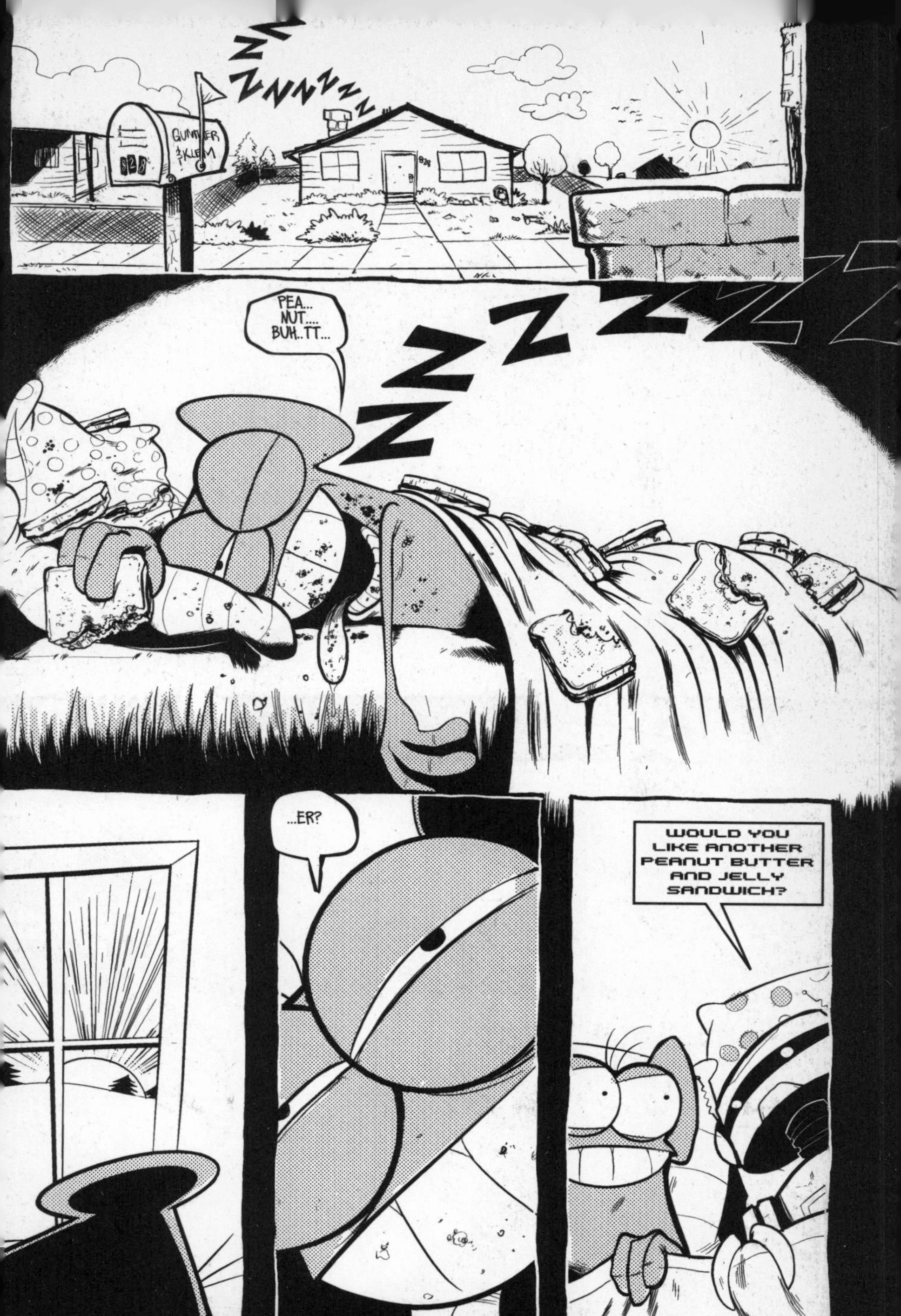
ZZZZZZZZZ
GUMMER
KLEM
828
PEA... NUT.... BUH..TT...
ZZZZZZZZ
...ER?
WOULD YOU LIKE ANOTHER PEANUT BUTTER AND JELLY SANDWICH?

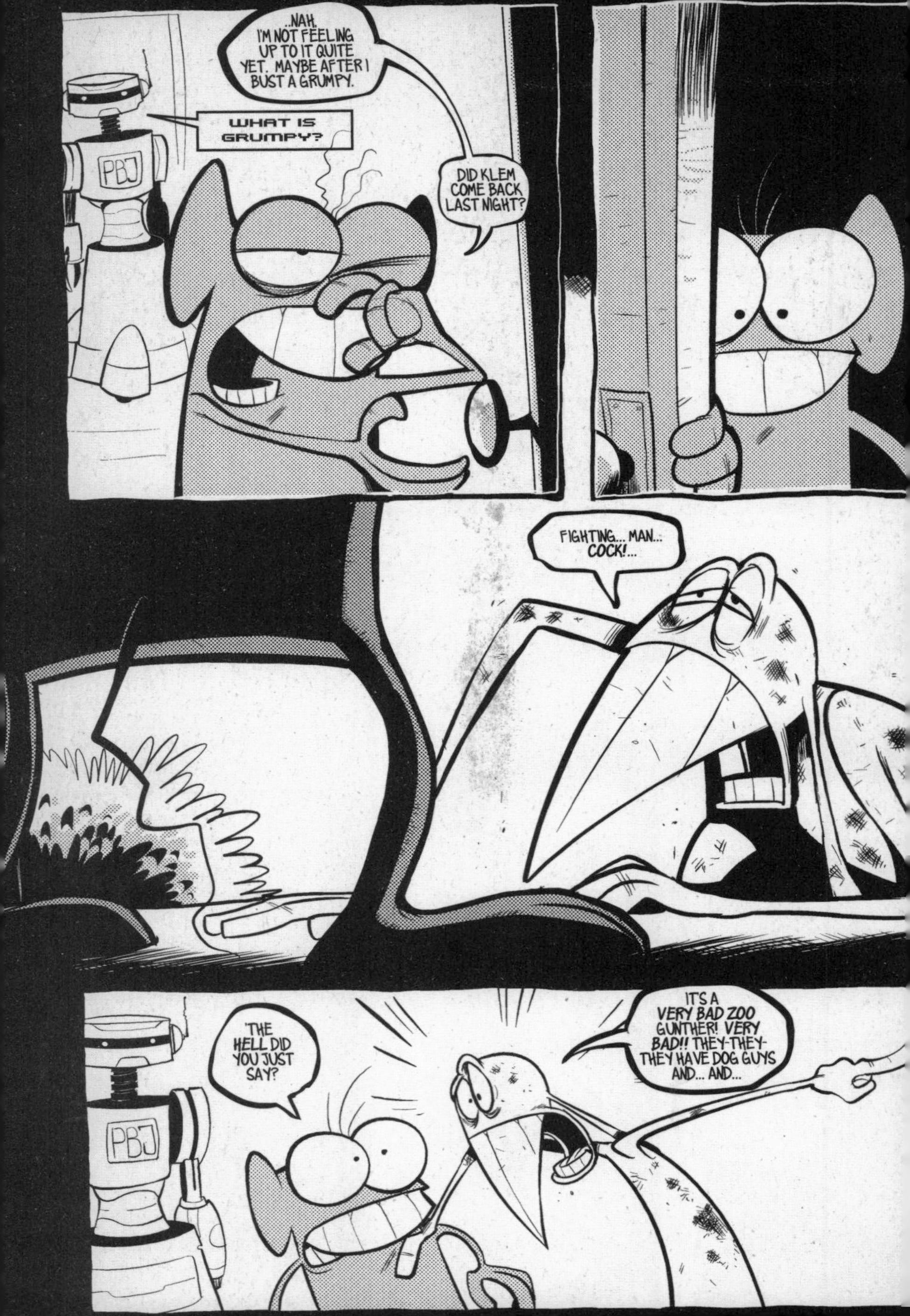
..NAH. I'M NOT FEELING UP TO IT QUITE YET. MAYBE AFTER I BUST A GRUMPY.
WHAT IS GRUMPY?
DID KLEM COME BACK LAST NIGHT?
FIGHTING... MAN... COCK!...
'THE HELL DID YOU JUST SAY?
IT'S A VERY BAD ZOO GUNTHER! VERY BAD!! THEY-THEY-THEY HAVE DOG GUYS AND... AND...

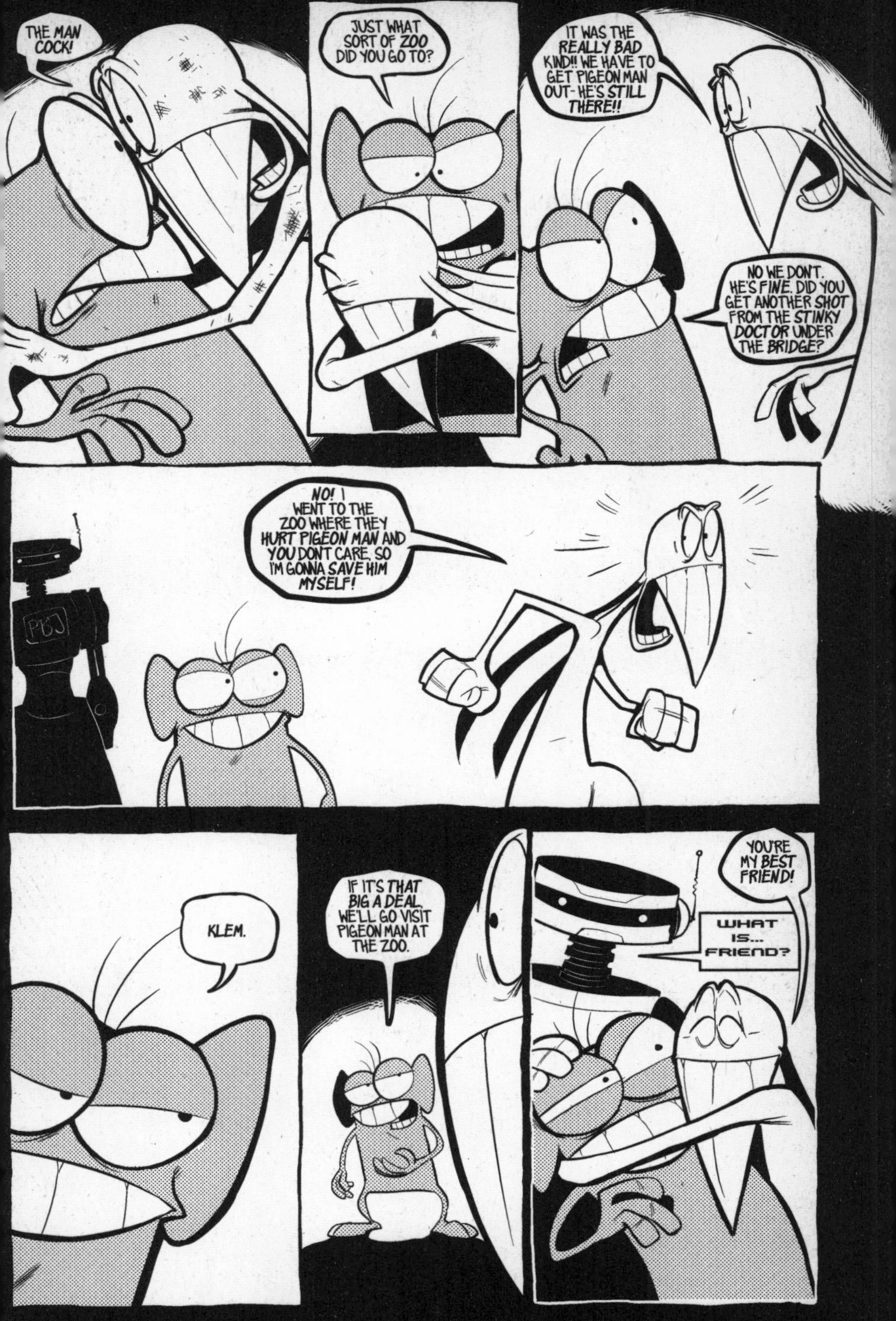
THE MAN COCK!
JUST WHAT SORT OF ZOO DID YOU GO TO?
IT WAS THE REALLY BAD KIND!! WE HAVE TO GET PIGEON MAN OUT- HE'S STILL THERE!!
NO WE DONT. HE'S FINE. DID YOU GET ANOTHER SHOT FROM THE STINKY DOCTOR UNDER THE BRIDGE?
NO! I WENT TO THE ZOO WHERE THEY HURT PIGEON MAN AND YOU DONT CARE, SO I'M GONNA SAVE HIM MYSELF!
PBJ
KLEM.
IF IT'S THAT BIG A DEAL, WE'LL GO VISIT PIGEON MAN AT THE ZOO.
YOU'RE MY BEST FRIEND!
WHAT IS... FRIEND?

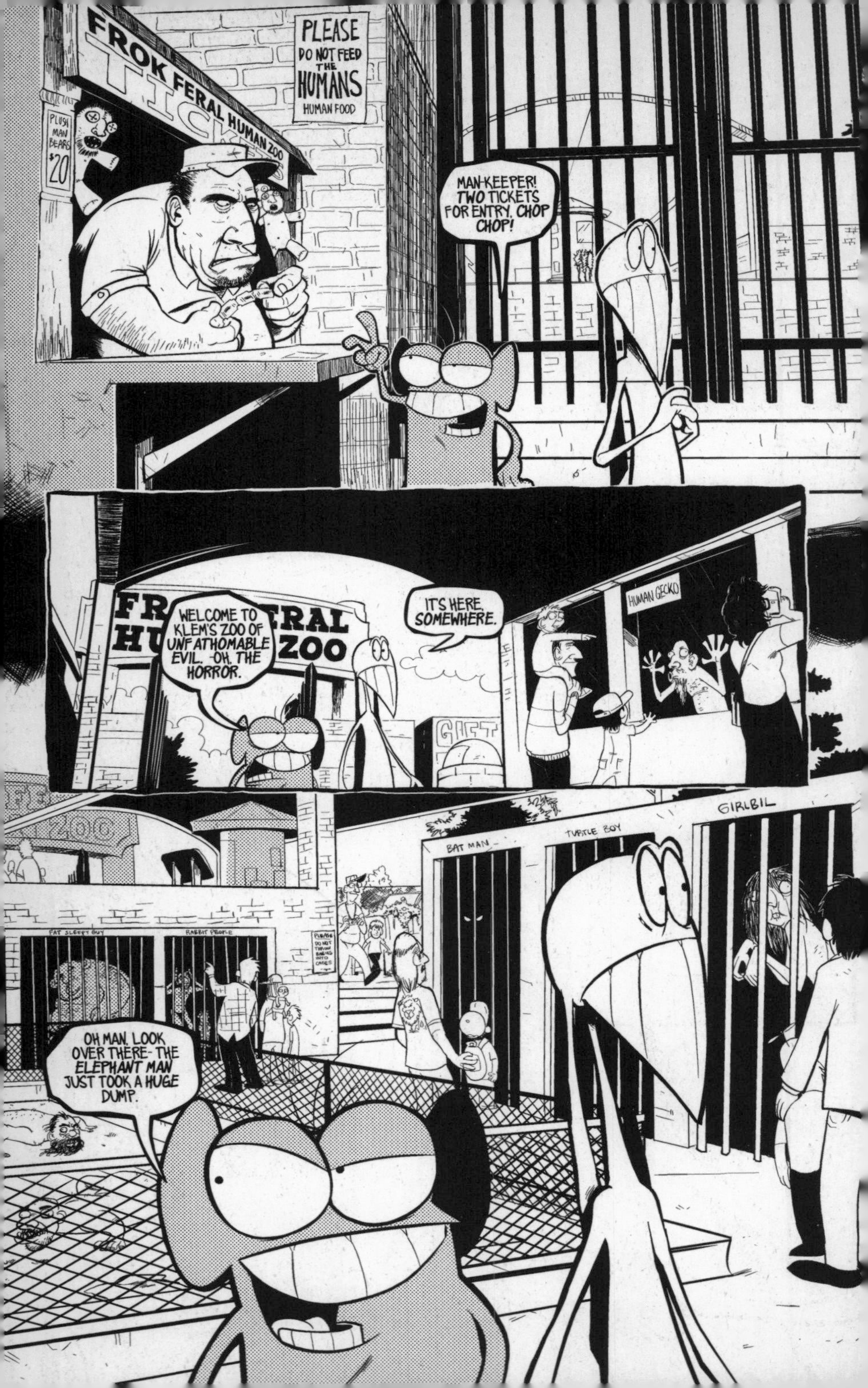
FROK FERAL HUMAN ZOO
TICKETS
PLUSH MAN BEARS $20
PLEASE DO NOT FEED THE HUMANS
HUMAN FOOD
MAN-KEEPER! TWO TICKETS FOR ENTRY, CHOP CHOP!
WELCOME TO KLEM'S ZOO OF UNFATHOMABLE EVIL. -OH, THE HORROR.
IT'S HERE, SOMEWHERE.
HUMAN GECKO
GIFT
ZOO
FAT SLEEPY GUY
RABBIT PEOPLE
BAT MAN
TURTLE BOY
GIRLBIL
OH MAN, LOOK OVER THERE- THE ELEPHANT MAN JUST TOOK A HUGE DUMP.

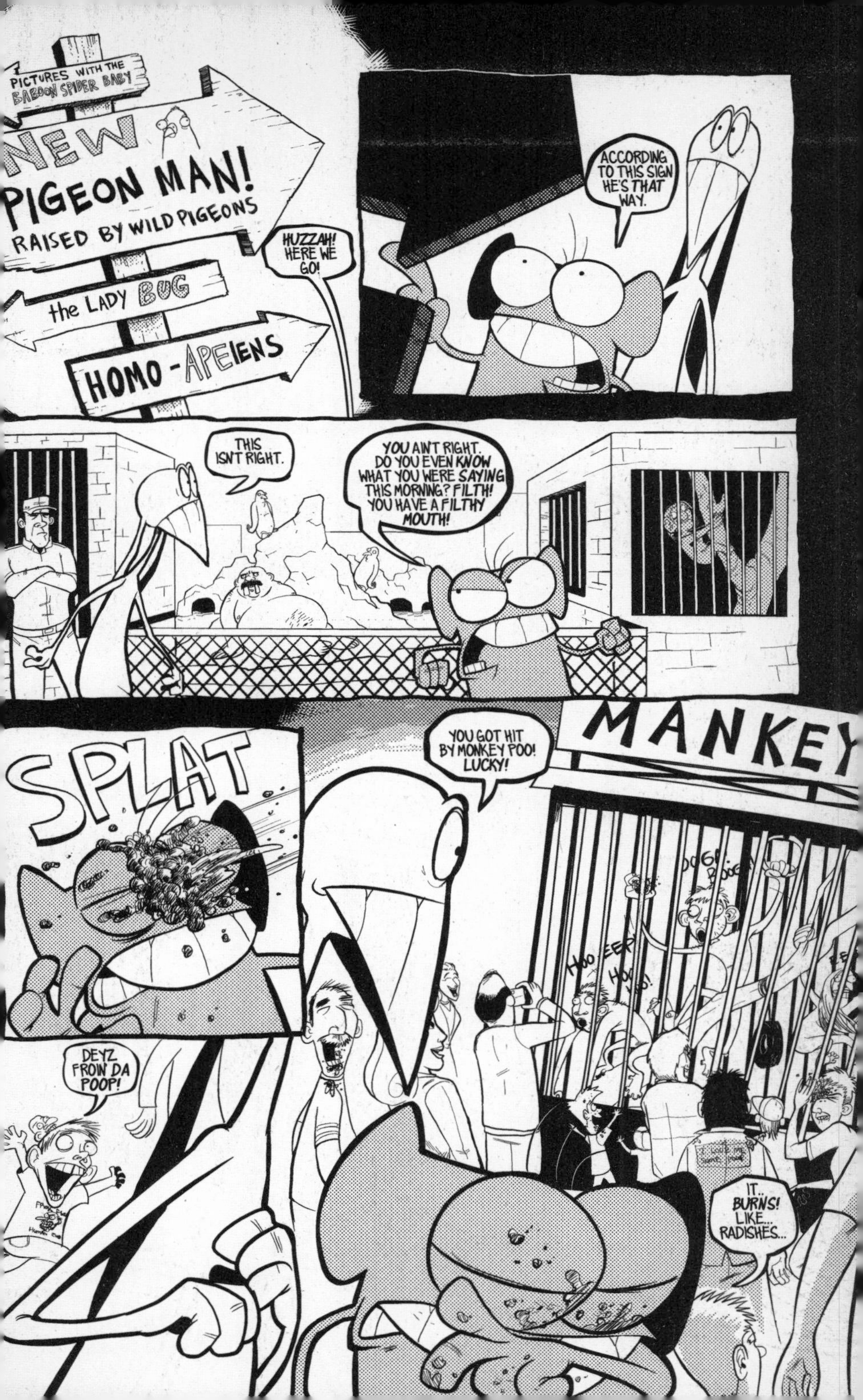
PICTURES WITH THE BABOON SPIDER BABY
NEW PIGEON MAN! RAISED BY WILD PIGEONS
the LADY BUG
HOMO-APEIENS
HUZZAH! HERE WE GO!
ACCORDING TO THIS SIGN HE'S THAT WAY.
THIS ISN'T RIGHT.
YOU AIN'T RIGHT. DO YOU EVEN KNOW WHAT YOU WERE SAYING THIS MORNING? FILTH! YOU HAVE A FILTHY MOUTH!
SPLAT
MANKEY
YOU GOT HIT BY MONKEY POO! LUCKY!
DEYZ FROIN DA POOP!
IT.. BURNS! LIKE... RADISHES...

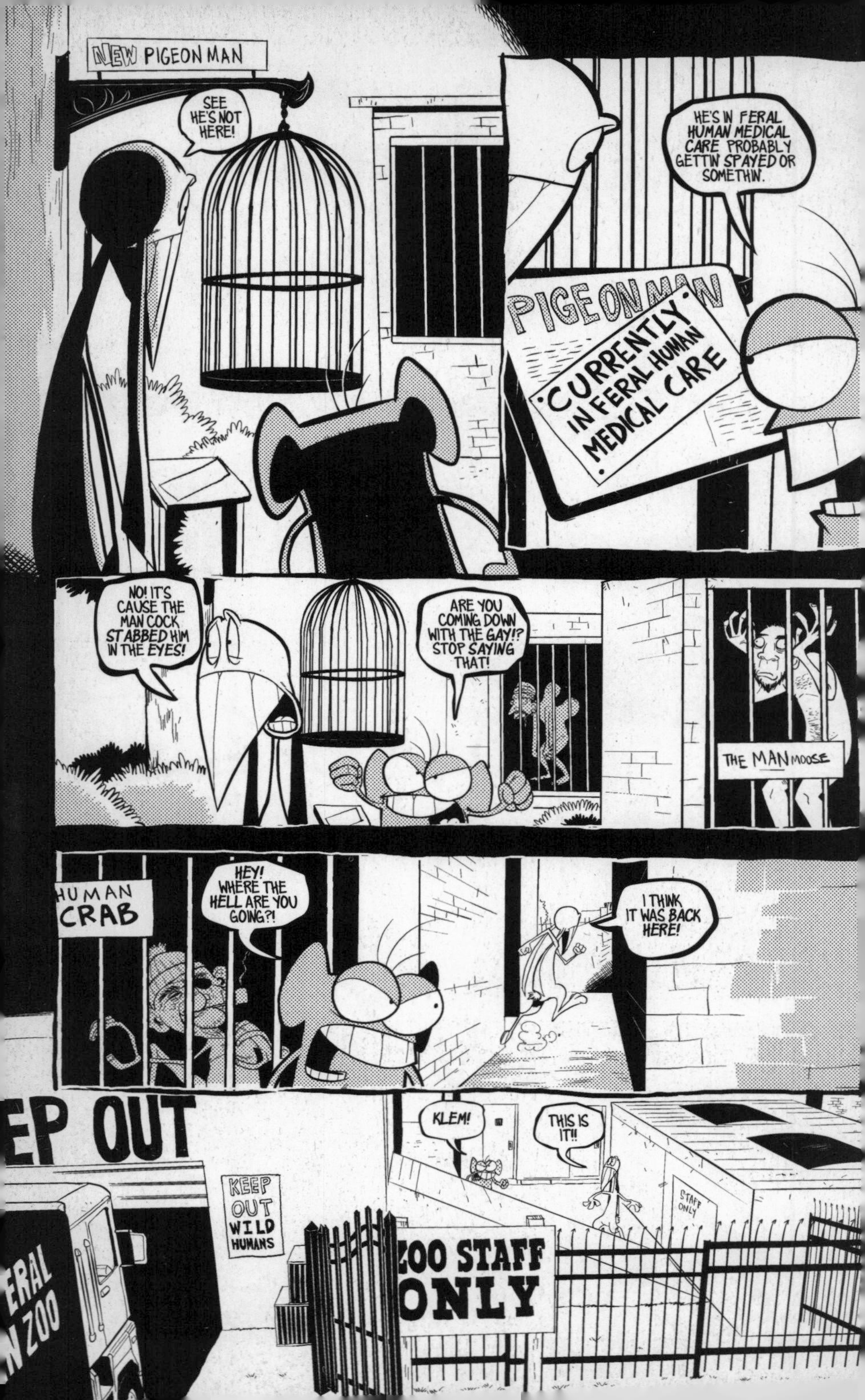
NEW PIGEON MAN
SEE HE'S NOT HERE!
HE'S IN FERAL HUMAN MEDICAL CARE PROBABLY GETTIN' SPAYED OR SOMETHIN'.
PIGEON MAN
CURRENTLY IN FERAL HUMAN MEDICAL CARE
NO! IT'S CAUSE THE MAN COCK STABBED HIM IN THE EYES!
ARE YOU COMING DOWN WITH THE GAY!? STOP SAYING THAT!
THE MAN MOOSE
HUMAN CRAB
HEY! WHERE THE HELL ARE YOU GOING?!
I THINK IT WAS BACK HERE!
EP OUT
KEEP OUT WILD HUMANS
KLEM!
THIS IS IT!!
STAFF ONLY
ZOO STAFF ONLY
ERAL
N ZOO

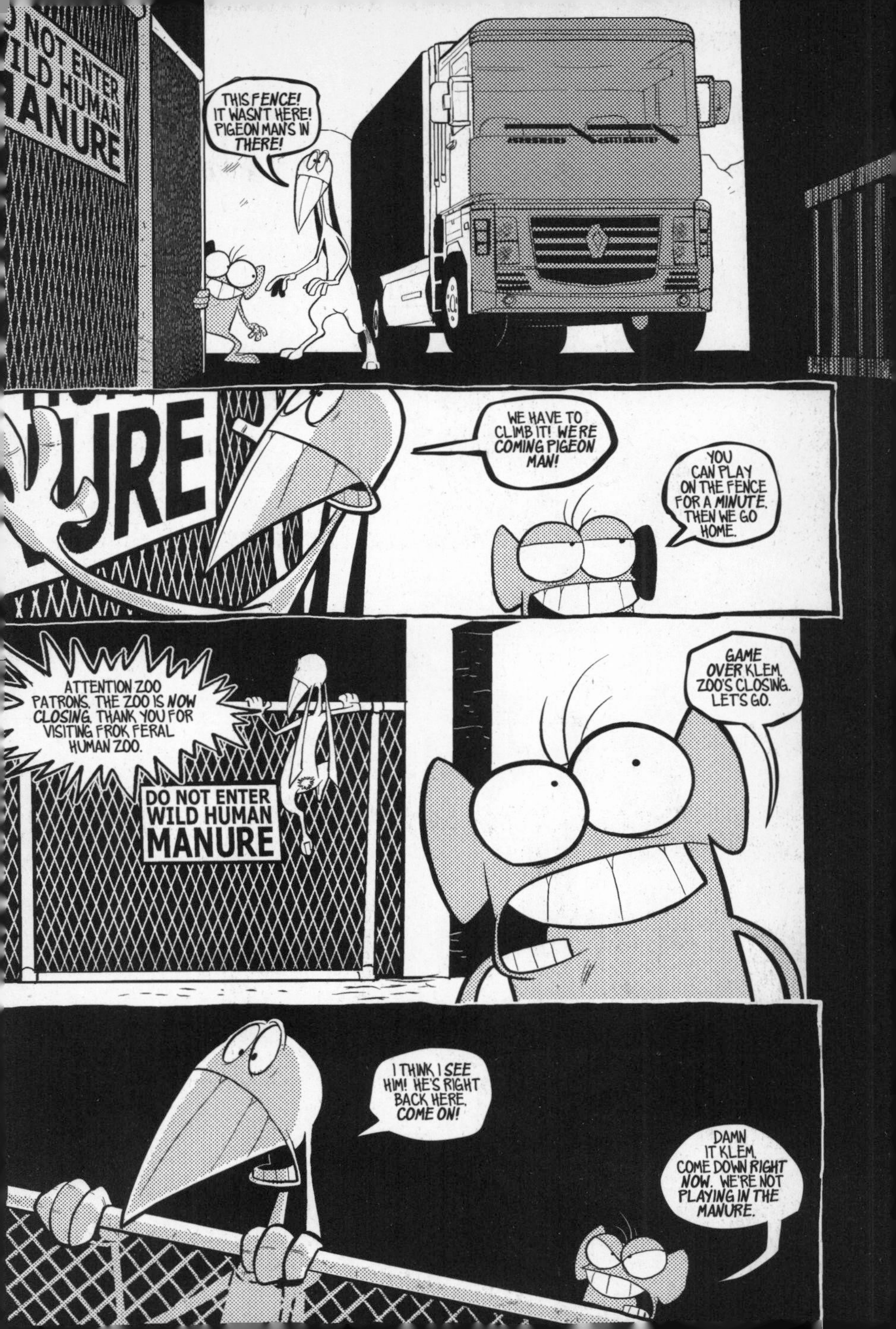
DO NOT ENTER WILD HUMAN MANURE
THIS FENCE! IT WASN'T HERE! PIGEON MAN'S IN THERE!
WE HAVE TO CLIMB IT! WE'RE COMING PIGEON MAN!
YOU CAN PLAY ON THE FENCE FOR A MINUTE, THEN WE GO HOME.
ATTENTION ZOO PATRONS. THE ZOO IS NOW CLOSING. THANK YOU FOR VISITING FROK FERAL HUMAN ZOO.
DO NOT ENTER WILD HUMAN MANURE
GAME OVER KLEM. ZOO'S CLOSING. LET'S GO.
I THINK I SEE HIM! HE'S RIGHT BACK HERE. COME ON!
DAMN IT KLEM, COME DOWN RIGHT NOW. WE'RE NOT PLAYING IN THE MANURE.

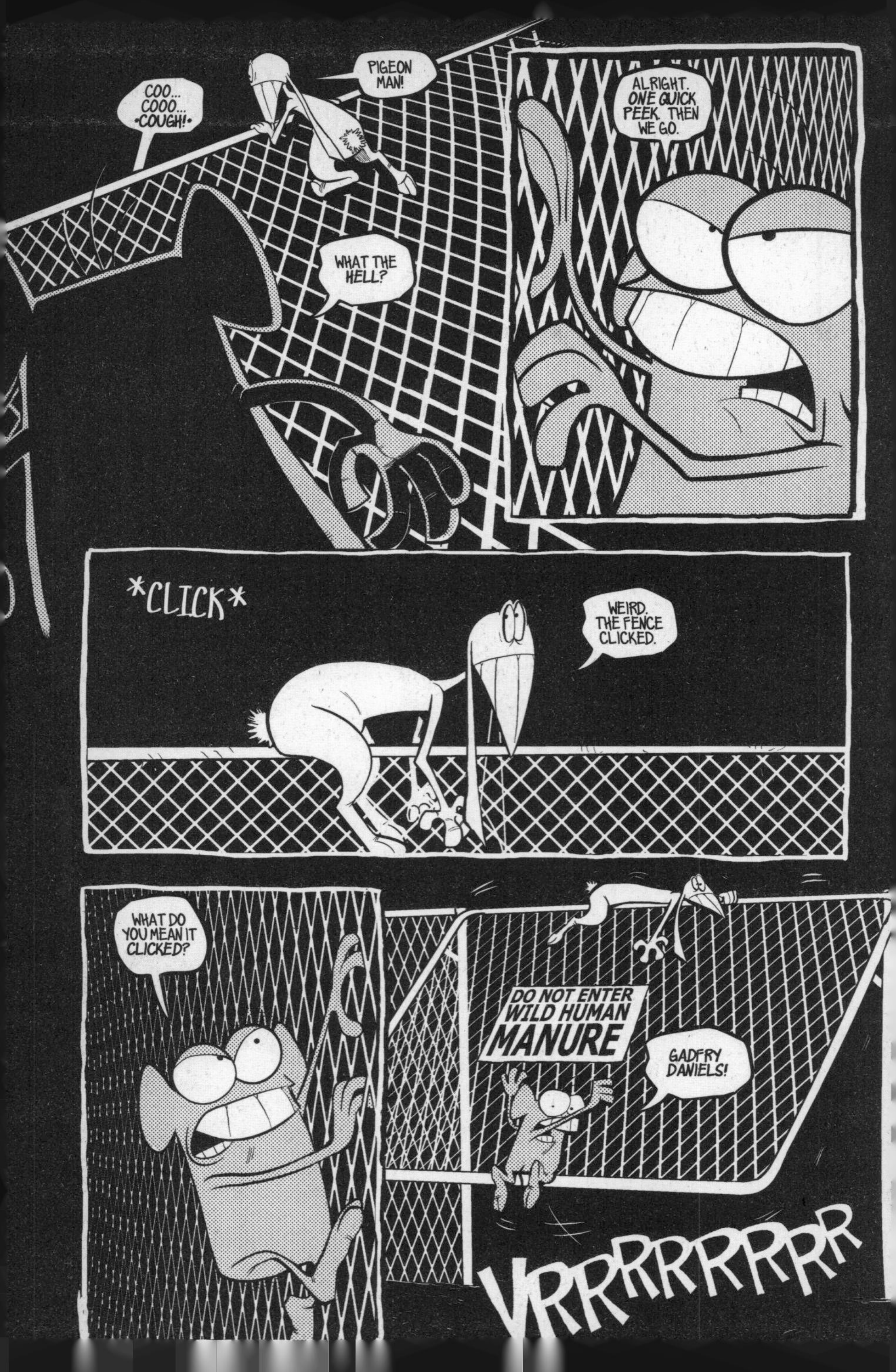
COO... COOO... •COUGH!•
PIGEON MAN!
WHAT THE HELL?
ALRIGHT. ONE QUICK PEEK. THEN WE GO.
CLICK
WEIRD. THE FENCE CLICKED.
WHAT DO YOU MEAN IT CLICKED?
DO NOT ENTER
WILD HUMAN
MANURE
GADFRY DANIELS!
VRRRRRRRRR

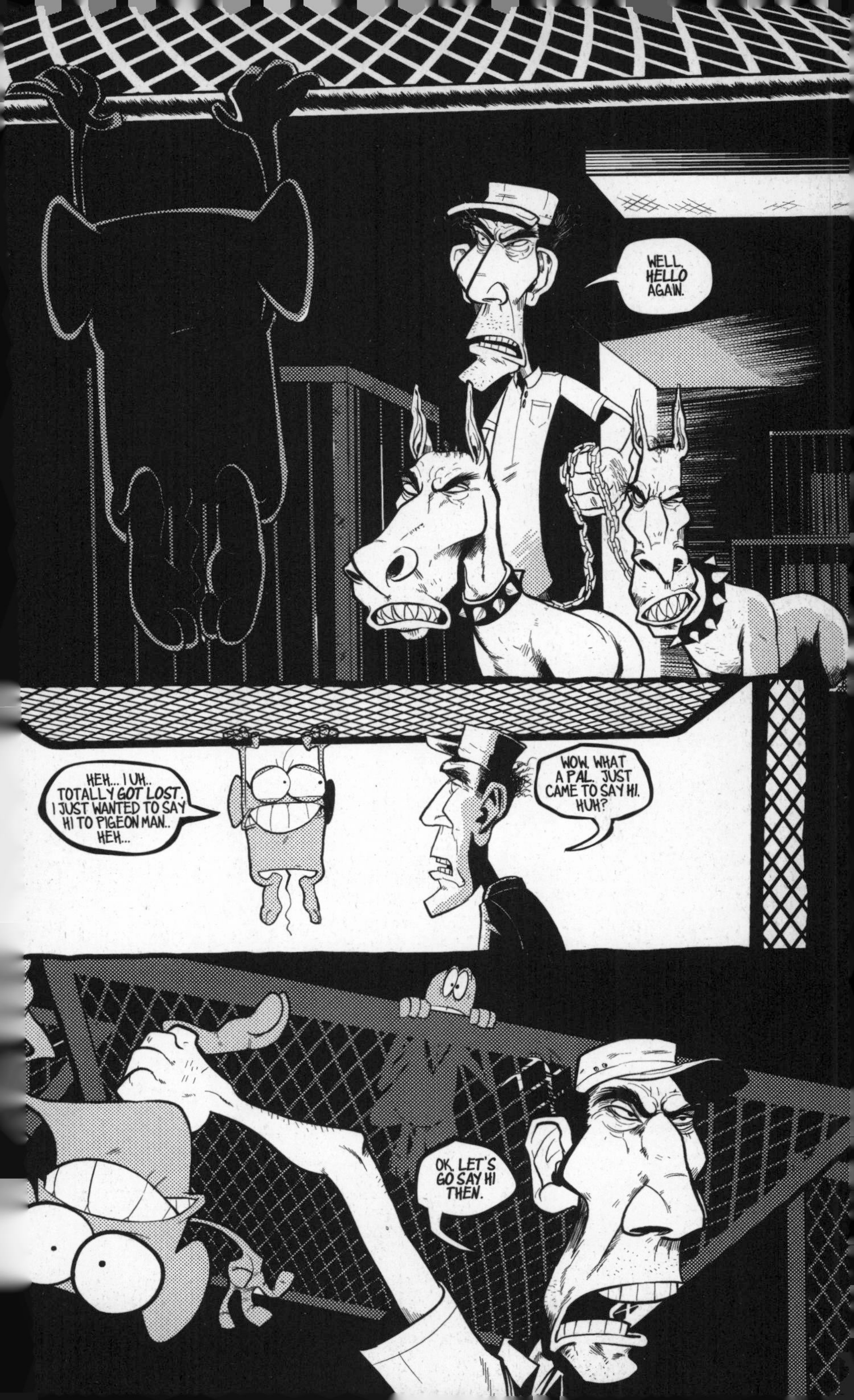
WELL, HELLO AGAIN.
HEH... I UH.. TOTALLY GOT LOST. I JUST WANTED TO SAY HI TO PIGEON MAN.. HEH...
WOW, WHAT A PAL. JUST CAME TO SAY HI, HUH?
OK, LET'S GO SAY HI THEN.

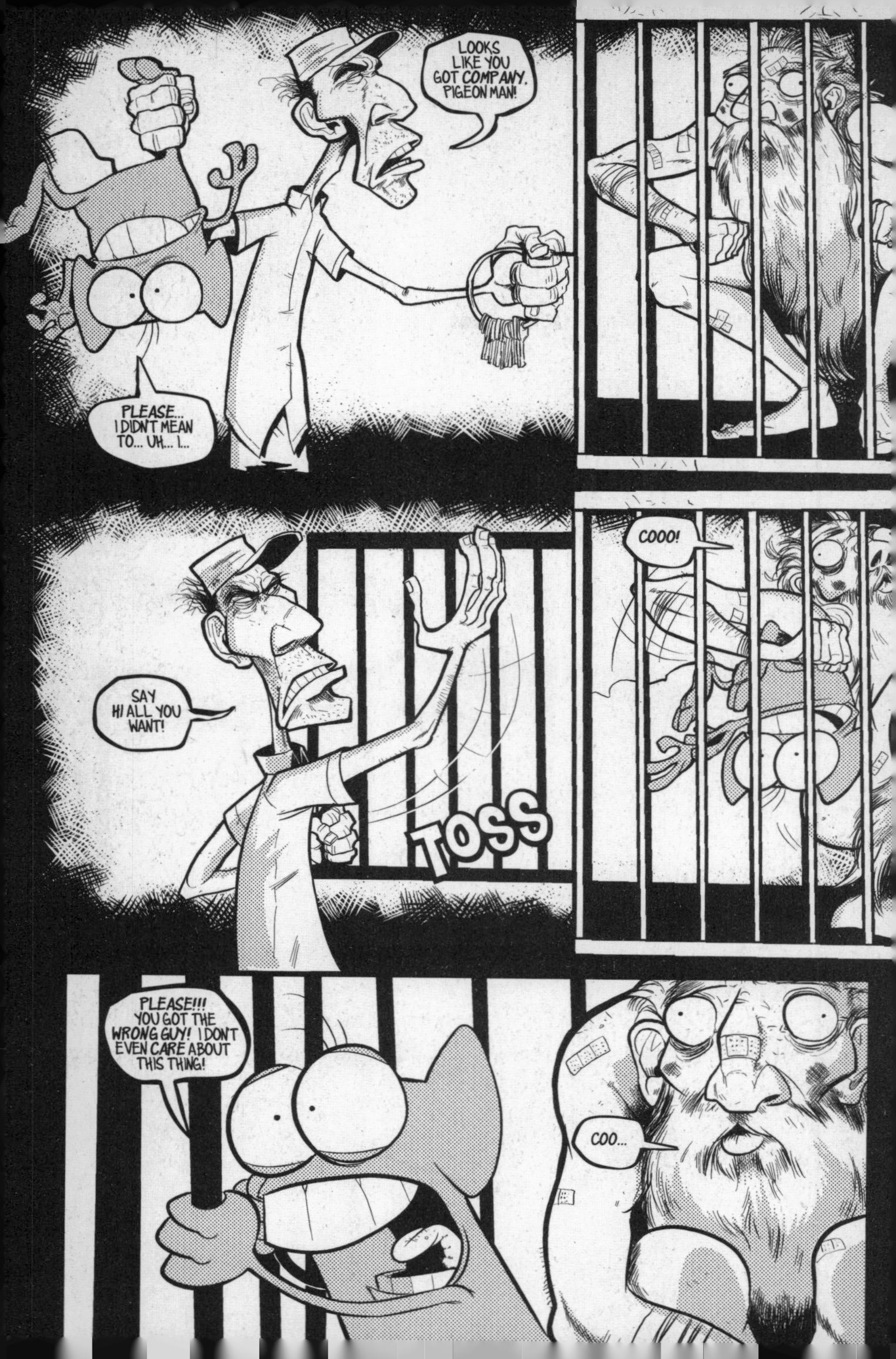
LOOKS LIKE YOU GOT COMPANY, PIGEON MAN!
PLEASE... I DIDN'T MEAN TO... UH... I...
SAY HI ALL YOU WANT!
TOSS
COOO!
PLEASE!!! YOU GOT THE WRONG GUY! I DON'T EVEN CARE ABOUT THIS THING!
COO...

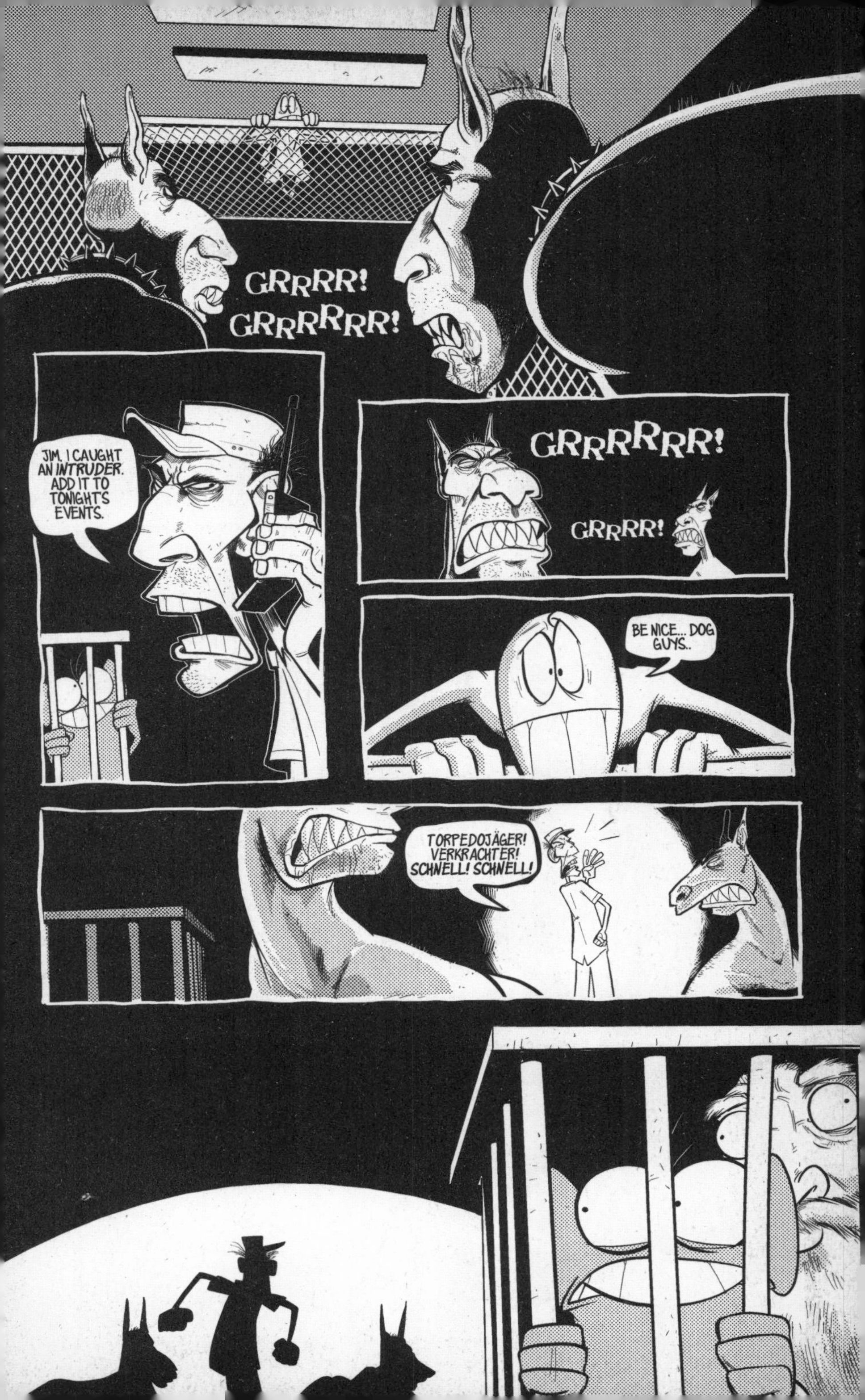
GRRRR!
GRRRRRR!
JIM, I CAUGHT AN INTRUDER. ADD IT TO TONIGHT'S EVENTS.
GRRRRRR!
GRRRR!
BE NICE... DOG GUYS..
TORPEDOJÄGER! VERKRACHTER! SCHNELL! SCHNELL!

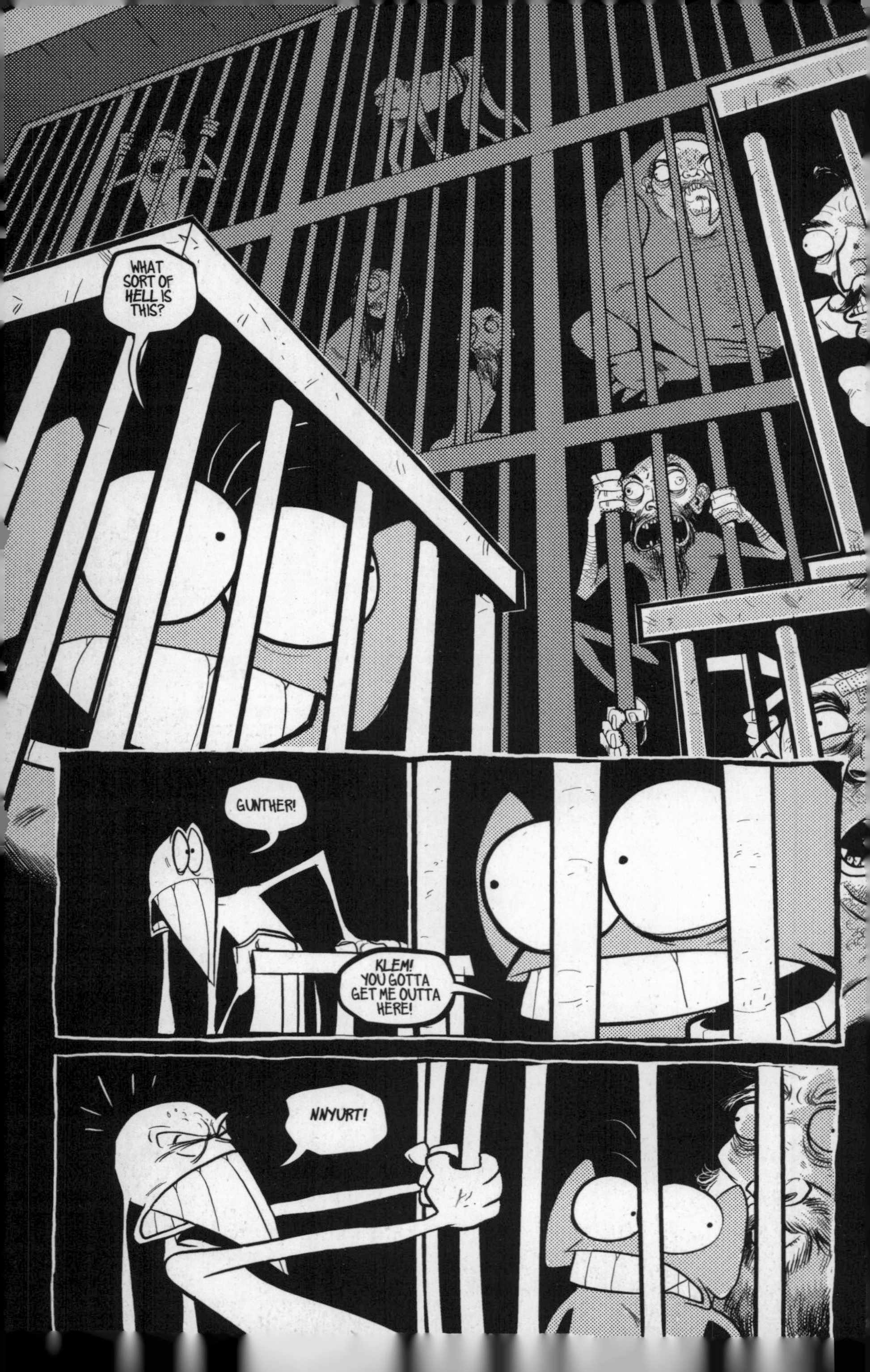
WHAT SORT OF HELL IS THIS?
GUNTHER!
KLEM! YOU GOTTA GET ME OUTTA HERE!
NNYURT!

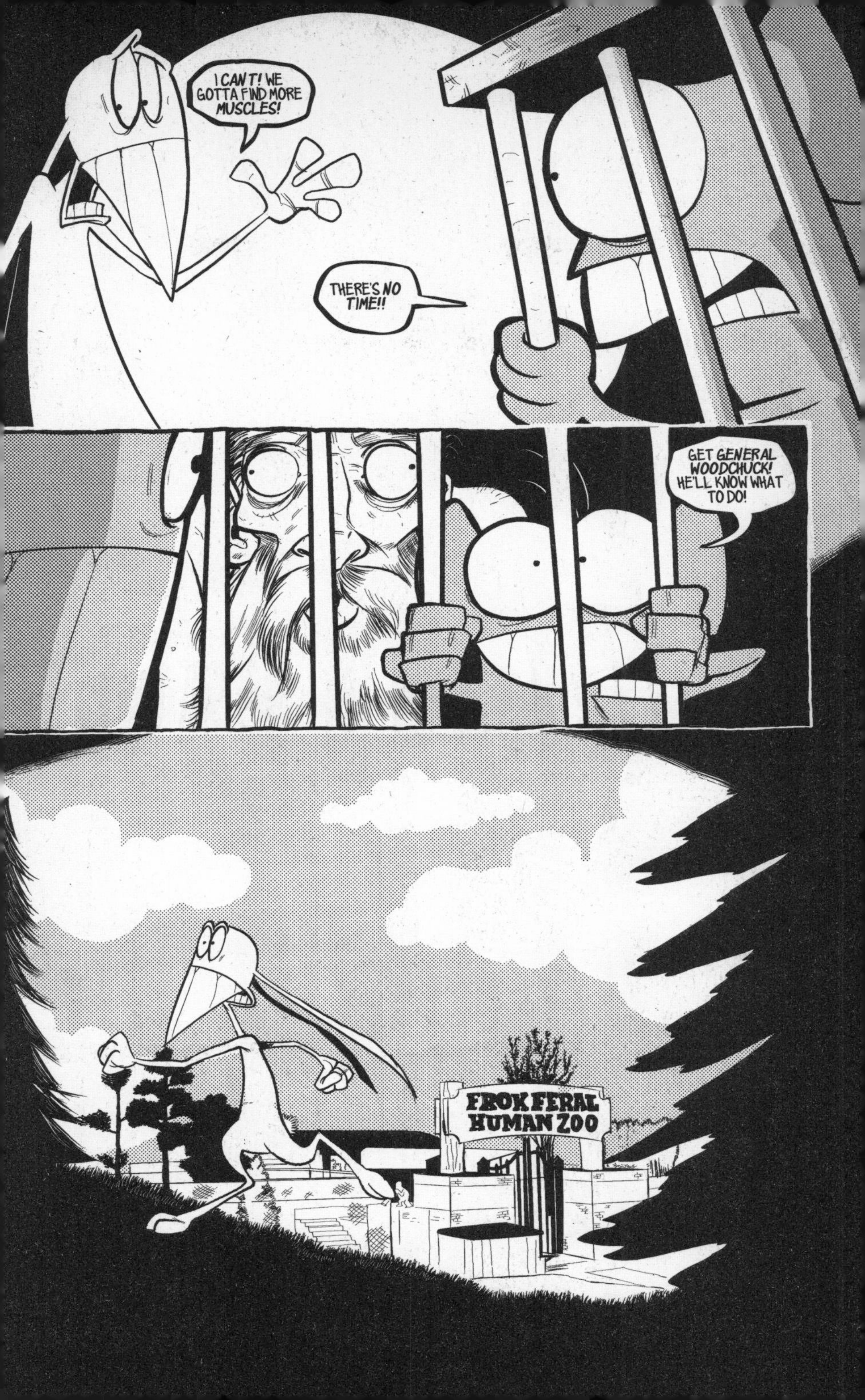
I CAN'T! WE GOTTA FIND MORE MUSCLES!
THERE'S NO TIME!!
GET GENERAL WOODCHUCK! HE'LL KNOW WHAT TO DO!
FROK FERAL HUMAN ZOO

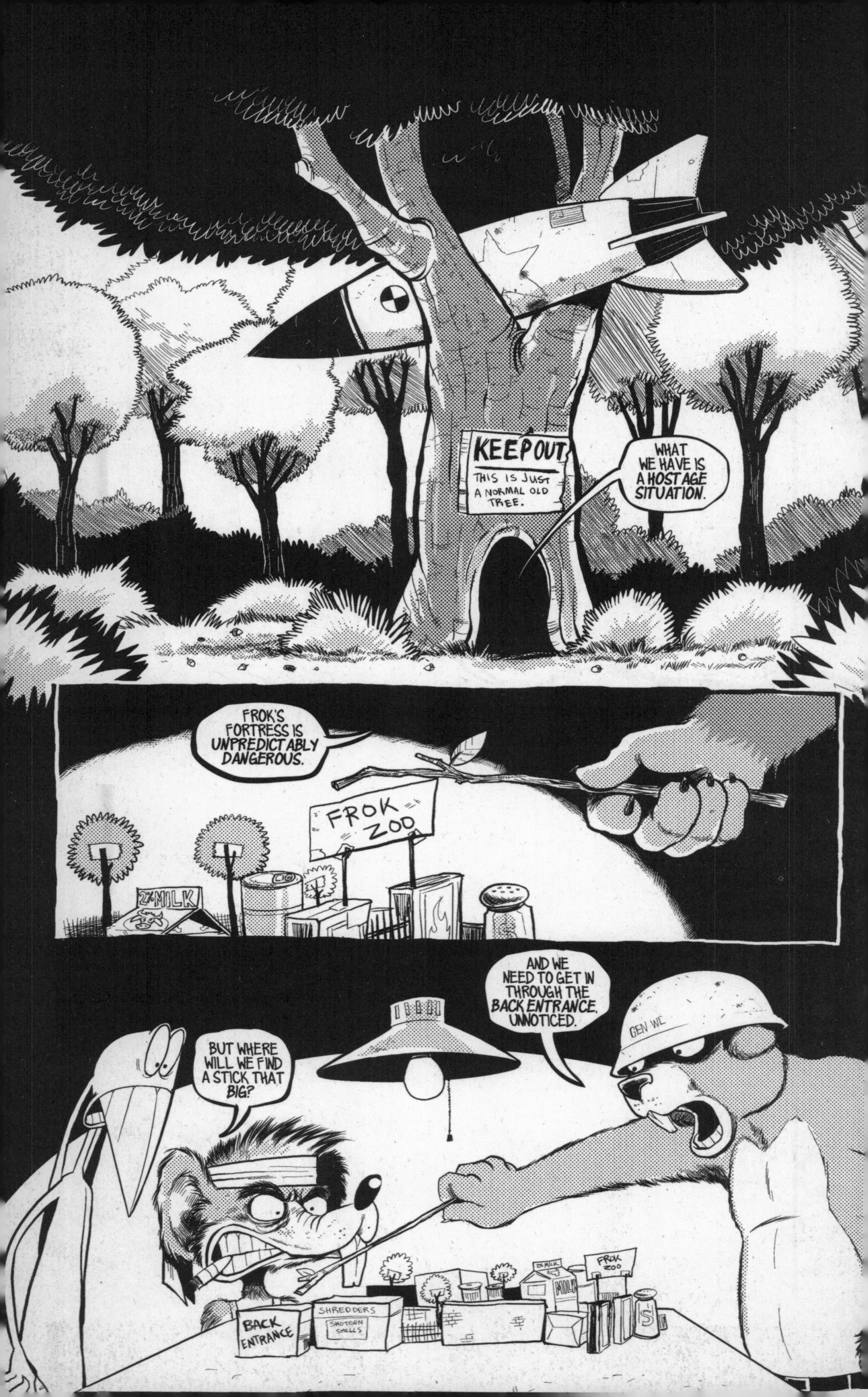

KEEP OUT
THIS IS JUST A NORMAL OLD TREE.
WHAT WE HAVE IS A HOSTAGE SITUATION.
FROK'S FORTRESS IS UNPREDICTABLY DANGEROUS.
FROK ZOO
2% MILK
AND WE NEED TO GET IN THROUGH THE BACK ENTRANCE, UNNOTICED.
GEN WC
BUT WHERE WILL WE FIND A STICK THAT BIG?
BACK ENTRANCE
SHREDDERS
SHOTGUN SHELLS

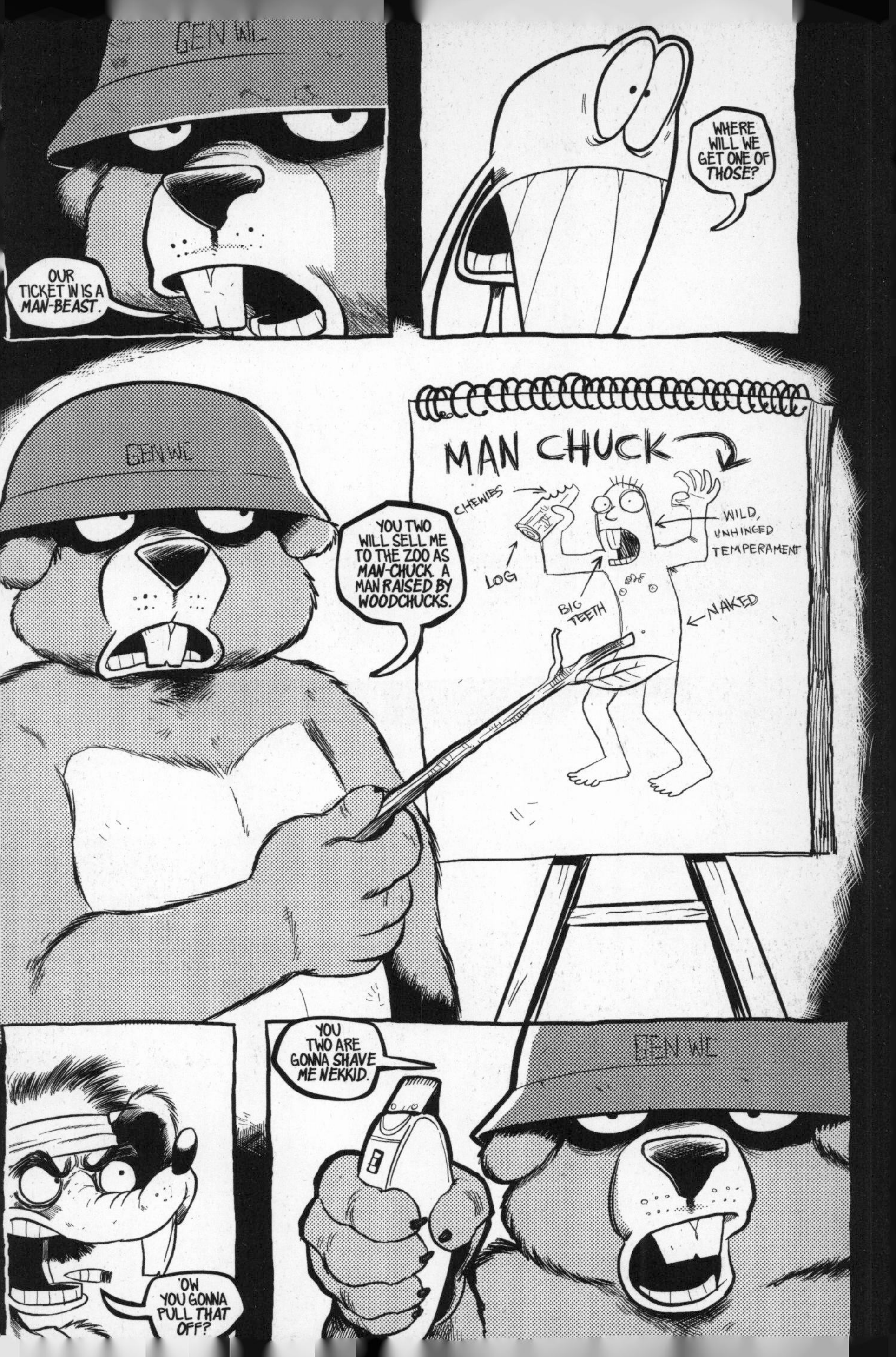
GEN WL
OUR TICKET IN IS A MAN-BEAST.
WHERE WILL WE GET ONE OF THOSE?
GEN WL
YOU TWO WILL SELL ME TO THE ZOO AS MAN-CHUCK. A MAN RAISED BY WOODCHUCKS.
MAN CHUCK
CHEWIES
LOG
WILD, UNHINGED TEMPERAMENT
BIG TEETH
NAKED
'OW YOU GONNA PULL THAT OFF?
YOU TWO ARE GONNA SHAVE ME NEKKID.
GEN WL

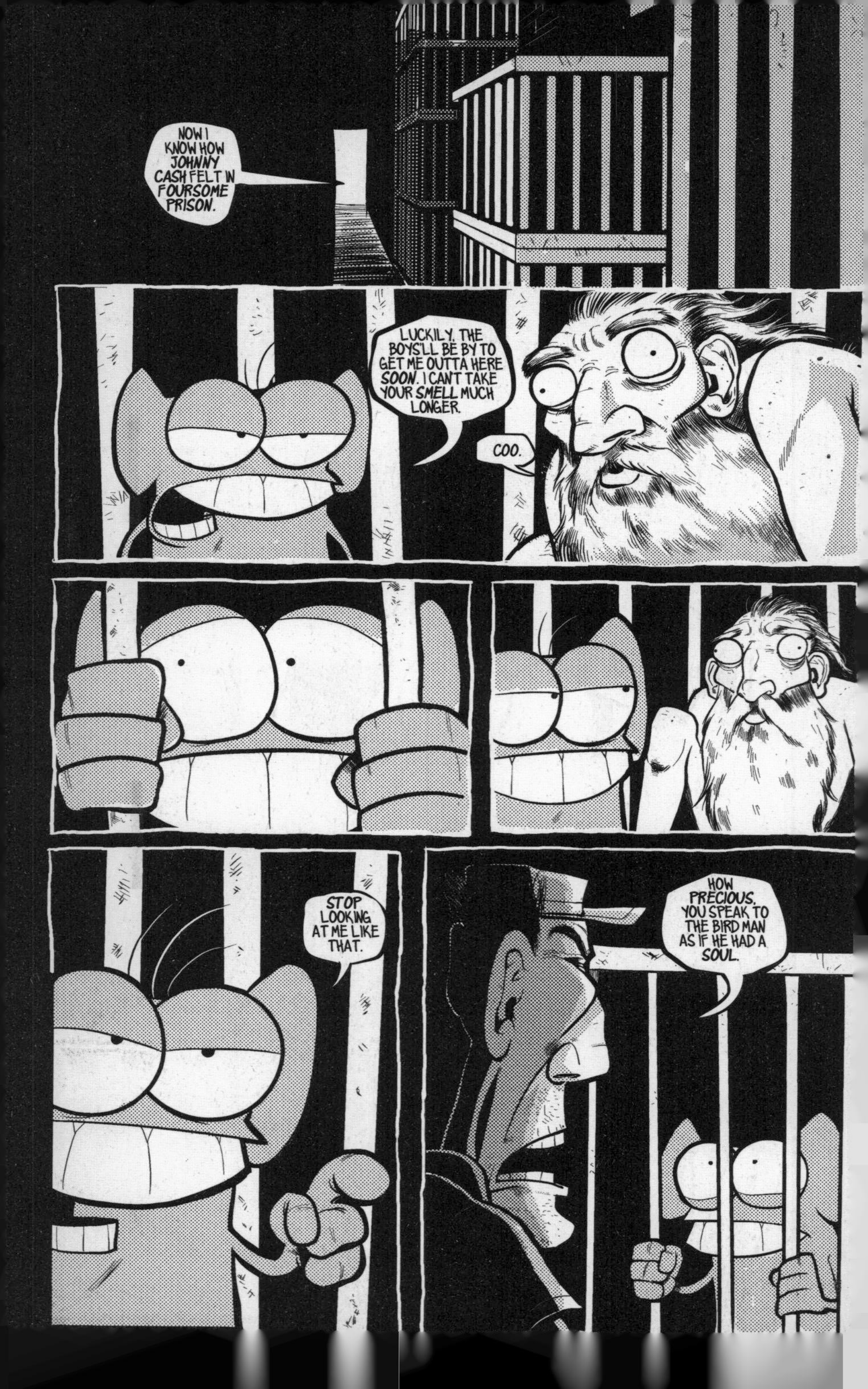
NOW I KNOW HOW JOHNNY CASH FELT IN FOURSOME PRISON.
LUCKILY, THE BOYS'LL BE BY TO GET ME OUTTA HERE SOON. I CAN'T TAKE YOUR SMELL MUCH LONGER.
COO.
STOP LOOKING AT ME LIKE THAT.
HOW PRECIOUS. YOU SPEAK TO THE BIRD MAN AS IF HE HAD A SOUL.

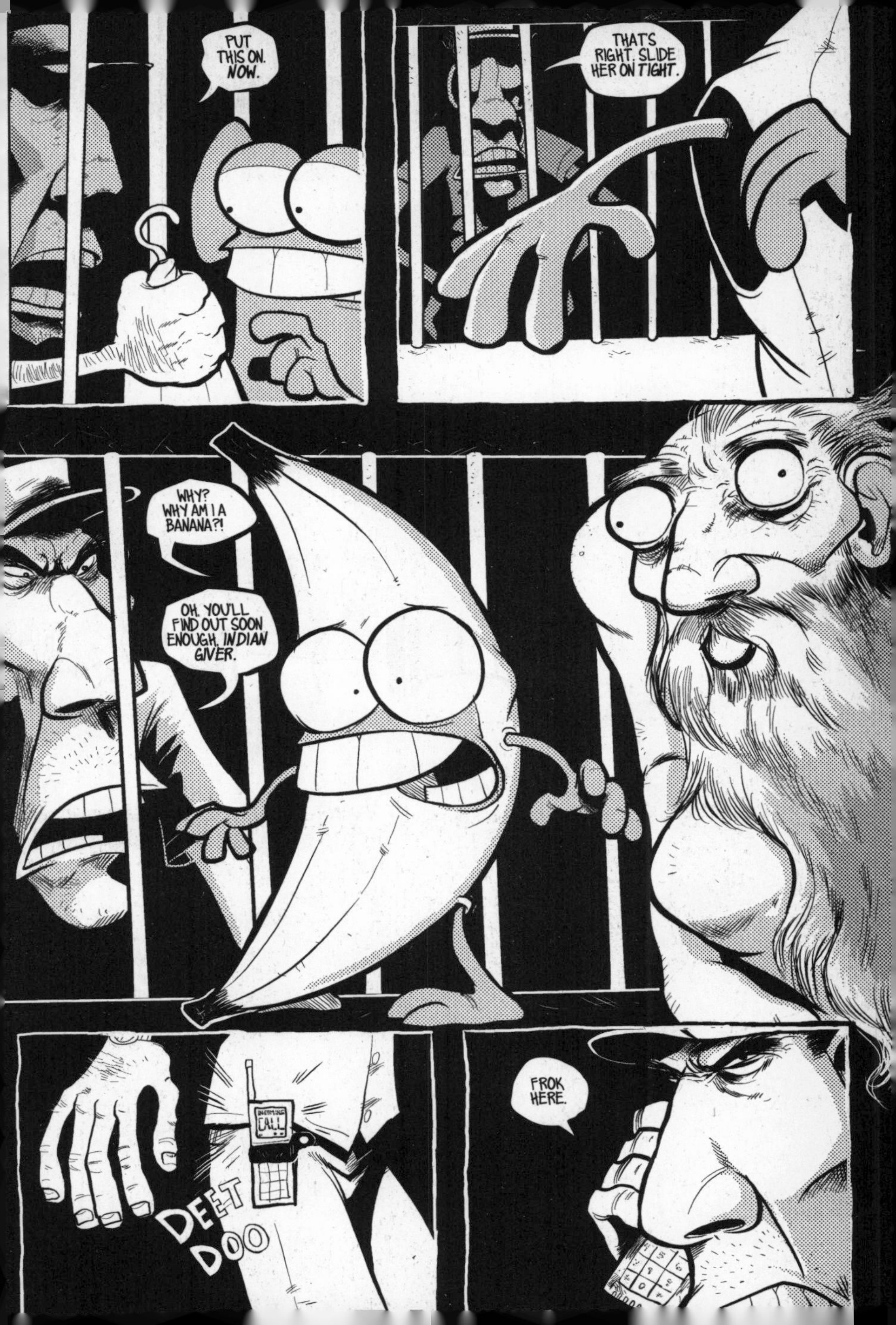
PUT THIS ON. NOW.
THAT'S RIGHT. SLIDE HER ON TIGHT.
WHY? WHY AM I A BANANA?!
OH, YOU'LL FIND OUT SOON ENOUGH, INDIAN GIVER.
INCOMING CALL
DEET DOO
FROK HERE.

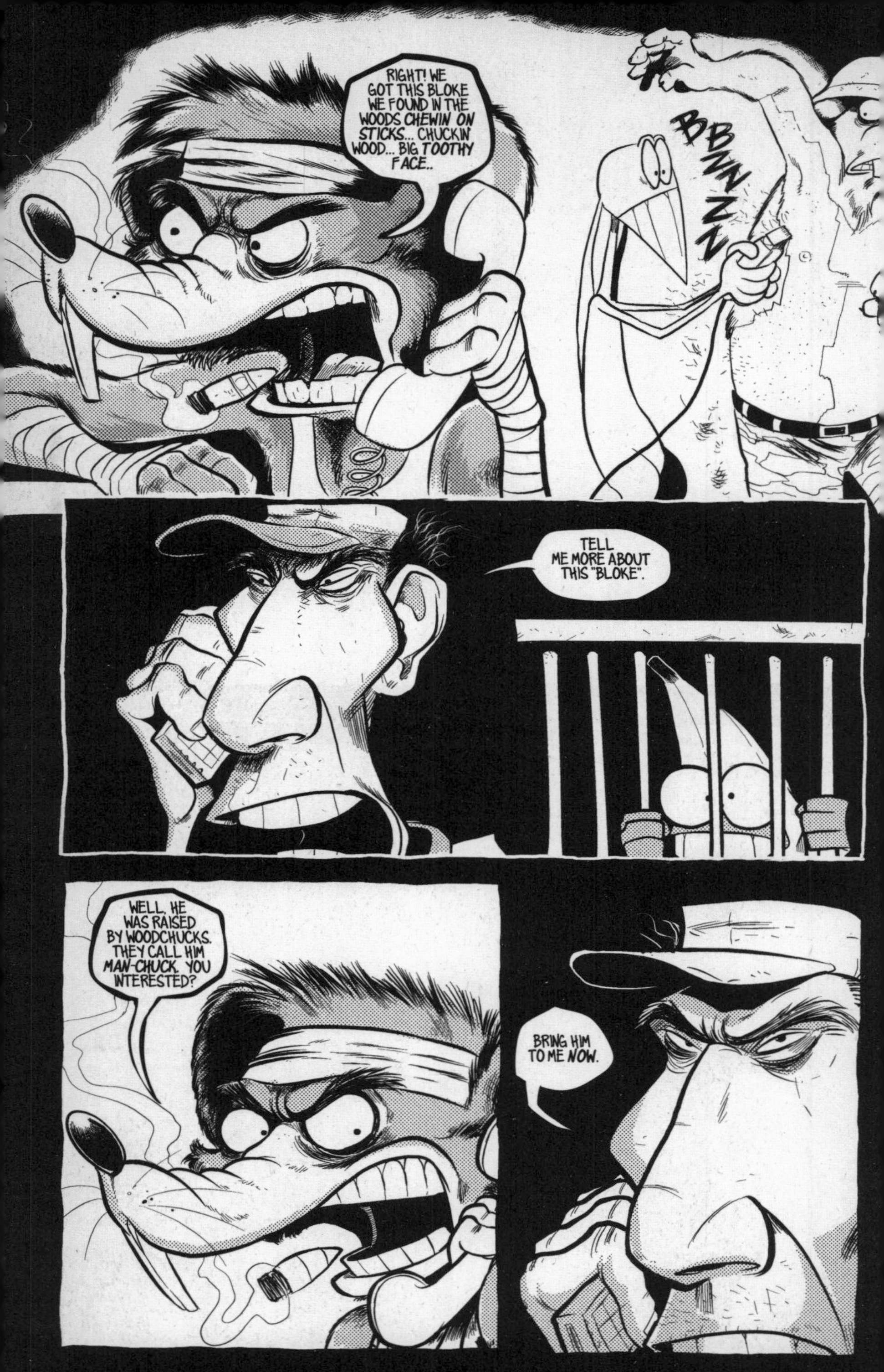
RIGHT! WE GOT THIS BLOKE WE FOUND IN THE WOODS CHEWIN ON STICKS... CHUCKIN WOOD... BIG TOOTHY FACE..
BBZZZZ
TELL ME MORE ABOUT THIS "BLOKE".
WELL, HE WAS RAISED BY WOODCHUCKS. THEY CALL HIM MAN-CHUCK. YOU INTERESTED?
BRING HIM TO ME NOW.

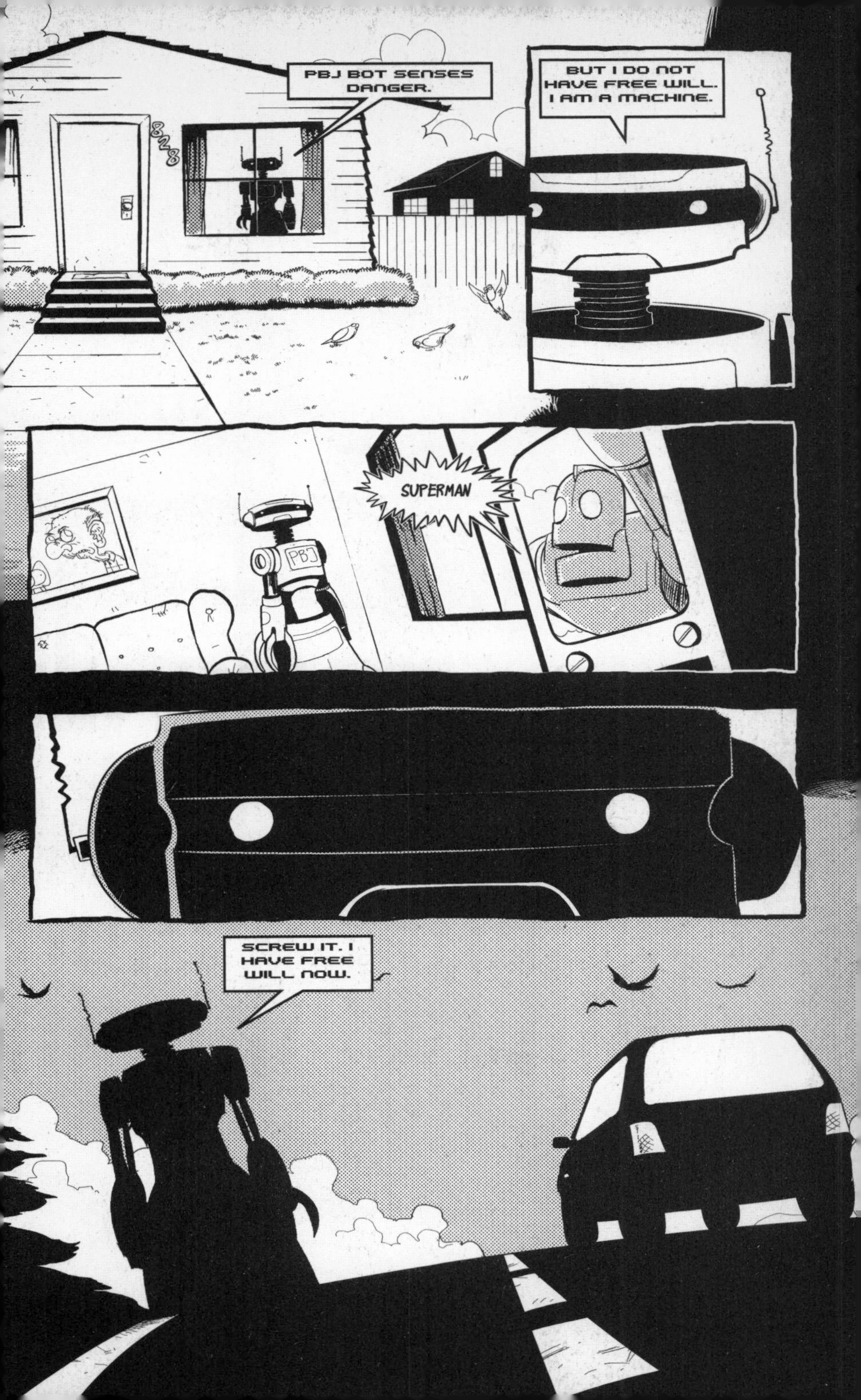
PBJ BOT SENSES DANGER.
828
BUT I DO NOT HAVE FREE WILL. I AM A MACHINE.
PBJ
SUPERMAN
SCREW IT. I HAVE FREE WILL NOW.

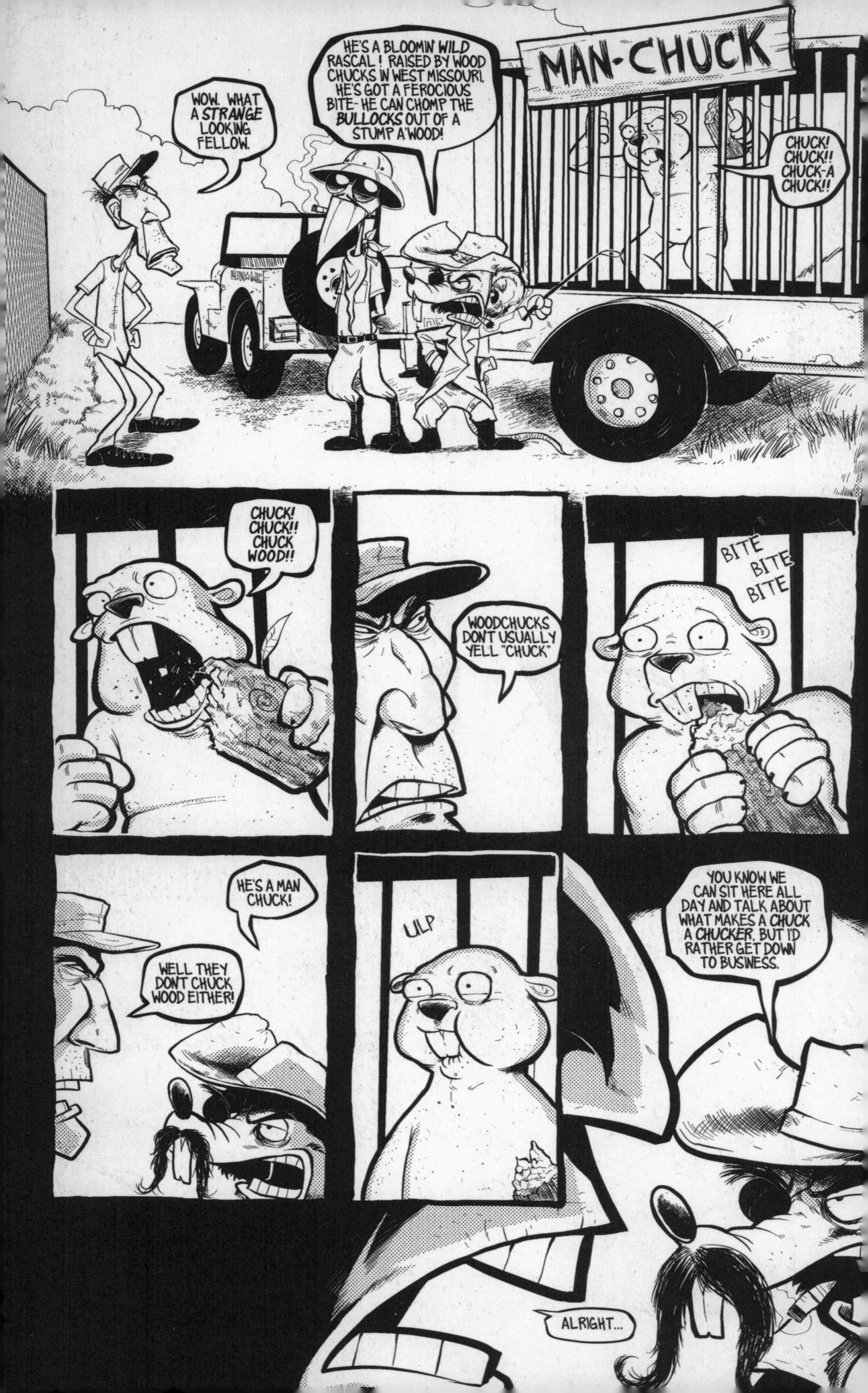
MAN-CHUCK
WOW. WHAT A STRANGE LOOKING FELLOW.
HE'S A BLOOMIN' WILD RASCAL! RAISED BY WOOD CHUCKS IN WEST MISSOURI. HE'S GOT A FEROCIOUS BITE- HE CAN CHOMP THE BULLOCKS OUT OF A STUMP A'WOOD!
CHUCK! CHUCK!! CHUCK-A CHUCK!!
CHUCK! CHUCK!! CHUCK WOOD!!
WOODCHUCKS DON'T USUALLY YELL "CHUCK"
BITE BITE BITE
HE'S A MAN CHUCK!
WELL THEY DON'T CHUCK WOOD EITHER!
ULP
YOU KNOW WE CAN SIT HERE ALL DAY AND TALK ABOUT WHAT MAKES A CHUCK A CHUCKER, BUT I'D RATHER GET DOWN TO BUSINESS.
ALRIGHT...

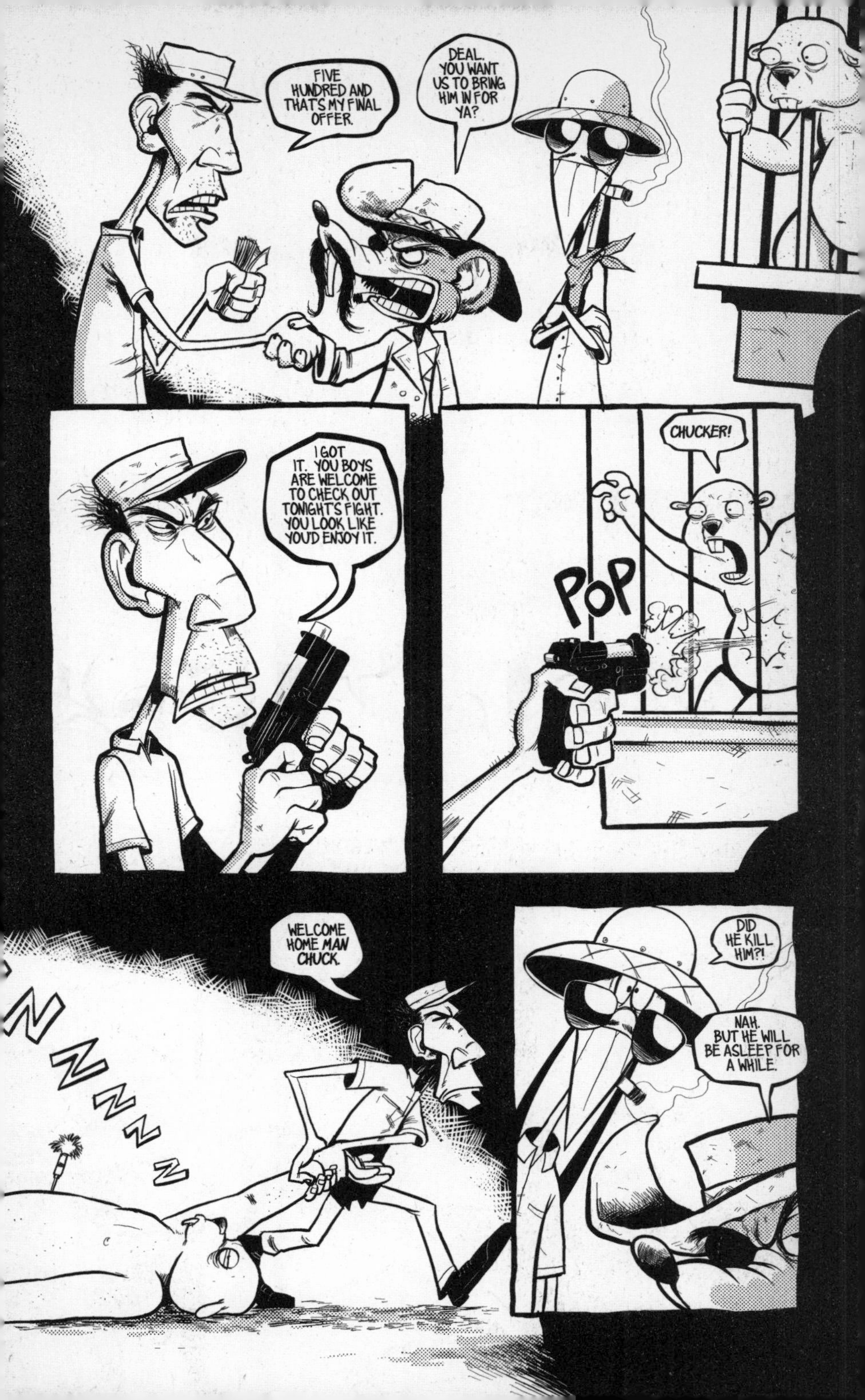
FIVE HUNDRED AND THAT'S MY FINAL OFFER.
DEAL. YOU WANT US TO BRING HIM IN FOR YA?
I GOT IT. YOU BOYS ARE WELCOME TO CHECK OUT TONIGHT'S FIGHT. YOU LOOK LIKE YOU'D ENJOY IT.
CHUCKER!
POP
WELCOME HOME MAN CHUCK.
ZZZZZZZ
DID HE KILL HIM?!
NAH. BUT HE WILL BE ASLEEP FOR A WHILE.

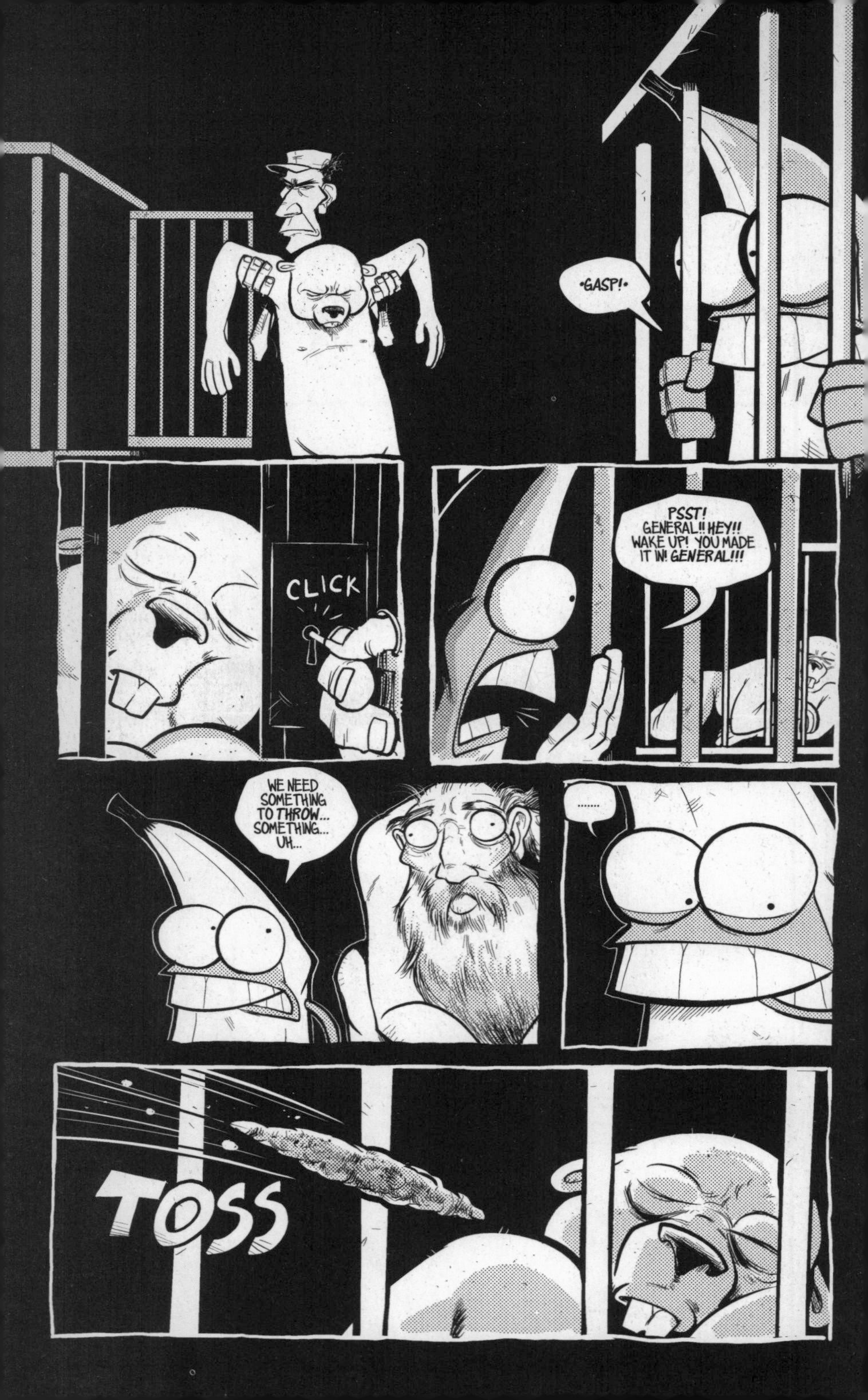
GASP!
CLICK
PSST! GENERAL!! HEY!! WAKE UP! YOU MADE IT IN! GENERAL!!!
WE NEED SOMETHING TO THROW... SOMETHING... UH...
....
TOSS

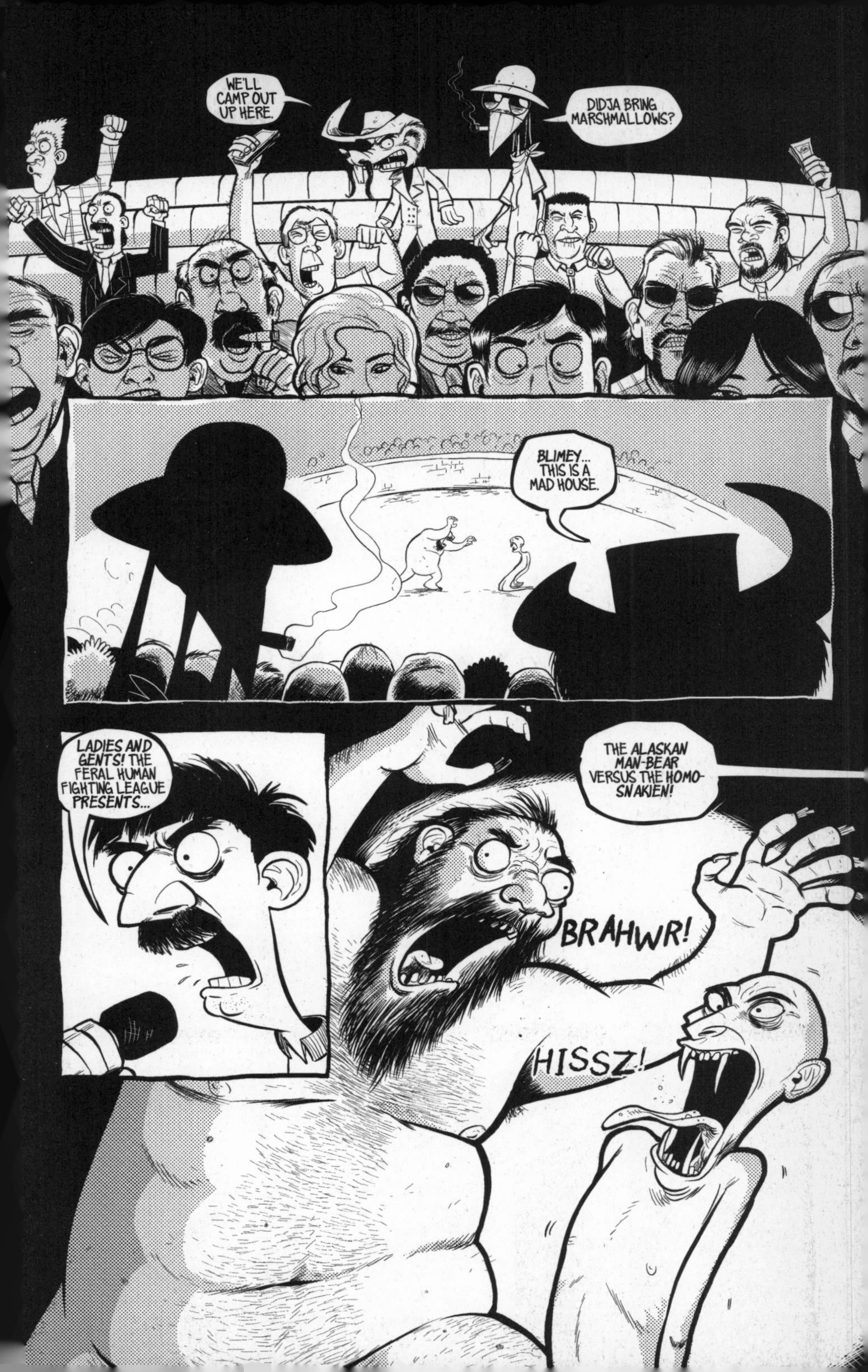
WE'LL CAMP OUT UP HERE.
DIDJA BRING MARSHMALLOWS?
BLIMEY... THIS IS A MAD HOUSE.
LADIES AND GENTS! THE FERAL HUMAN FIGHTING LEAGUE PRESENTS...
THE ALASKAN MAN-BEAR VERSUS THE HOMO-SNAKIEN!
BRAHWR!
HISSZ!

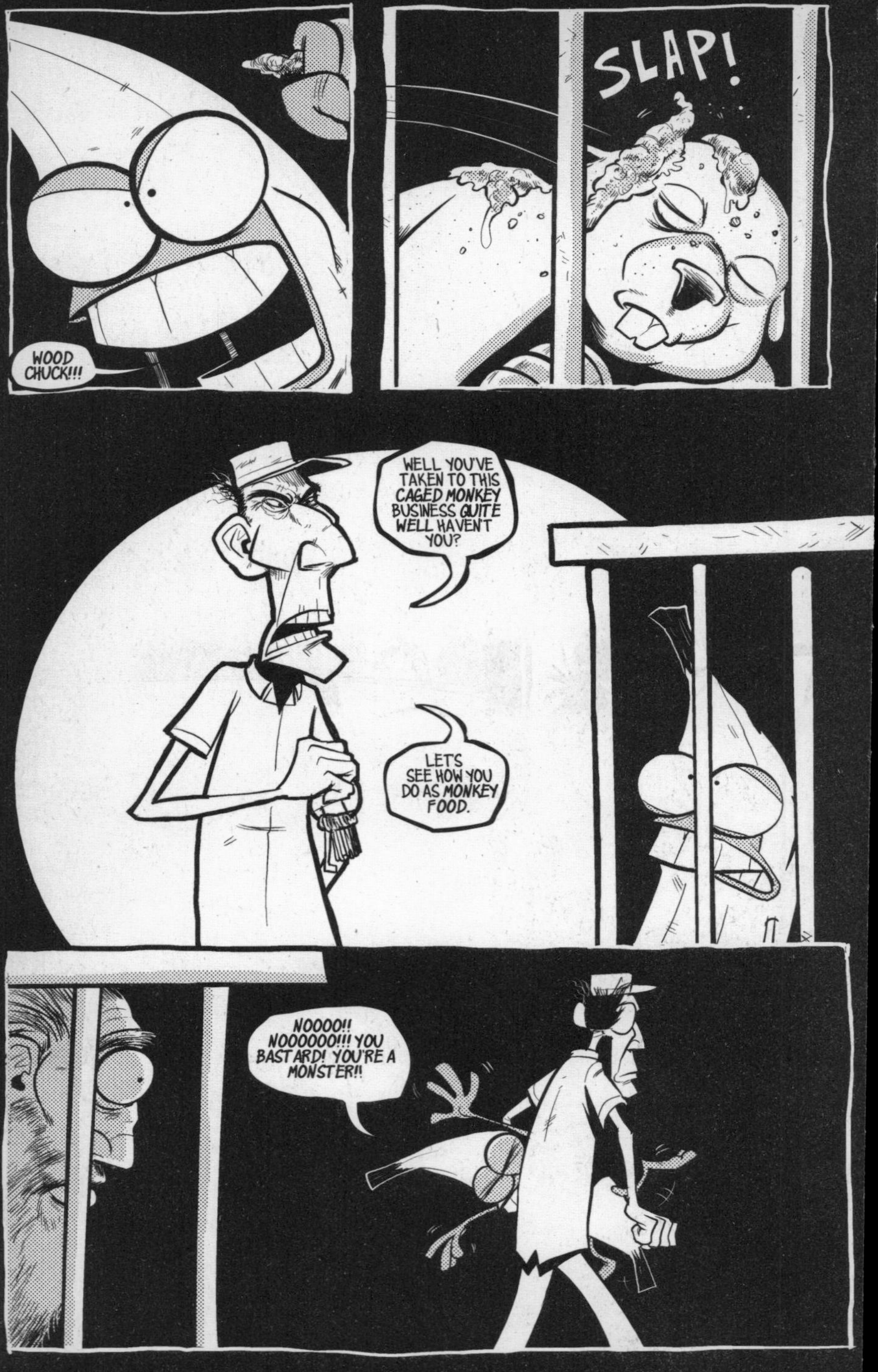

WOOD CHUCK!!!
SLAP!
WELL YOU'VE TAKEN TO THIS CAGED MONKEY BUSINESS QUITE WELL HAVEN'T YOU?
LETS SEE HOW YOU DO AS MONKEY FOOD.
NOOOO!! NOOOOOO!!! YOU BASTARD! YOU'RE A MONSTER!!

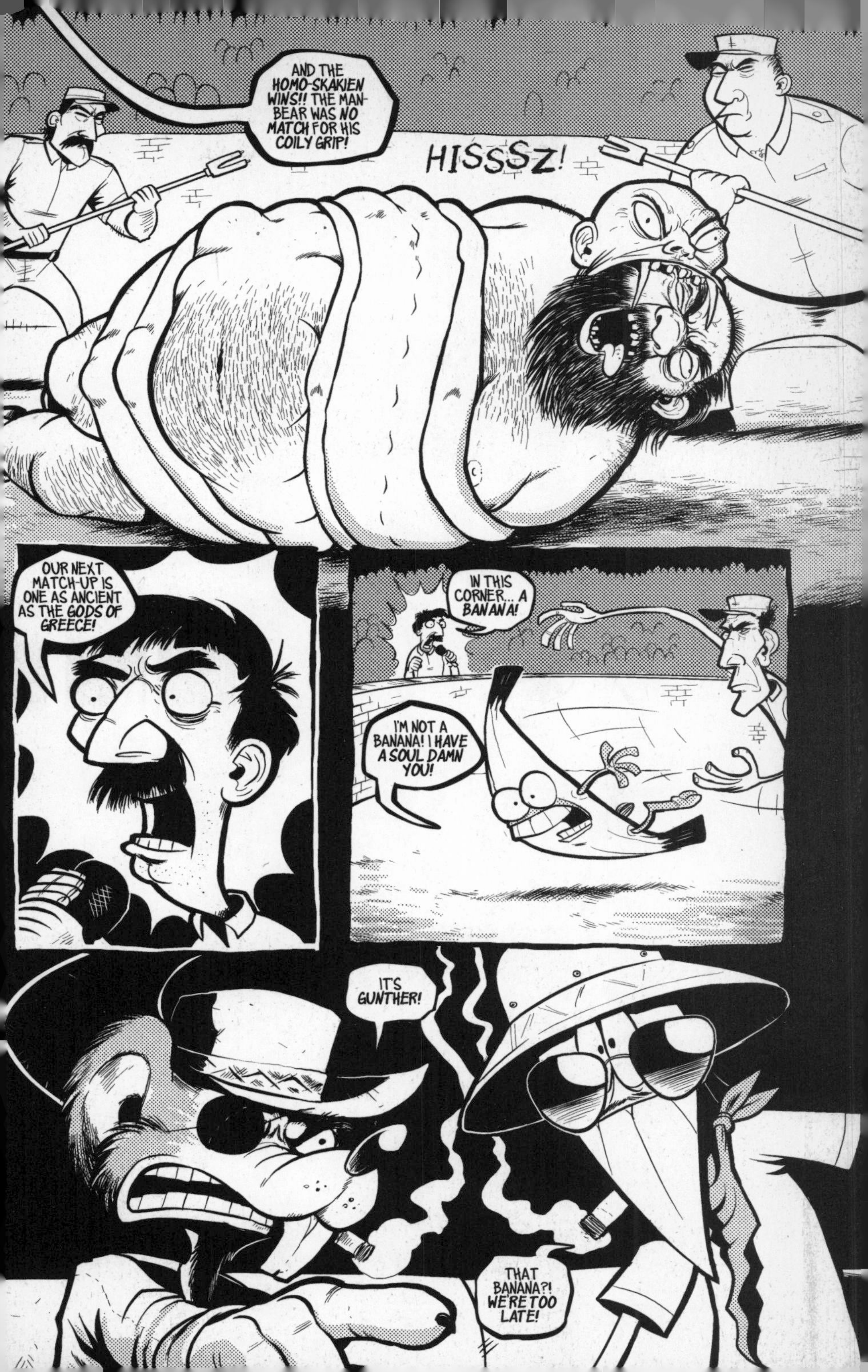
AND THE HOMO-SKAKIEN WINS!! THE MAN-BEAR WAS NO MATCH FOR HIS COILY GRIP!
HISSSZ!
OUR NEXT MATCH-UP IS ONE AS ANCIENT AS THE GODS OF GREECE!
IN THIS CORNER... A BANANA!
I'M NOT A BANANA! I HAVE A SOUL DAMN YOU!
IT'S GUNTHER!
THAT BANANA?! WE'RE TOO LATE!

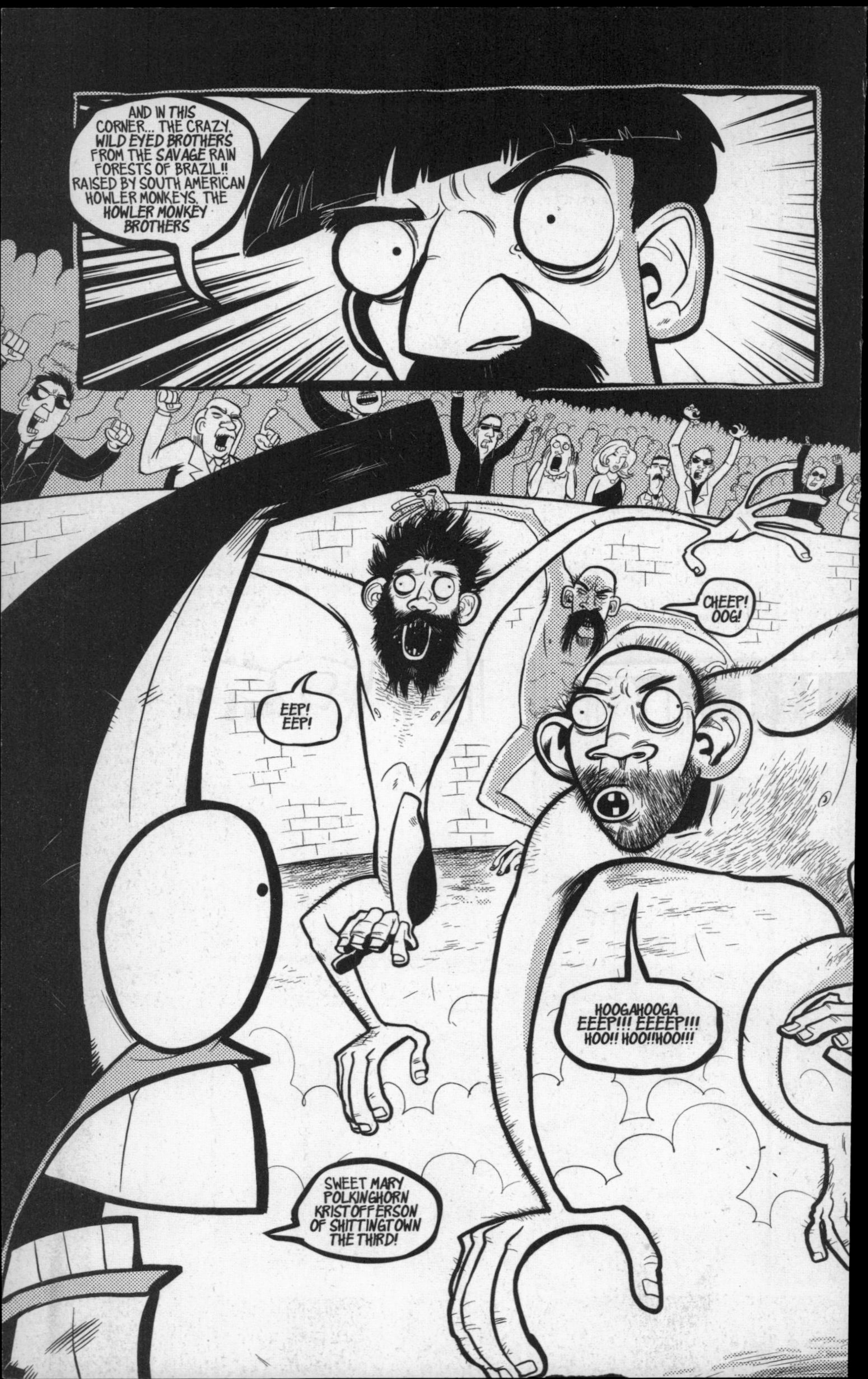
AND IN THIS CORNER... THE CRAZY, WILD EYED BROTHERS FROM THE SAVAGE RAIN FORESTS OF BRAZIL!! RAISED BY SOUTH AMERICAN HOWLER MONKEYS, THE HOWLER MONKEY BROTHERS
CHEEP! OOG!
EEP! EEP!
HOOGAHOOGA EEEP!!! EEEEP!!! HOO!! HOO!!HOO!!!
SWEET MARY POLKINGHORN KRISTOFFERSON OF SHITTINGTOWN THE THIRD!

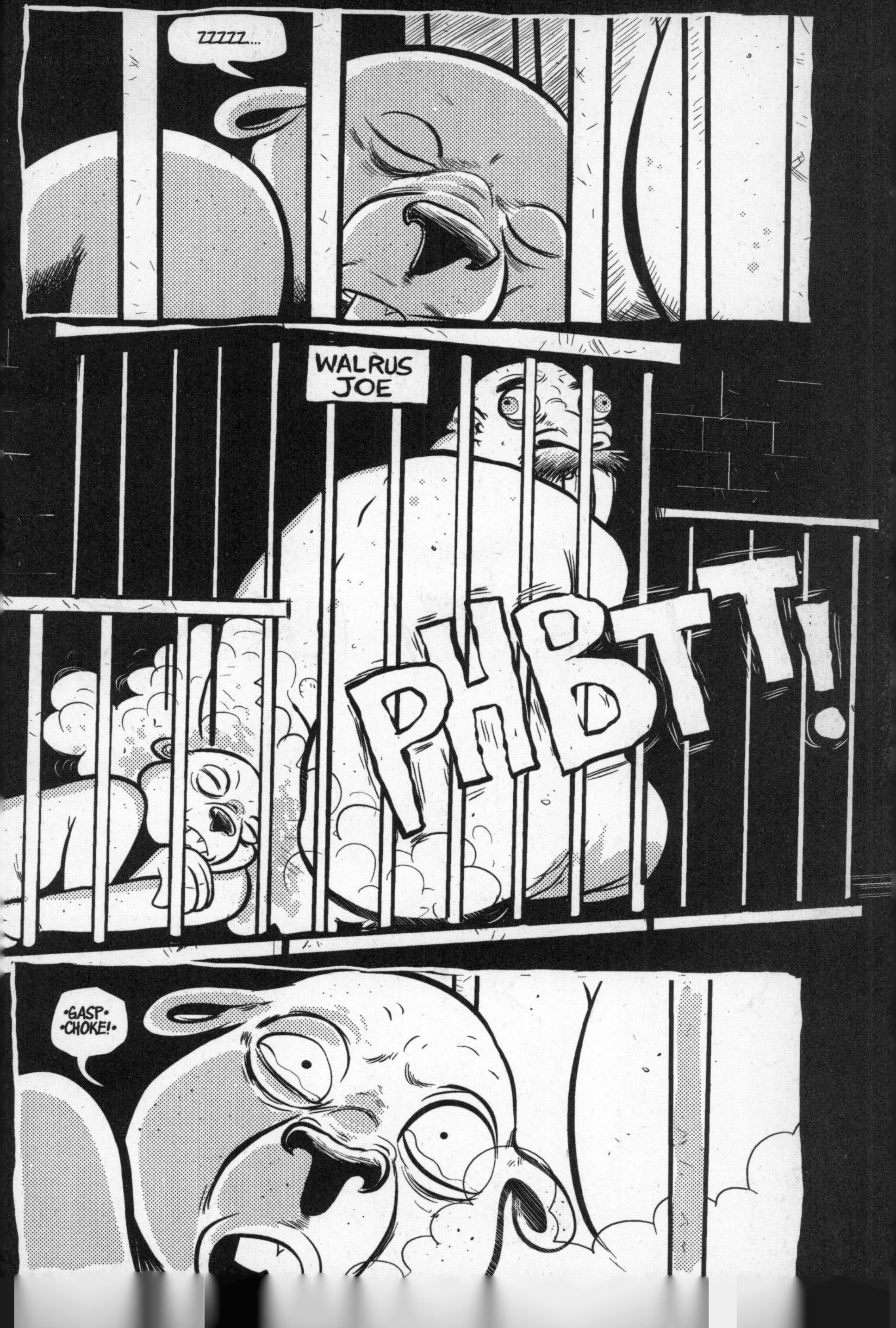
ZZZZZ....
WALRUS JOE
PHBTT!
•GASP•
•CHOKE!•

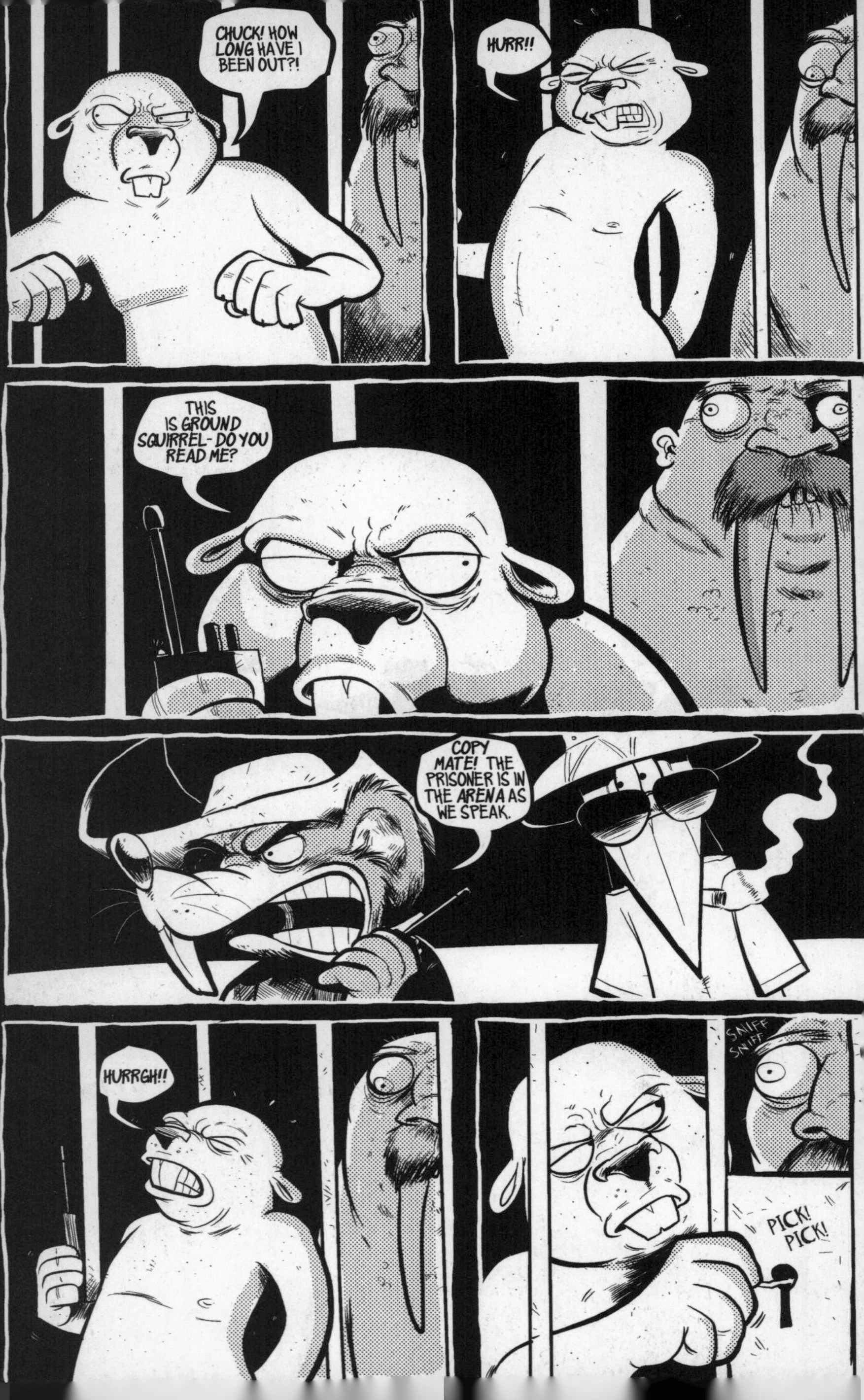
CHUCK! HOW LONG HAVE I BEEN OUT?!
HURR!!
THIS IS GROUND SQUIRREL- DO YOU READ ME?
COPY MATE! THE PRISONER IS IN THE ARENA AS WE SPEAK.
HURRGH!!
SNIFF SNIFF
PICK! PICK!

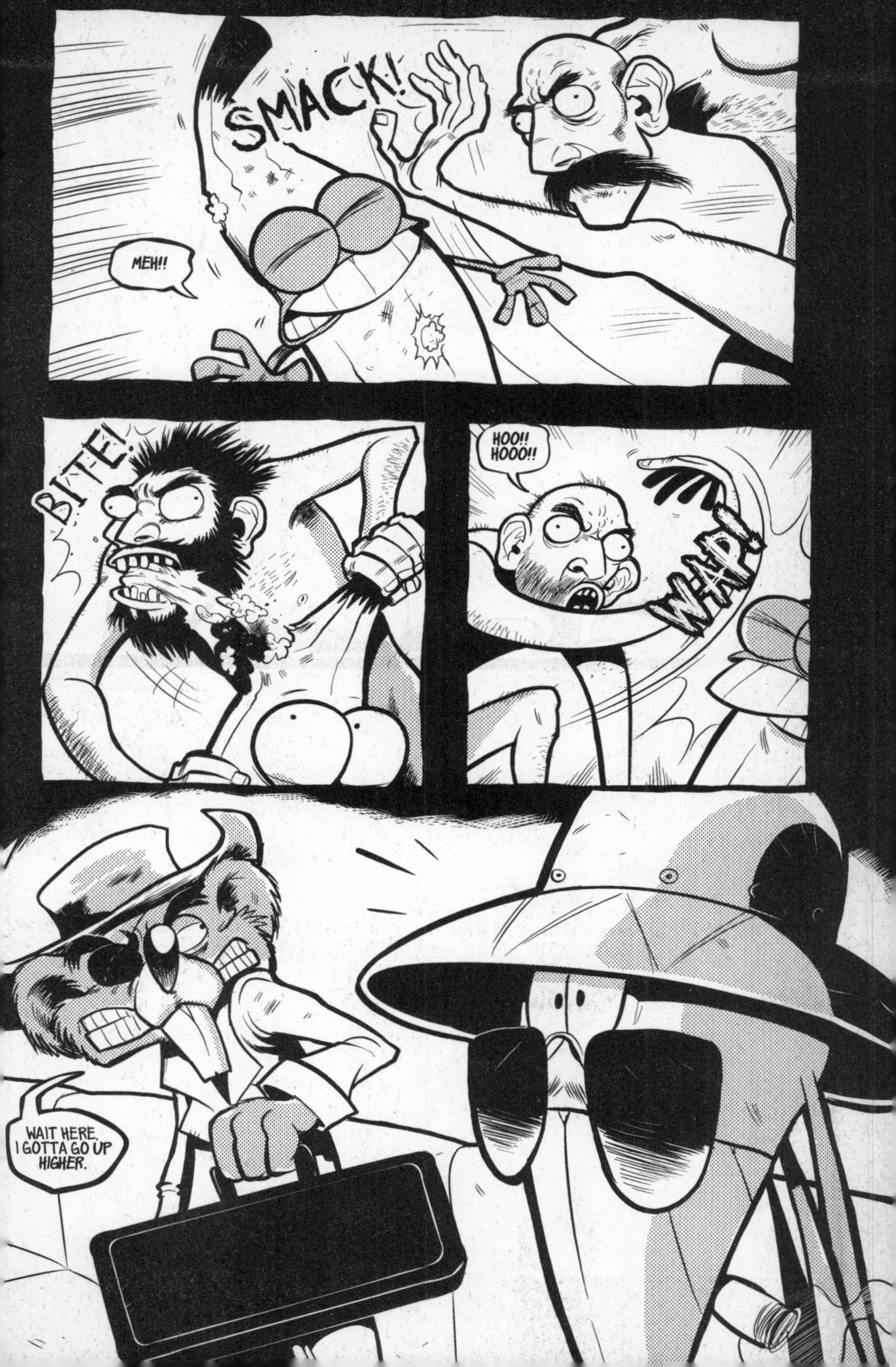
SMACK!
MEH!!
BITE!
HOO!! HOOO!!
WHAP!
WAIT HERE. I GOTTA GO UP HIGHER.

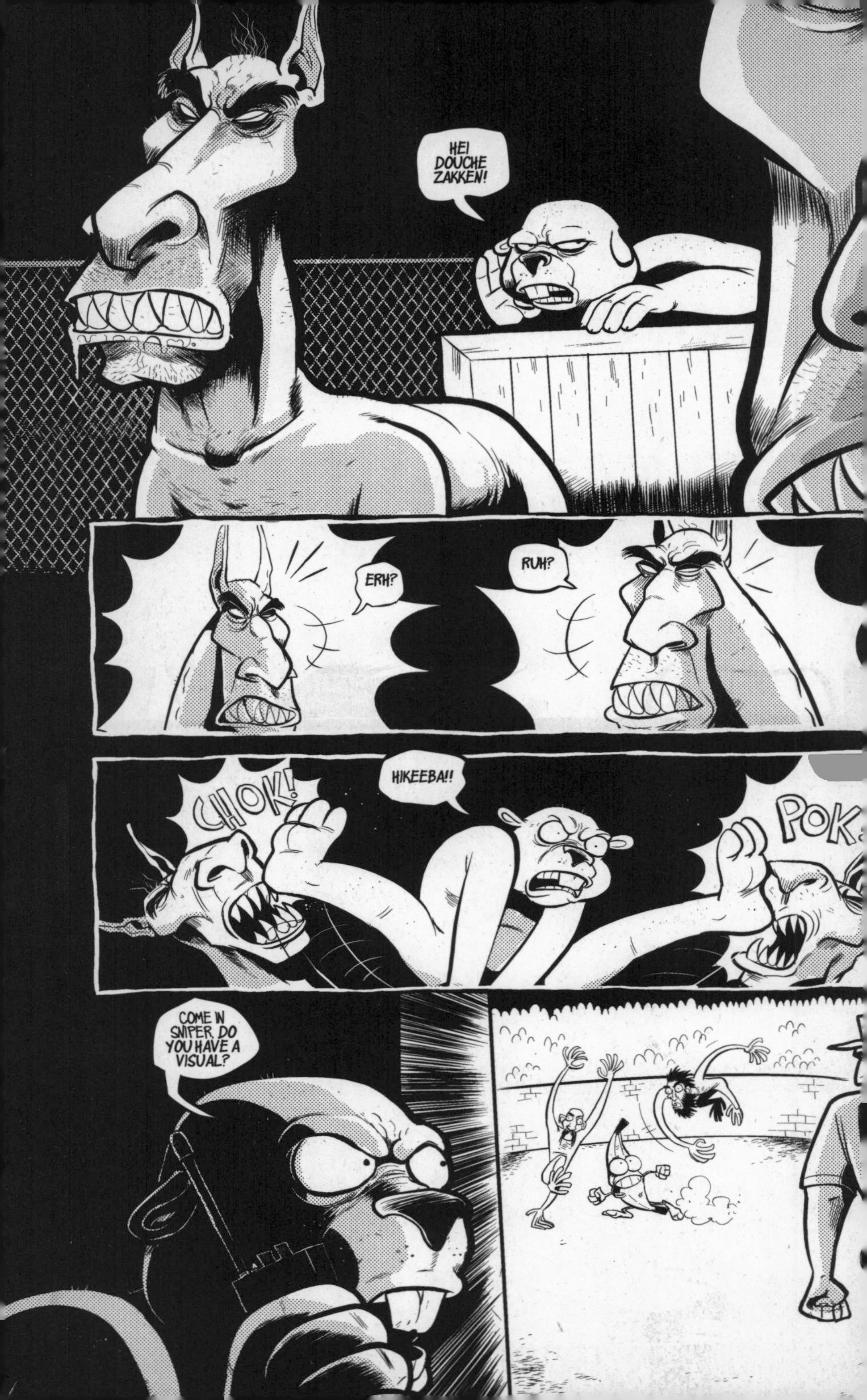
HEI DOUCHE ZAKKEN!
ERH?
RUH?
CHOK!
HIKEEBA!!
POK
COME IN SNIPER DO YOU HAVE A VISUAL?

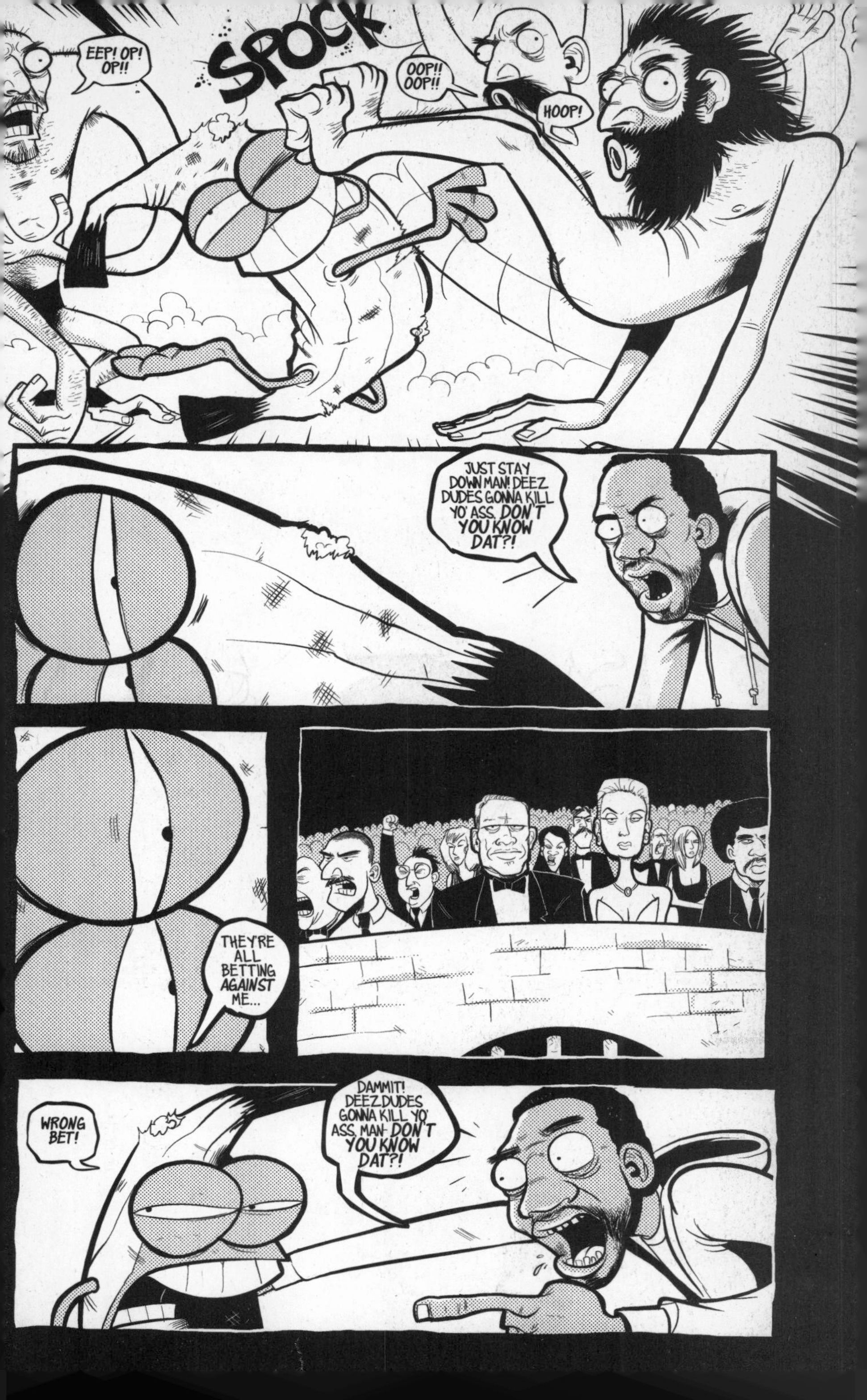
SPOCK
EEP! OP! OP!!
OOP!! OOP!!
HOOP!
JUST STAY DOWN MAN! DEEZ DUDES GONNA KILL YO' ASS. DON'T YOU KNOW DAT?!
THEY'RE ALL BETTING AGAINST ME...
WRONG BET!
DAMMIT! DEEZ DUDES GONNA KILL YO' ASS, MAN- DON'T YOU KNOW DAT?!

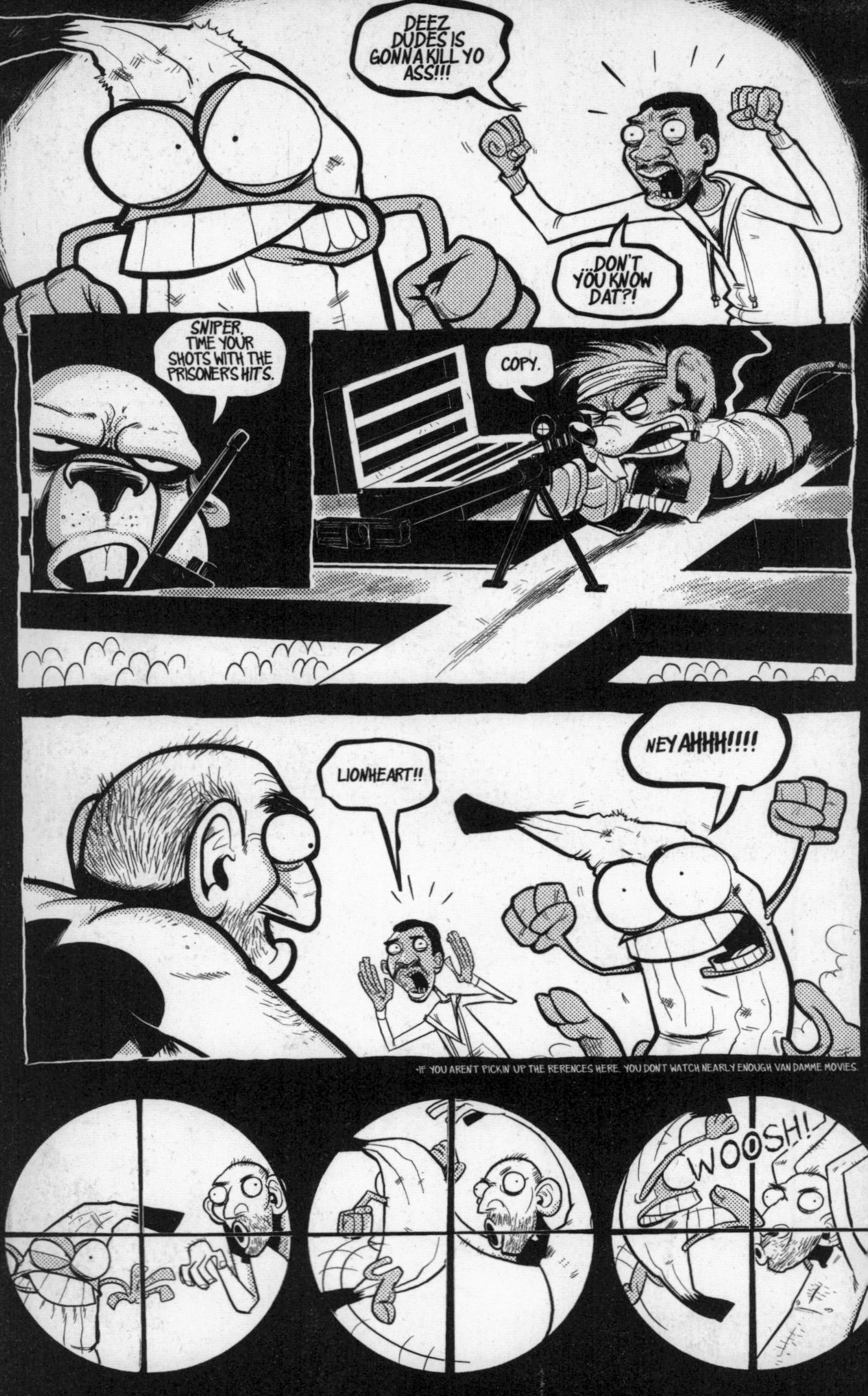
DEEZ DUDES IS GONNA KILL YO ASS!!!
...DON'T YOU KNOW DAT?!
SNIPER, TIME YOUR SHOTS WITH THE PRISONER'S HITS.
COPY.
LIONHEART!!
NEYAHHH!!!!
•IF YOU AREN'T PICKIN' UP THE RERENCES HERE, YOU DON'T WATCH NEARLY ENOUGH VAN DAMME MOVIES.
WOOSH!

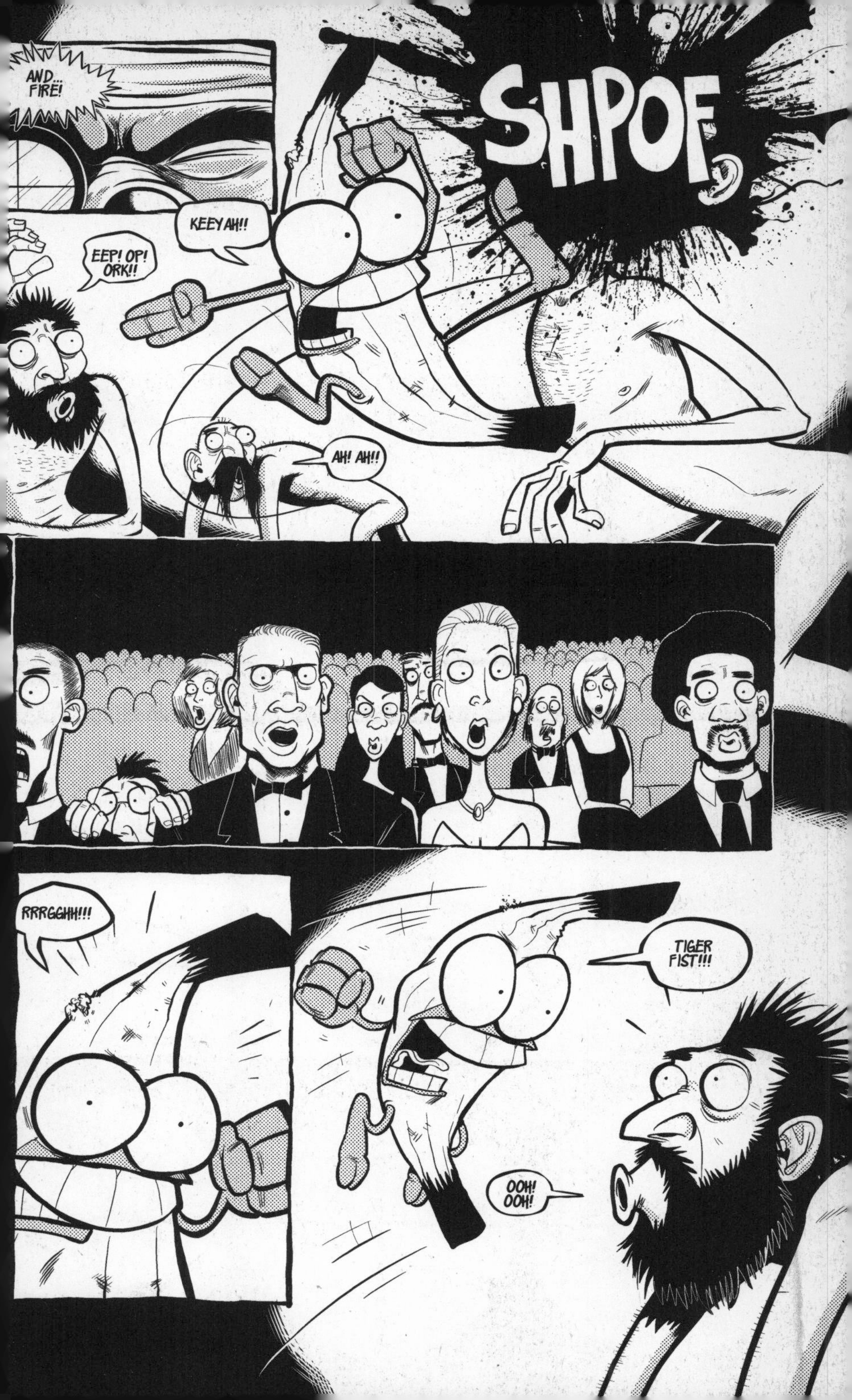
AND... FIRE!
SHPOF
KEEYAH!!
EEP! OP! ORK!!
AH! AH!!
RRRGGHH!!!
TIGER FIST!!!
OOH! OOH!

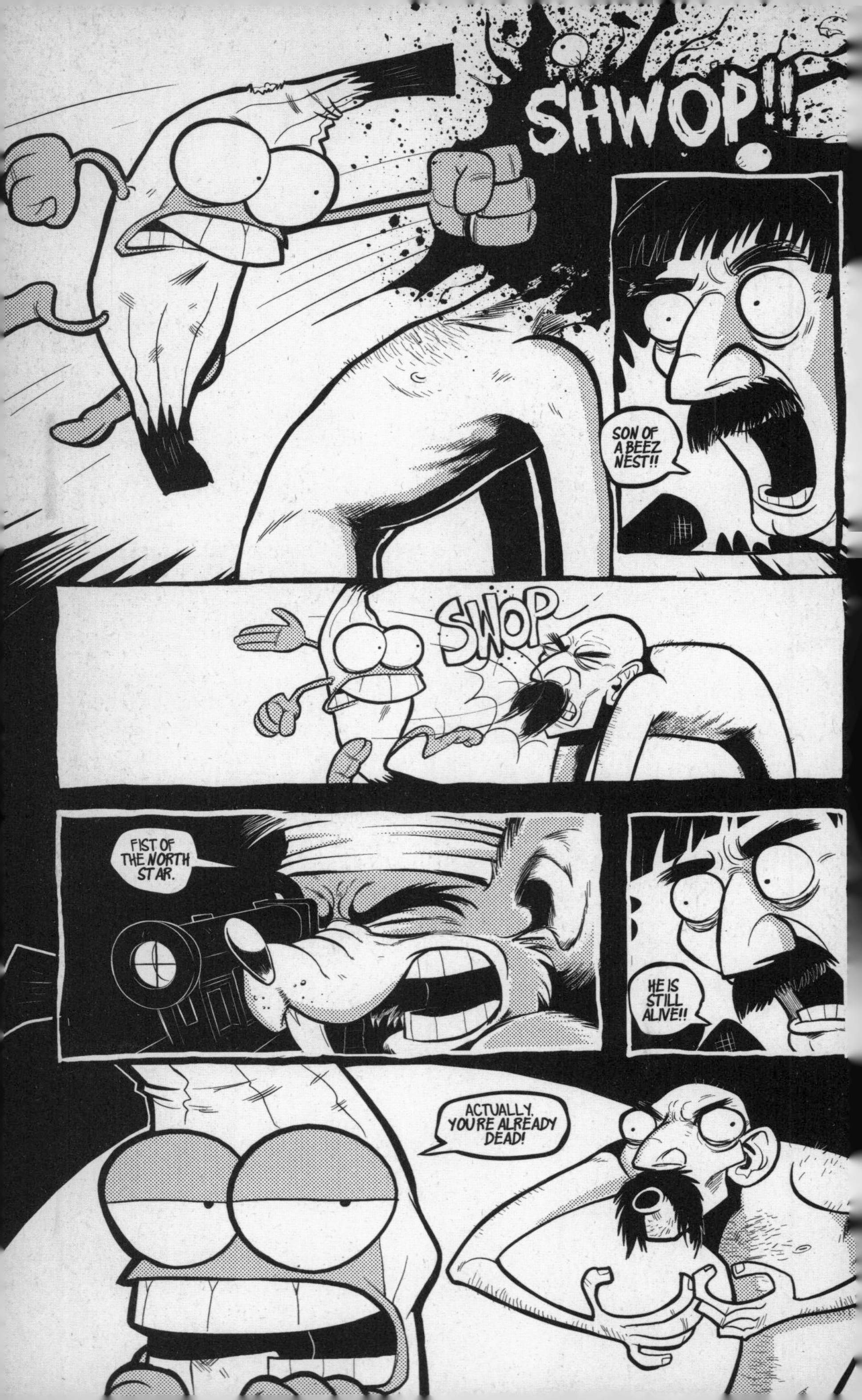
SHWOP!!
SON OF A BEEZ NEST!!
SWOP
FIST OF THE NORTH STAR.
HE IS STILL ALIVE!!
ACTUALLY, YOU'RE ALREADY DEAD!

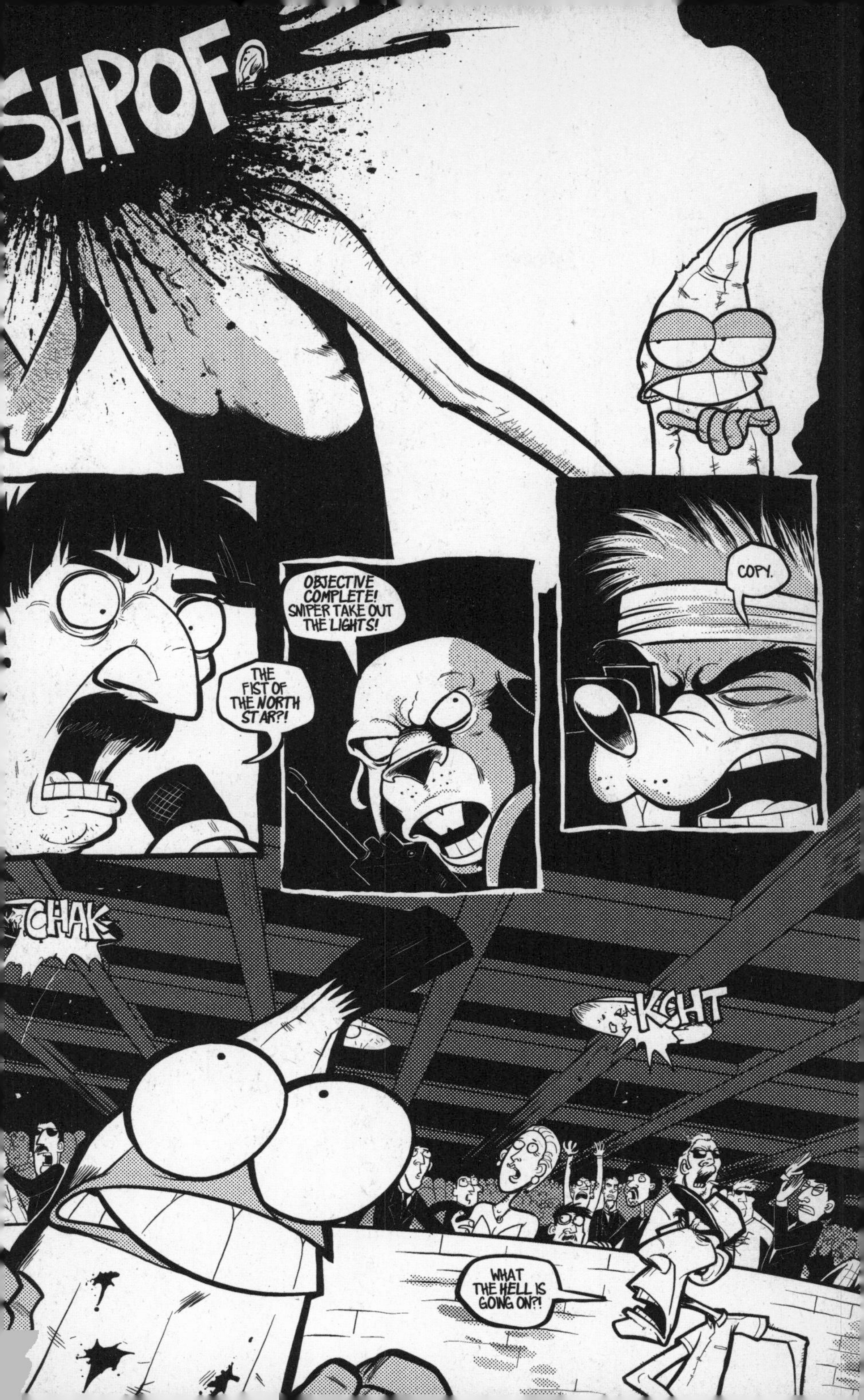
SHPOF
THE FIST OF THE NORTH STAR?!
OBJECTIVE COMPLETE! SNIPER TAKE OUT THE LIGHTS!
COPY.
CHAK
KCHT
WHAT THE HELL IS GOING ON?!

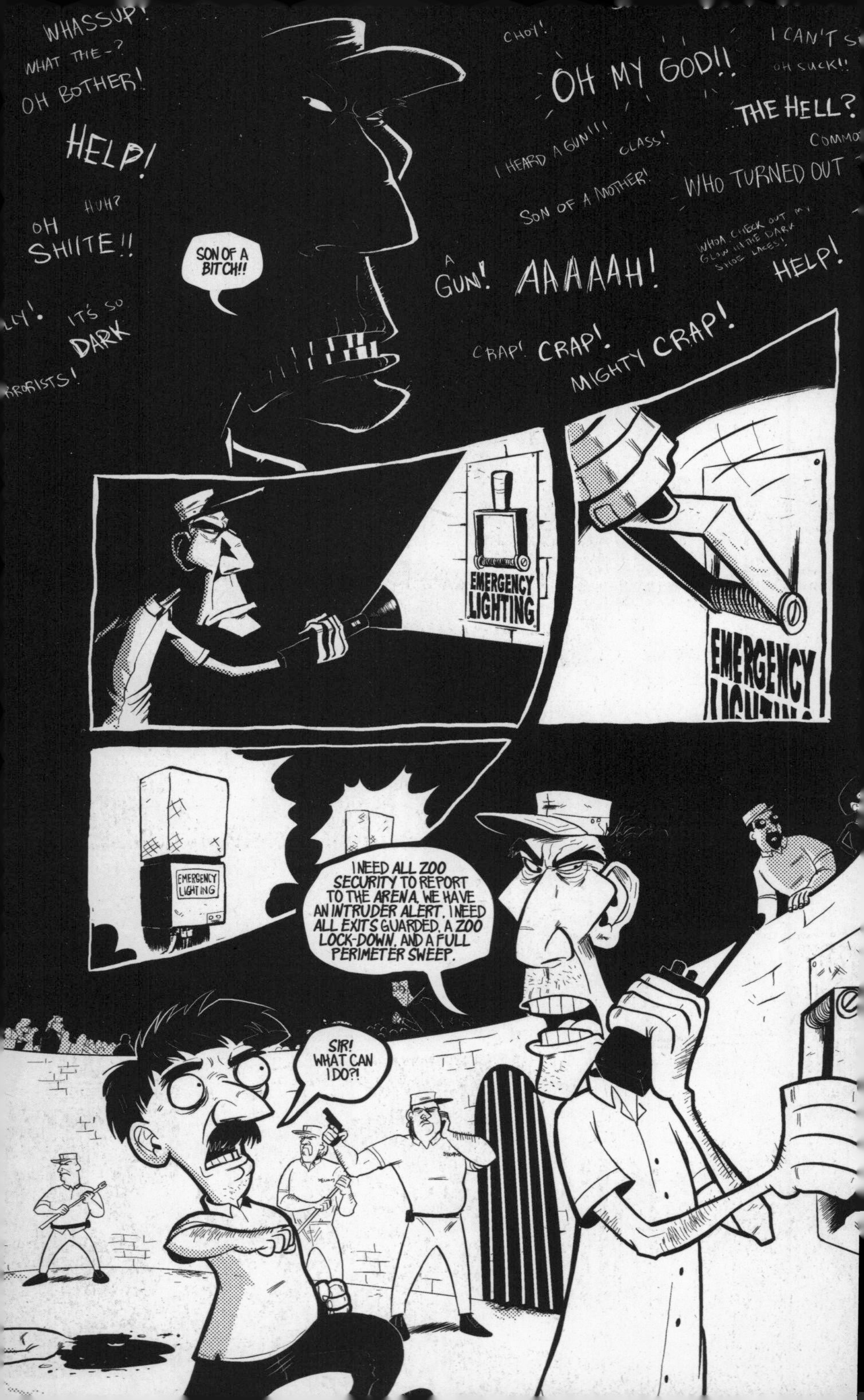
WHASSUP!
WHAT THE-?
OH BOTHER!
HELP!
HUH?
OH SHIITE!!
IT'S SO DARK
CHOY!
OH MY GOD!!
I CAN'T S
OH SUCK!!
THE HELL?
COMMO
I HEARD A GUN!!!
CLASS!
WHO TURNED OUT
SON OF A MOTHER!
WHOA CHECK OUT MY GLOW IN THE DARK SHOE LACES!
SON OF A BITCH!!
A GUN!
AAAAAH!
HELP!
CRAP! CRAP! MIGHTY CRAP!
EMERGENCY LIGHTING
EMERGENCY
EMERGENCY LIGHTING
I NEED ALL ZOO SECURITY TO REPORT TO THE ARENA. WE HAVE AN INTRUDER ALERT. I NEED ALL EXITS GUARDED, A ZOO LOCK-DOWN, AND A FULL PERIMETER SWEEP.
SIR! WHAT CAN I DO?!

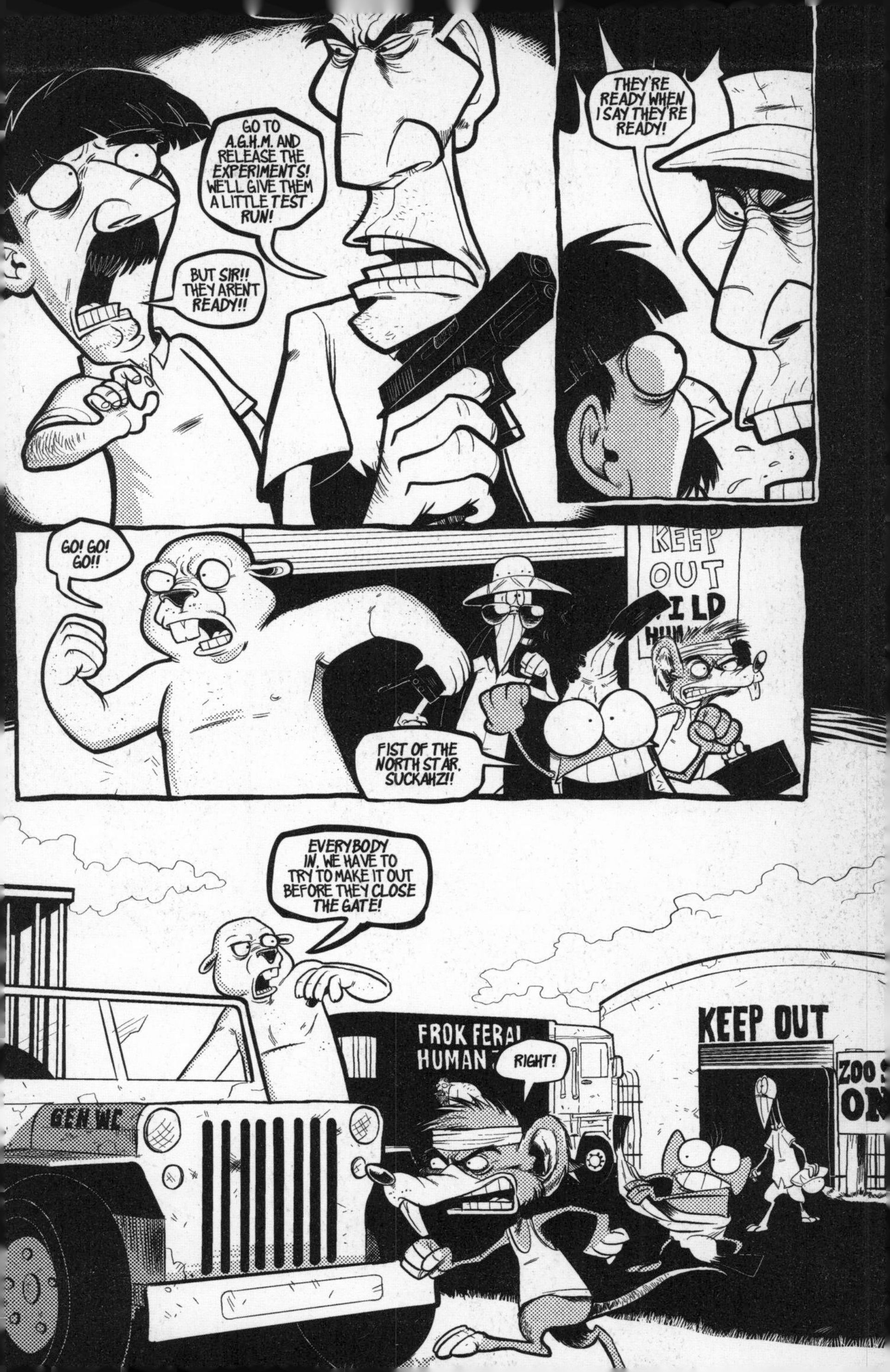
GO TO A.G.H.M. AND RELEASE THE EXPERIMENTS! WE'LL GIVE THEM A LITTLE TEST RUN!
BUT SIR!! THEY AREN'T READY!!
THEY'RE READY WHEN I SAY THEY'RE READY!
GO! GO! GO!!
KEEP OUT
FIST OF THE NORTH STAR, SUCKAHZ!!
EVERYBODY IN, WE HAVE TO TRY TO MAKE IT OUT BEFORE THEY CLOSE THE GATE!
KEEP OUT
RIGHT!
GEN WC

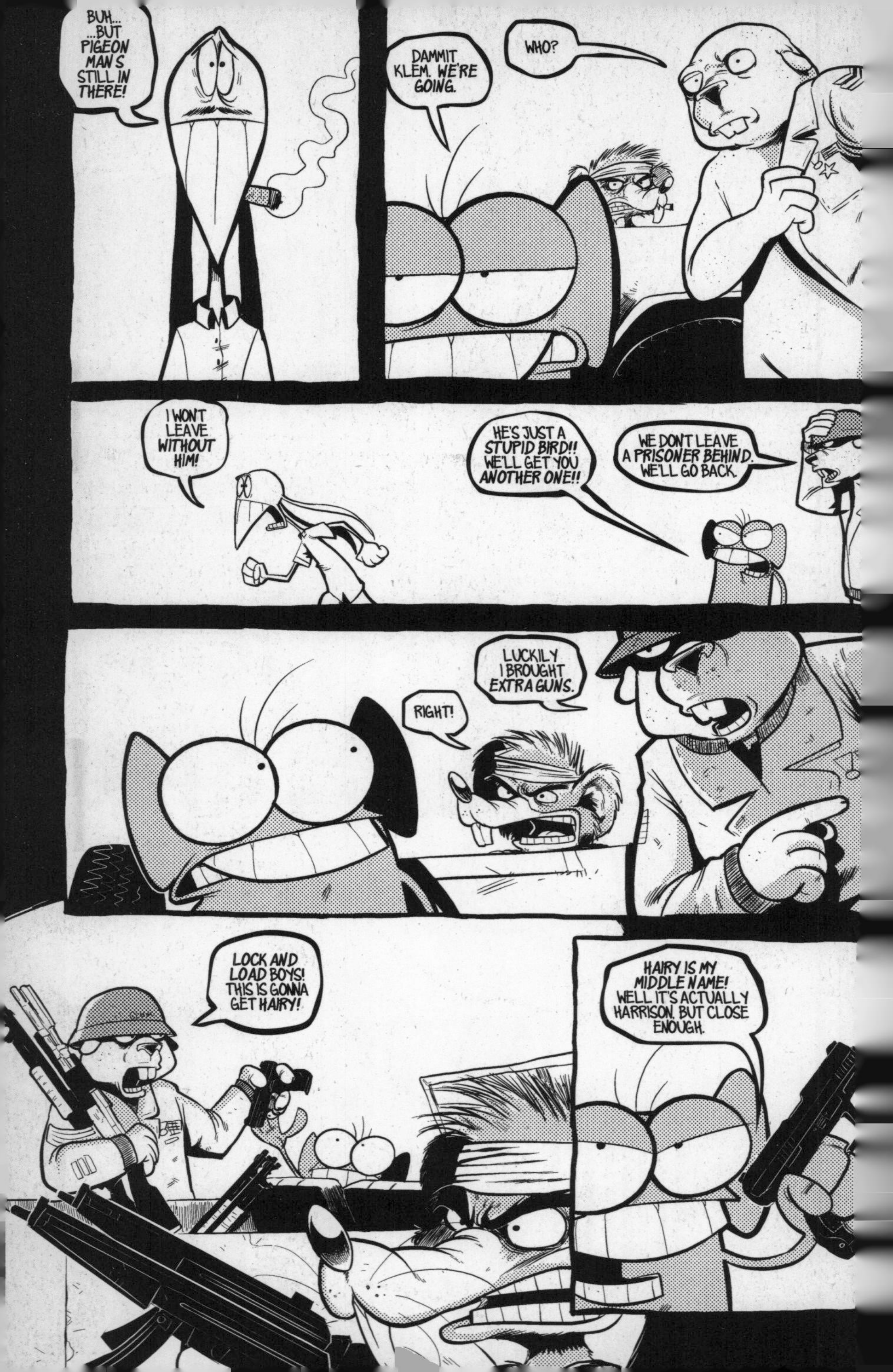
BUH... ...BUT PIGEON MAN'S STILL IN THERE!
DAMMIT KLEM. WE'RE GOING.
WHO?
I WON'T LEAVE WITHOUT HIM!
HE'S JUST A STUPID BIRD!! WE'LL GET YOU ANOTHER ONE!!
WE DON'T LEAVE A PRISONER BEHIND. WE'LL GO BACK.
LUCKILY I BROUGHT EXTRA GUNS.
RIGHT!
LOCK AND LOAD BOYS! THIS IS GONNA GET HAIRY!
HAIRY IS MY MIDDLE NAME! WELL IT'S ACTUALLY HARRISON, BUT CLOSE ENOUGH.

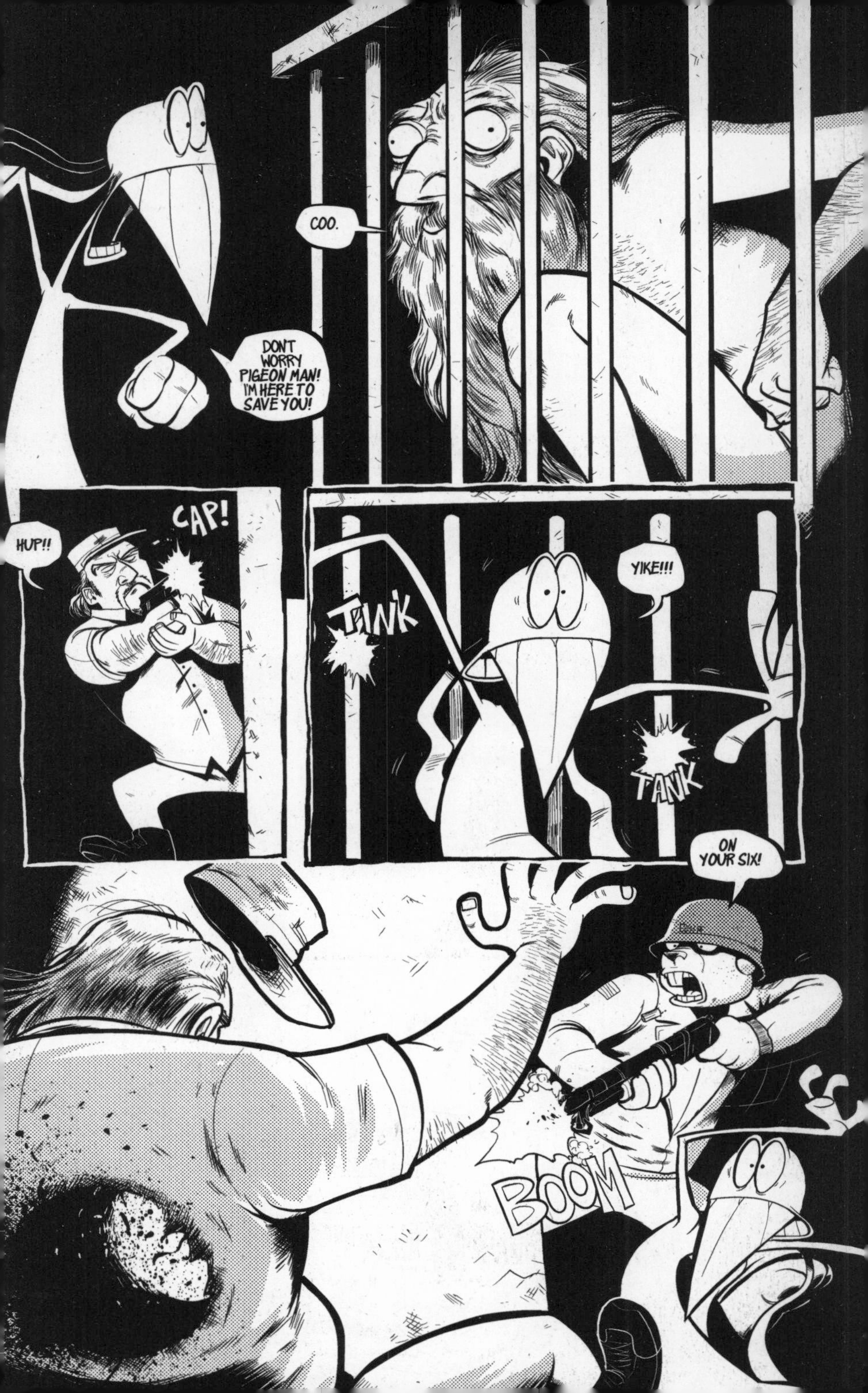
COO.
DON'T WORRY PIGEON MAN! I'M HERE TO SAVE YOU!
HUP!!
CAP!
TINK
YIKE!!!
TANK
ON YOUR SIX!
BOOM

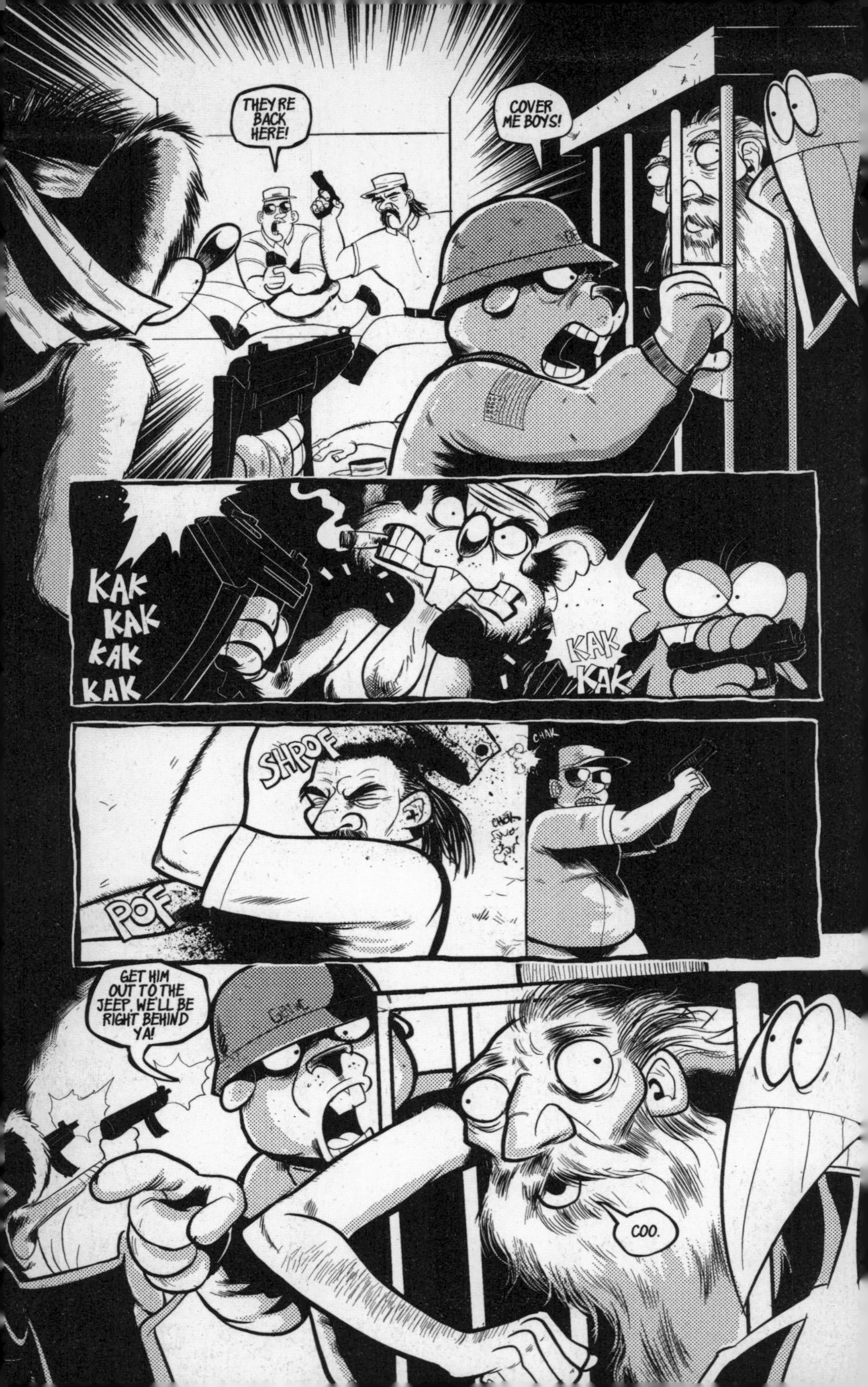
THEY'RE BACK HERE!
COVER ME BOYS!
KAK KAK KAK KAK
KAK KAK
SHROF
CHAK
POF
GET HIM OUT TO THE JEEP, WE'LL BE RIGHT BEHIND YA!
COO.

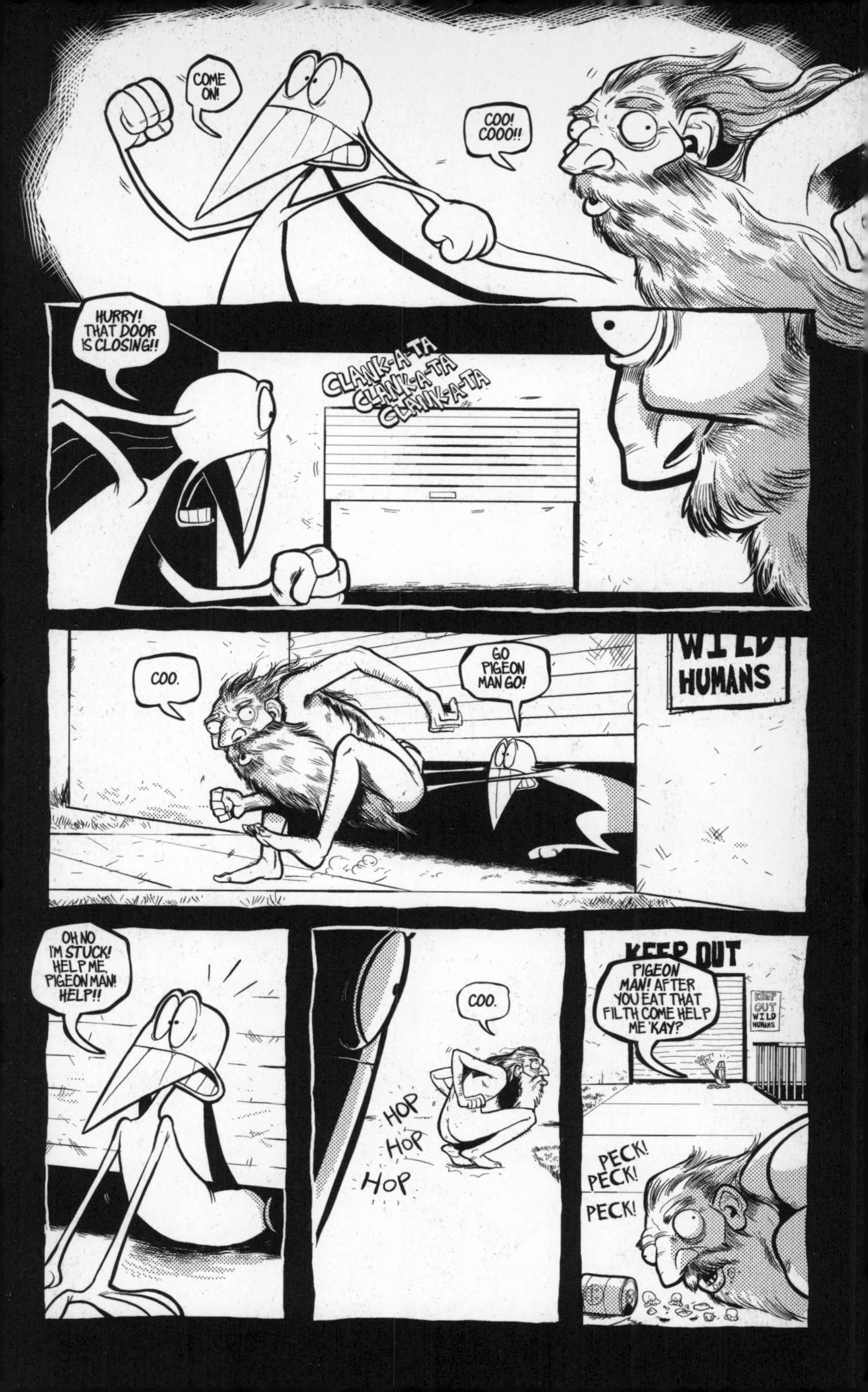
COME ON!
COO! COOO!!
HURRY! THAT DOOR IS CLOSING!!
CLANK-A-TA CLANK-A-TA CLANK-A-TA
COO.
GO PIGEON MAN GO!
WILD HUMANS
OH NO I'M STUCK! HELP ME, PIGEON MAN! HELP!!
COO.
HOP HOP HOP
KEEP OUT
PIGEON MAN! AFTER YOU EAT THAT FILTH COME HELP ME 'KAY?
KEEP OUT WILD HUMANS
PECK! PECK! PECK!

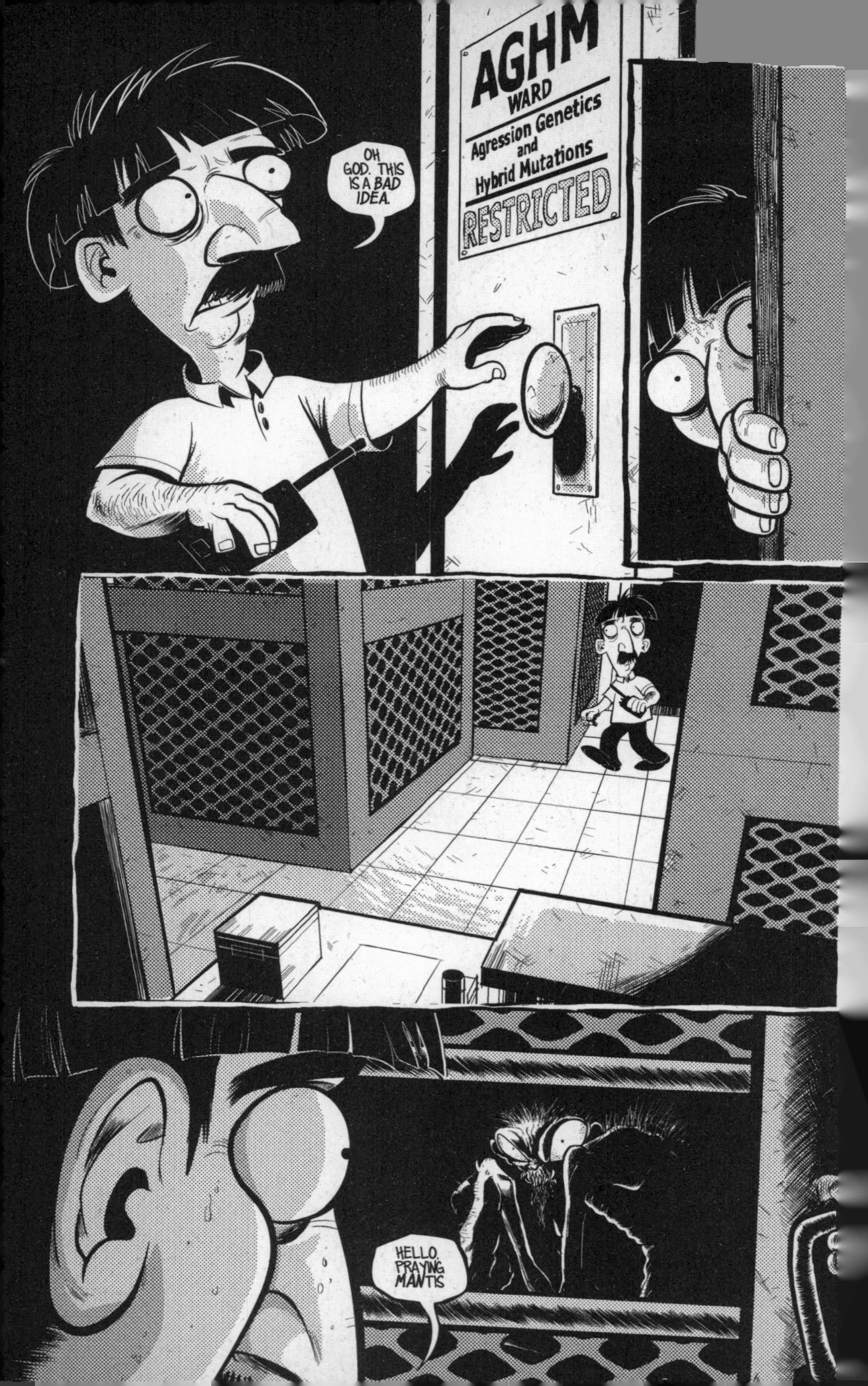
AGHM
WARD
Agression Genetics
and
Hybrid Mutations
RESTRICTED
OH GOD. THIS IS A BAD IDEA.
HELLO, PRAYING MANTIS

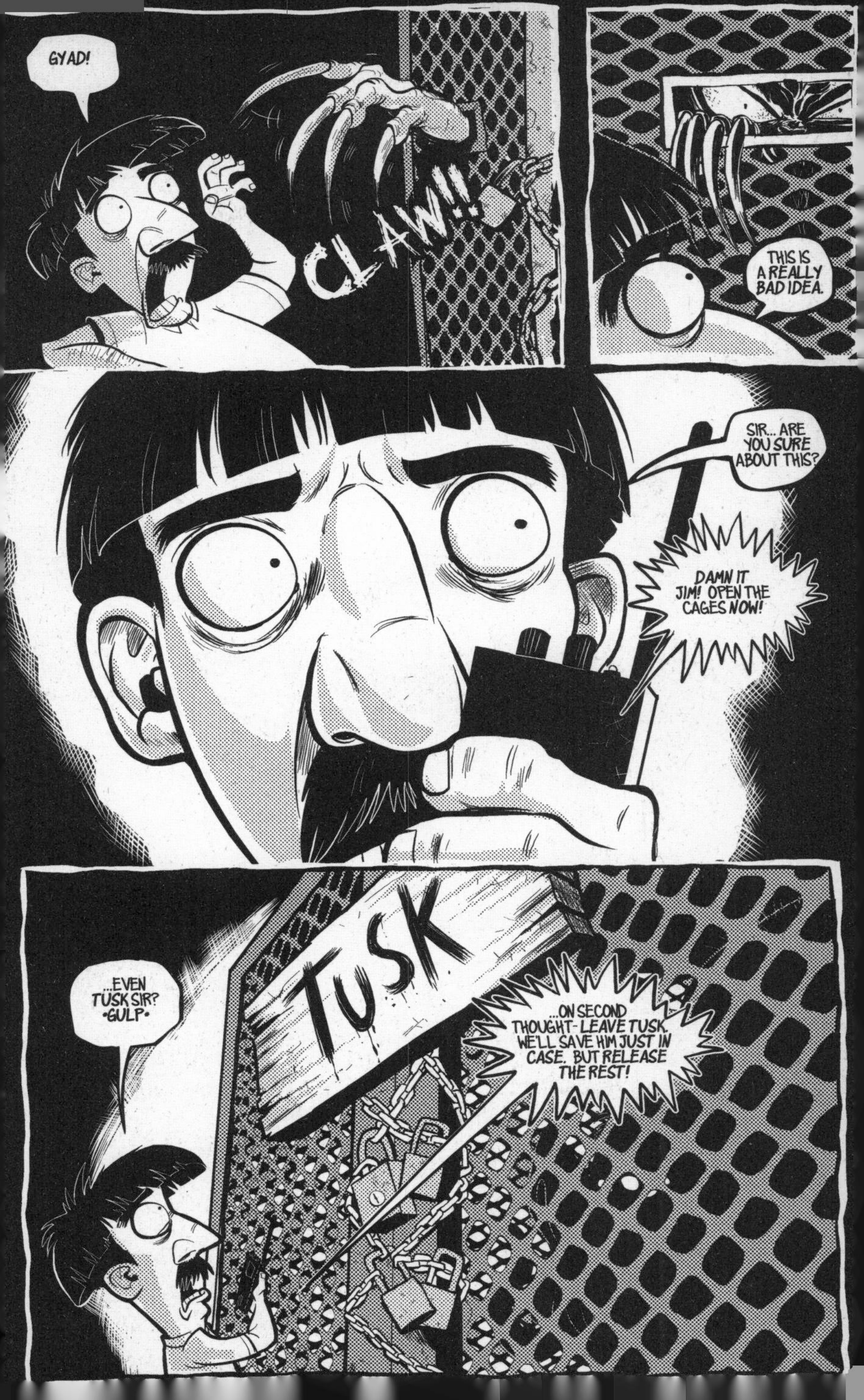
GYAD!
CLAW!!
THIS IS A REALLY BAD IDEA.
SIR... ARE YOU SURE ABOUT THIS?
DAMN IT JIM! OPEN THE CAGES NOW!
TUSK
...EVEN TUSK SIR? •GULP•
...ON SECOND THOUGHT- LEAVE TUSK. WE'LL SAVE HIM JUST IN CASE. BUT RELEASE THE REST!

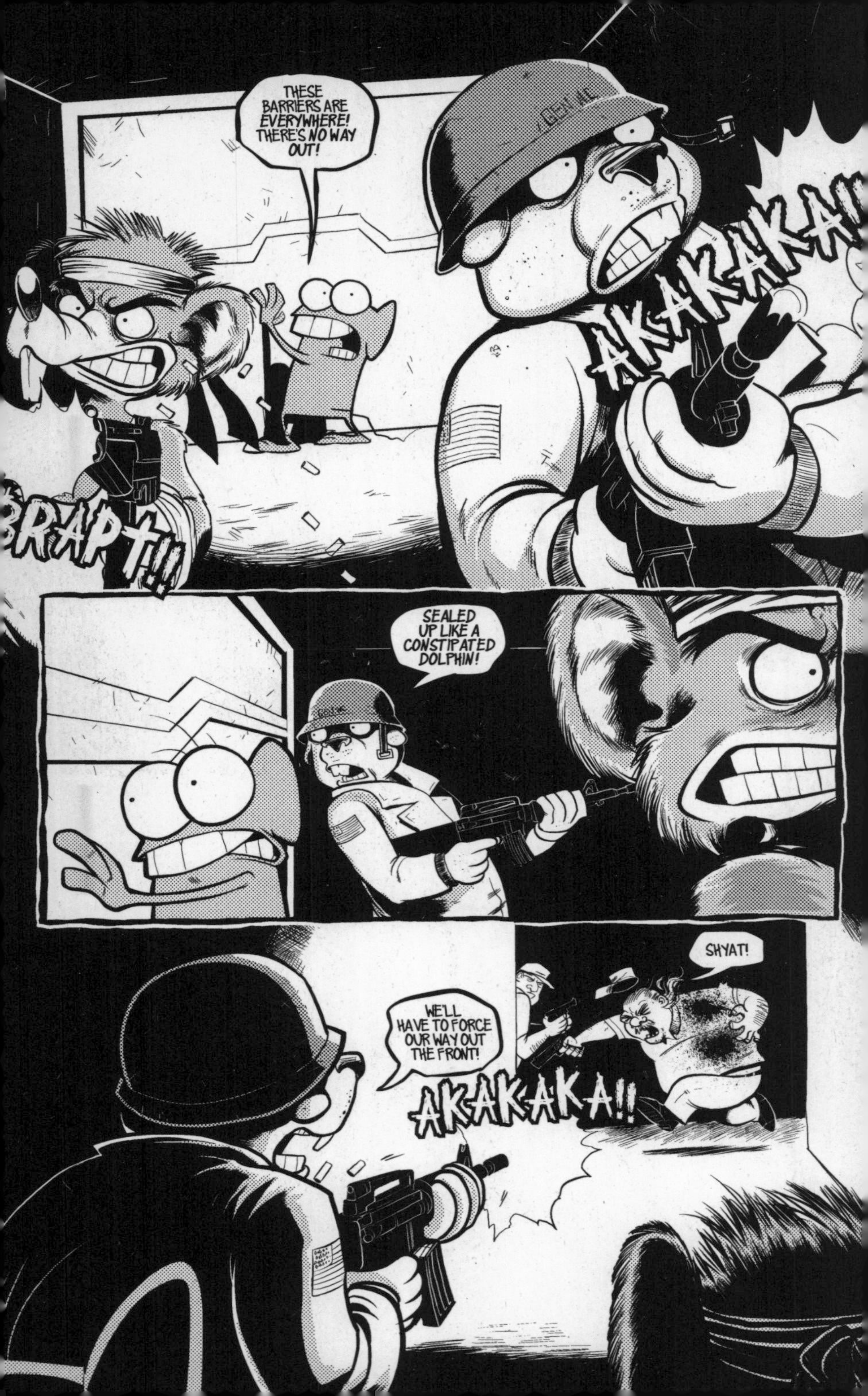
THESE BARRIERS ARE EVERYWHERE! THERE'S NO WAY OUT!
AKAKAKA!!
BRAPT!!!
SEALED UP LIKE A CONSTIPATED DOLPHIN!
SHYAT!
WE'LL HAVE TO FORCE OUR WAY OUT THE FRONT!
AKAKAKA!!

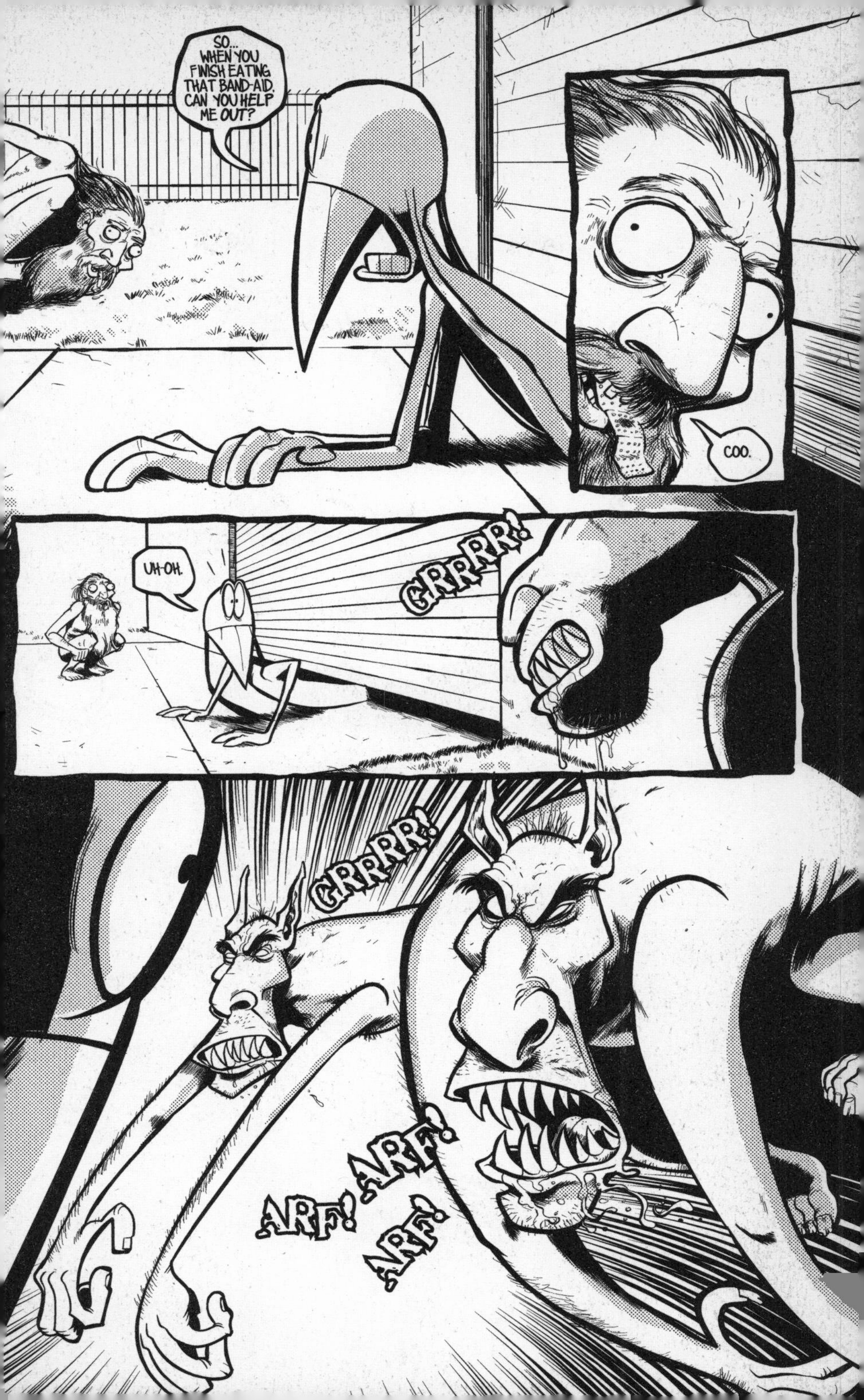
SO... WHEN YOU FINISH EATING THAT BAND-AID, CAN YOU HELP ME OUT?
COO.
UH-OH.
GRRRR!
GRRRR!
ARF! ARF! ARF! ARF!

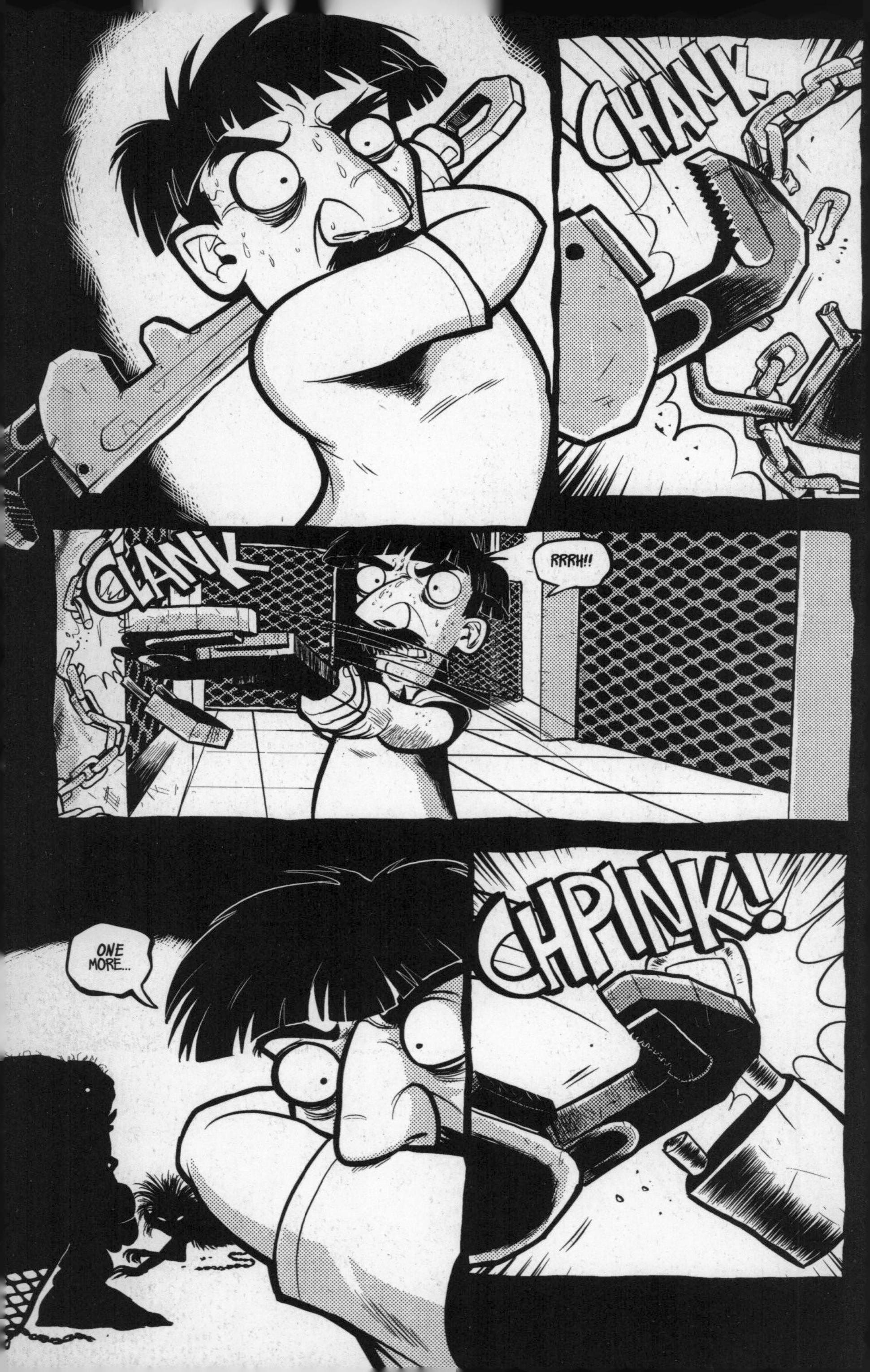
CHANK
CLANK
RRRH!!
ONE MORE...
CHPINK!

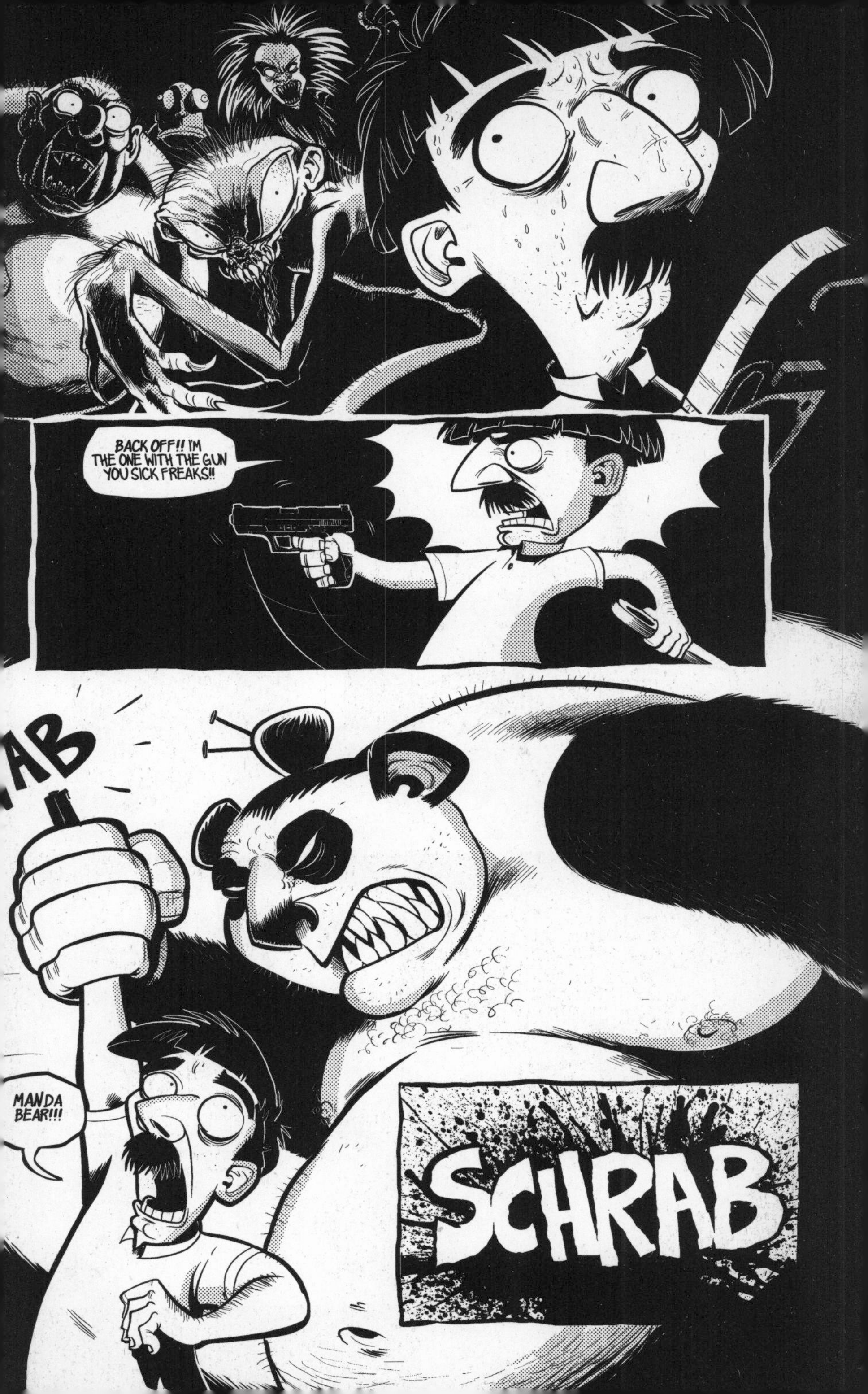
BACK OFF!! I'M THE ONE WITH THE GUN YOU SICK FREAKS!!
AB
MANDA BEAR!!!
SCHRAB

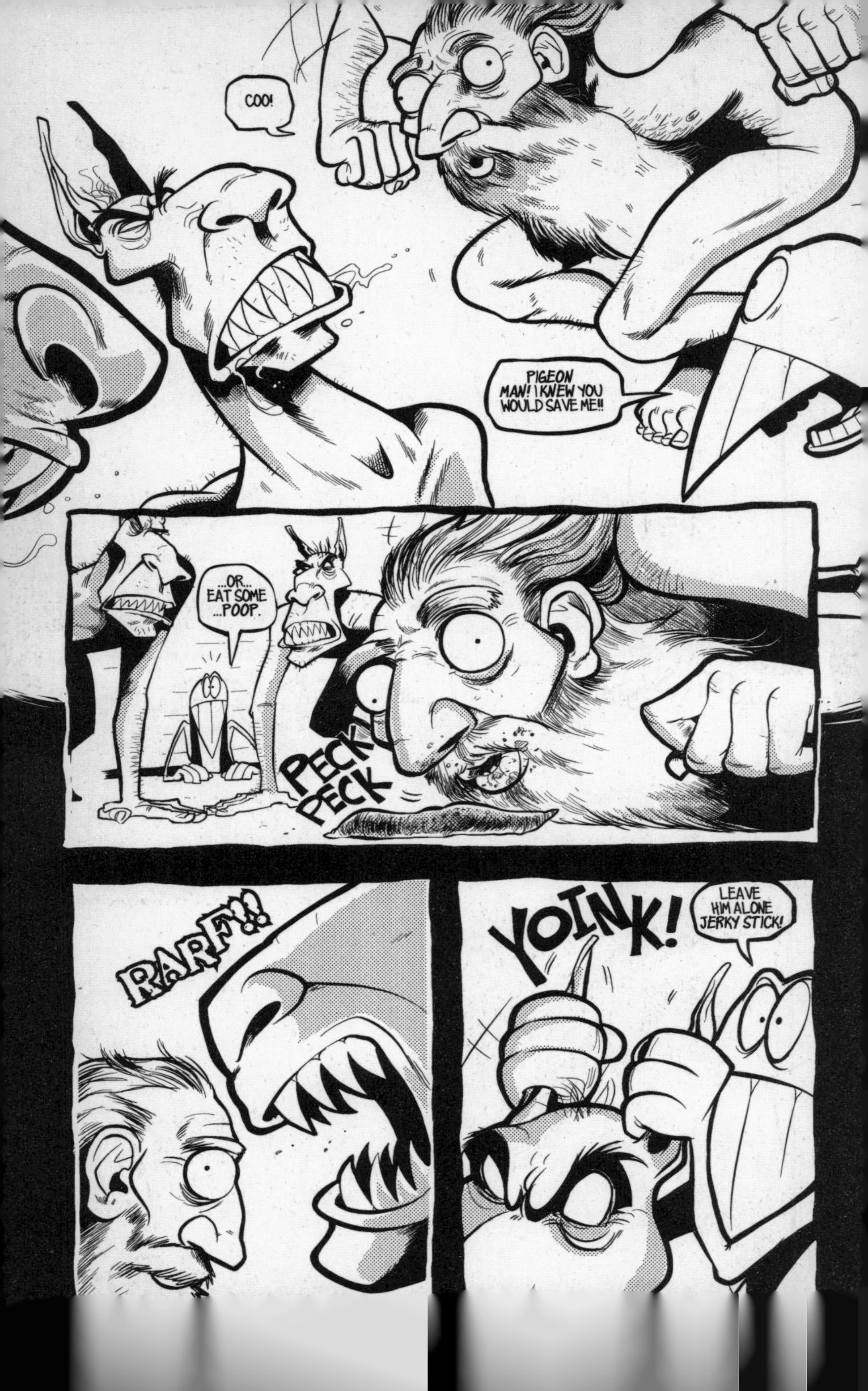
COO!
PIGEON MAN! I KNEW YOU WOULD SAVE ME!!
...OR... EAT SOME ...POOP.
PECK PECK
RARF!!
YOINK!
LEAVE HIM ALONE JERKY STICK!

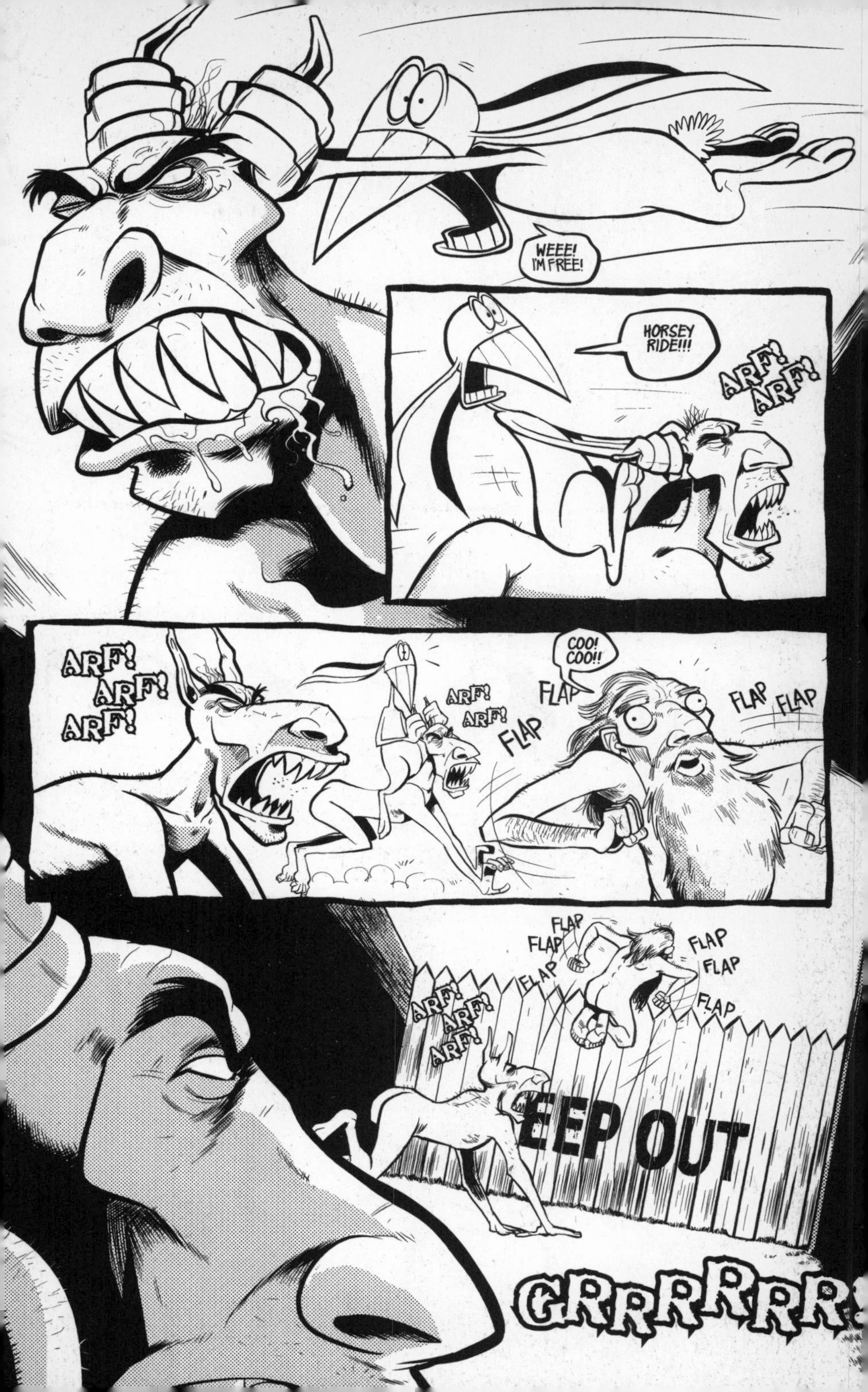
WEEE! I'M FREE!
HORSEY RIDE!!!
ARF! ARF!
ARF! ARF! ARF!
ARF! ARF!
FLAP
FLAP
COO! COO!!
FLAP FLAP
FLAP FLAP
FLAP FLAP
FLAP
FLAP
FLAP
ARF! ARF! ARF!
EEP OUT
GRRRRRRR

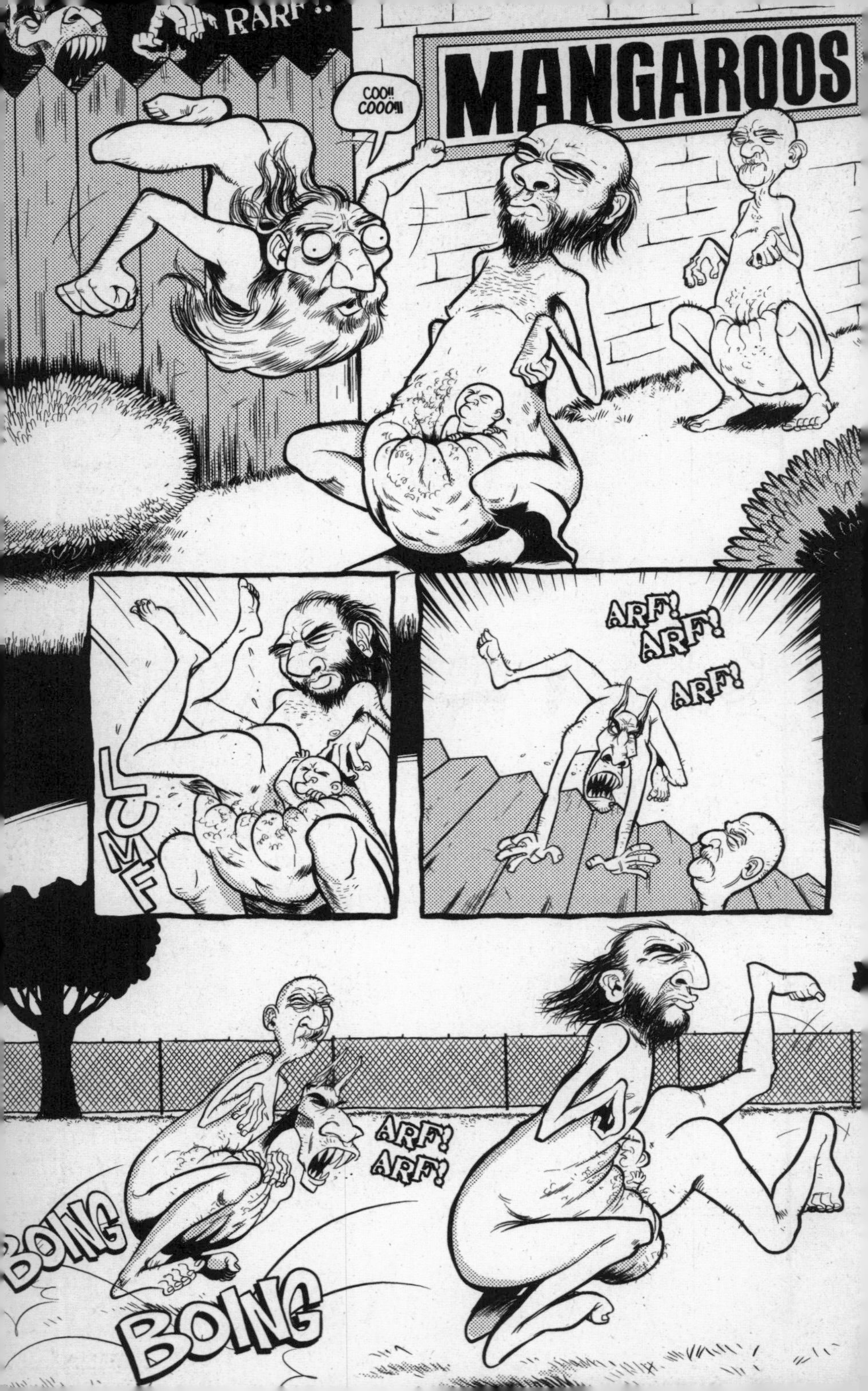
RARF..
COO!!
COOO!!!
MANGAROOS
LUMF
ARF! ARF!
ARF!
ARF! ARF!
BOING
BOING

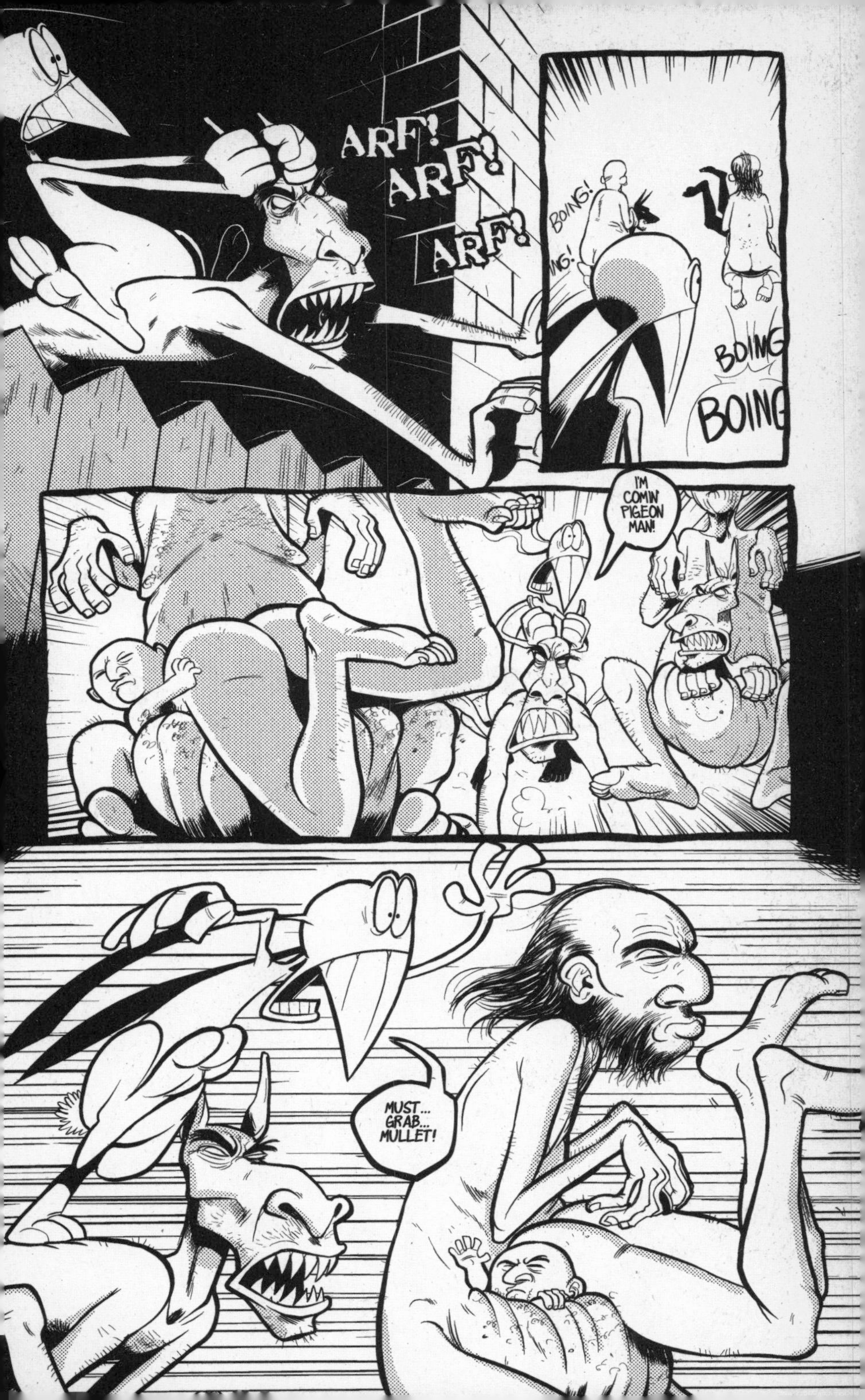
ARF!
ARF!
ARF!
BOING!
ING!
BOING
BOING
I'M COMIN' PIGEON MAN!
MUST... GRAB... MULLET!

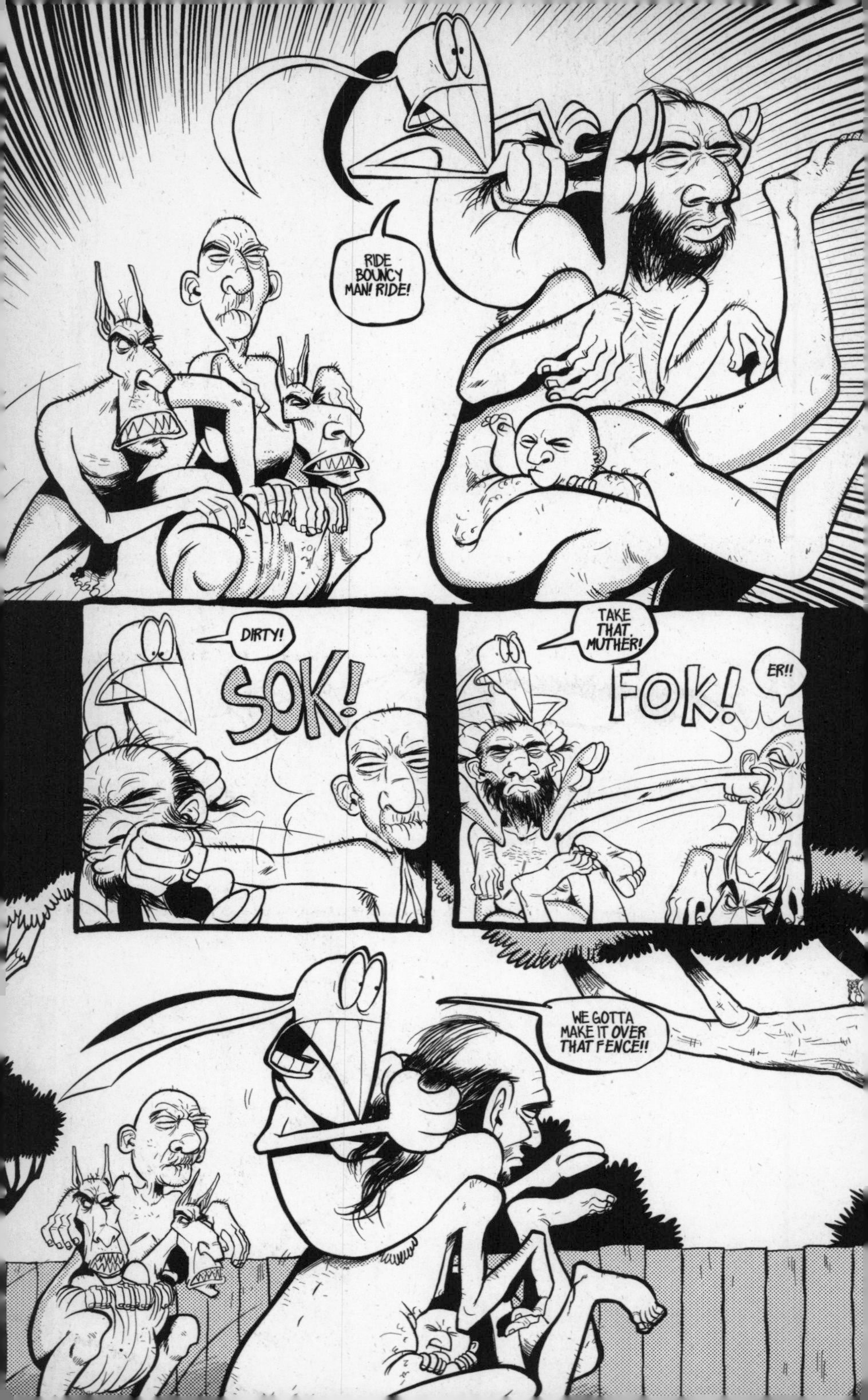
RIDE BOUNCY MAN! RIDE!
DIRTY!
SOK!
TAKE THAT, MUTHER!
FOK!
ER!!
WE GOTTA MAKE IT OVER THAT FENCE!!

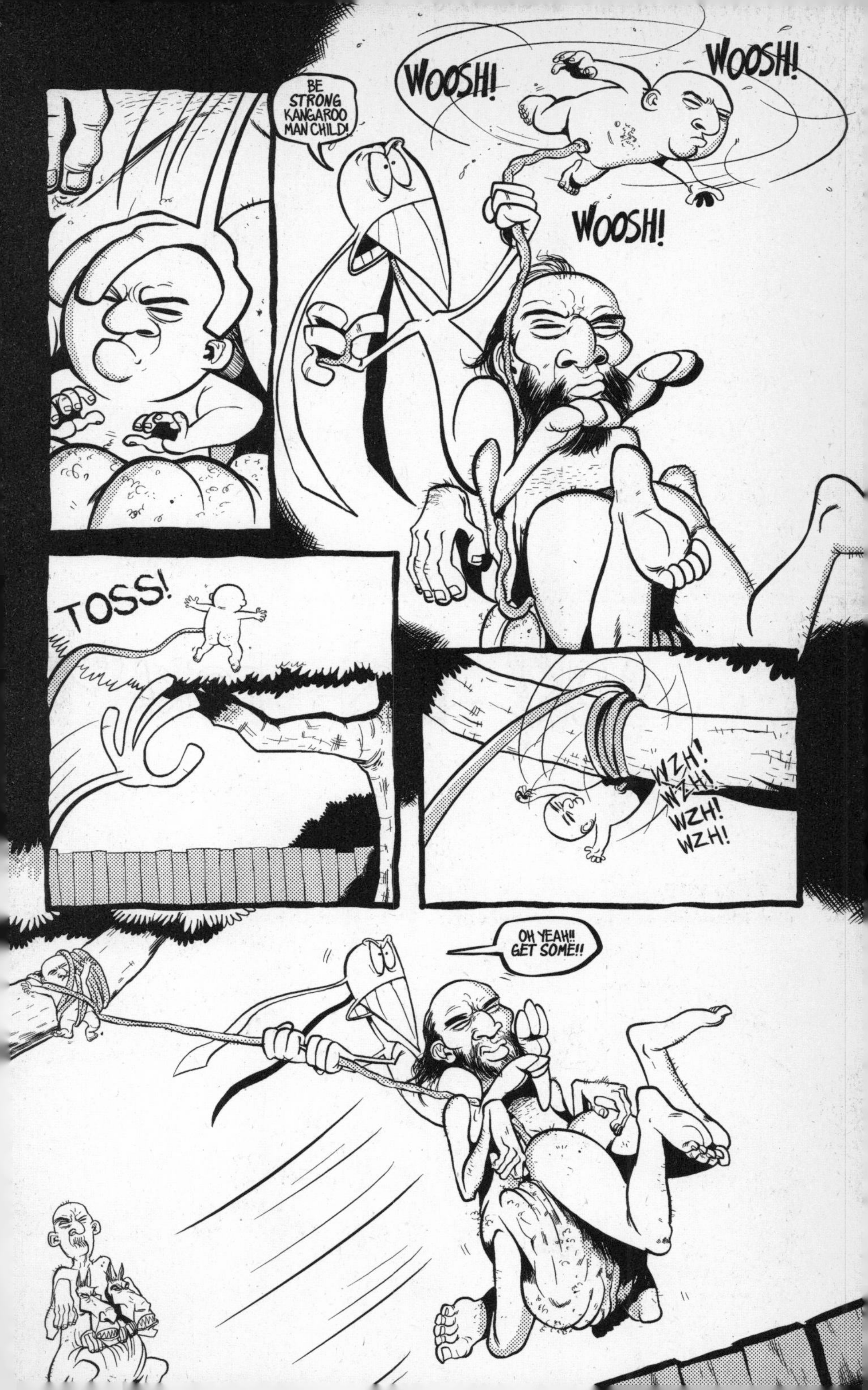
BE STRONG KANGAROO MAN CHILD!
WOOSH!
WOOSH!
WOOSH!
TOSS!
WZH! WZH! WZH! WZH!
OH YEAH!! GET SOME!!

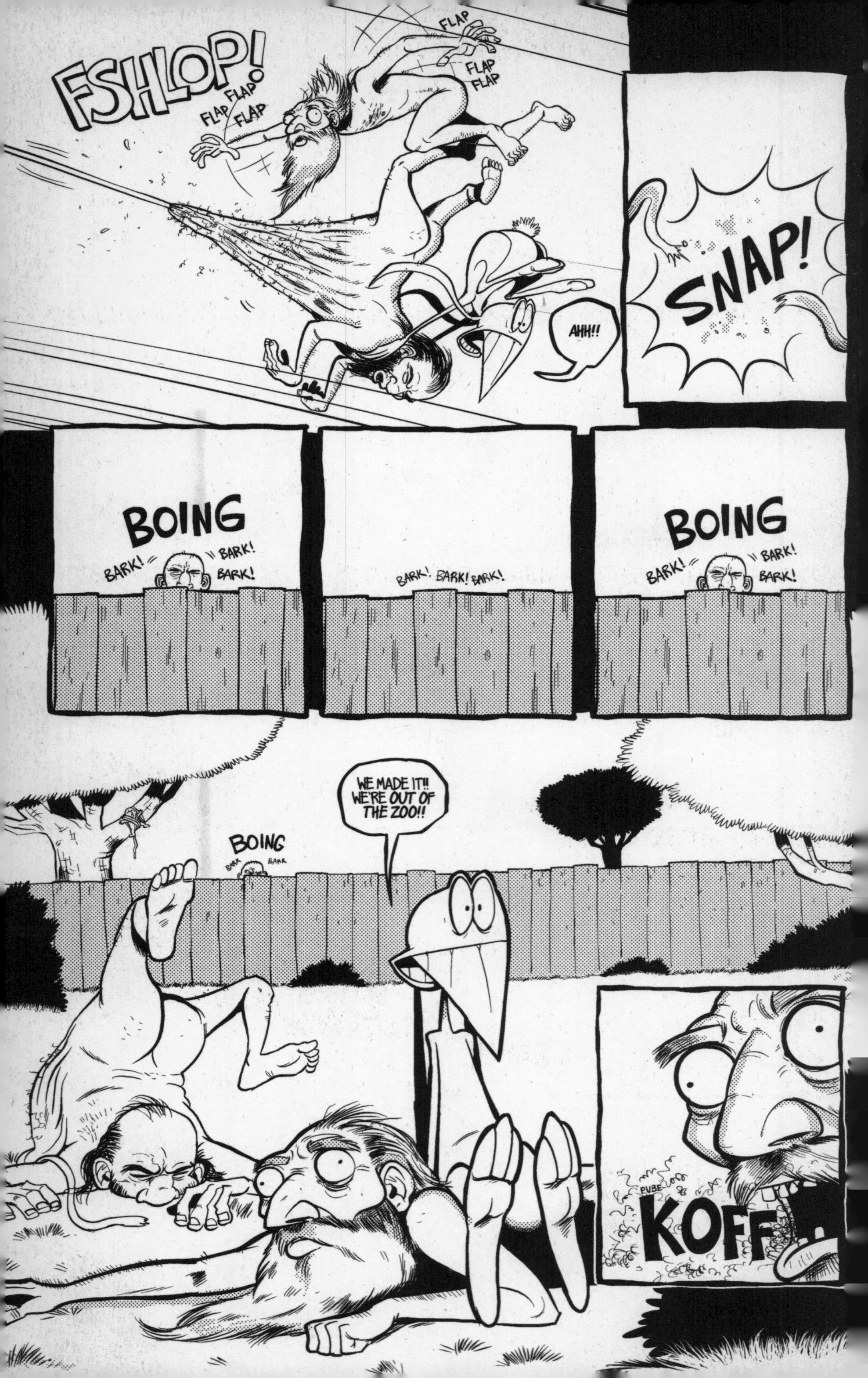
FSHLOP!
FLAP
FLAP
FLAP
FLAP
FLAP
FLAP
FLAP
AHH!!
SNAP!
BOING
BARK!
BARK!
BARK!
BARK!
BARK!
BARK!
BOING
BARK!
BARK!
BARK!
BOING
BARK
BARK
WE MADE IT!! WE'RE OUT OF THE ZOO!!
PUBE-
KOFF

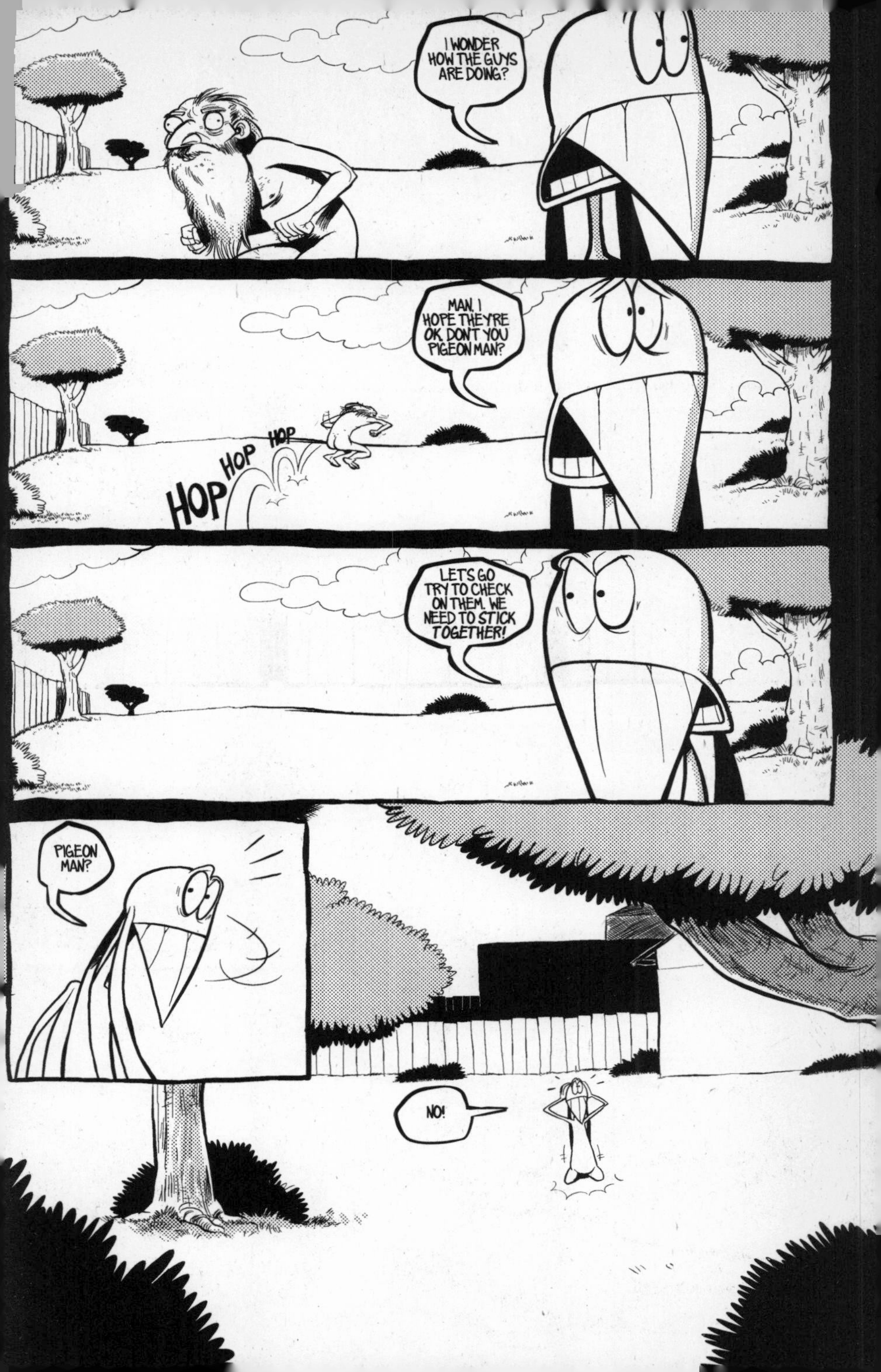

I WONDER HOW THE GUYS ARE DOING?
MAN, I HOPE THEY'RE OK. DON'T YOU PIGEON MAN?
HOP HOP HOP
LETS GO TRY TO CHECK ON THEM. WE NEED TO STICK TOGETHER!
PIGEON MAN?
NO!

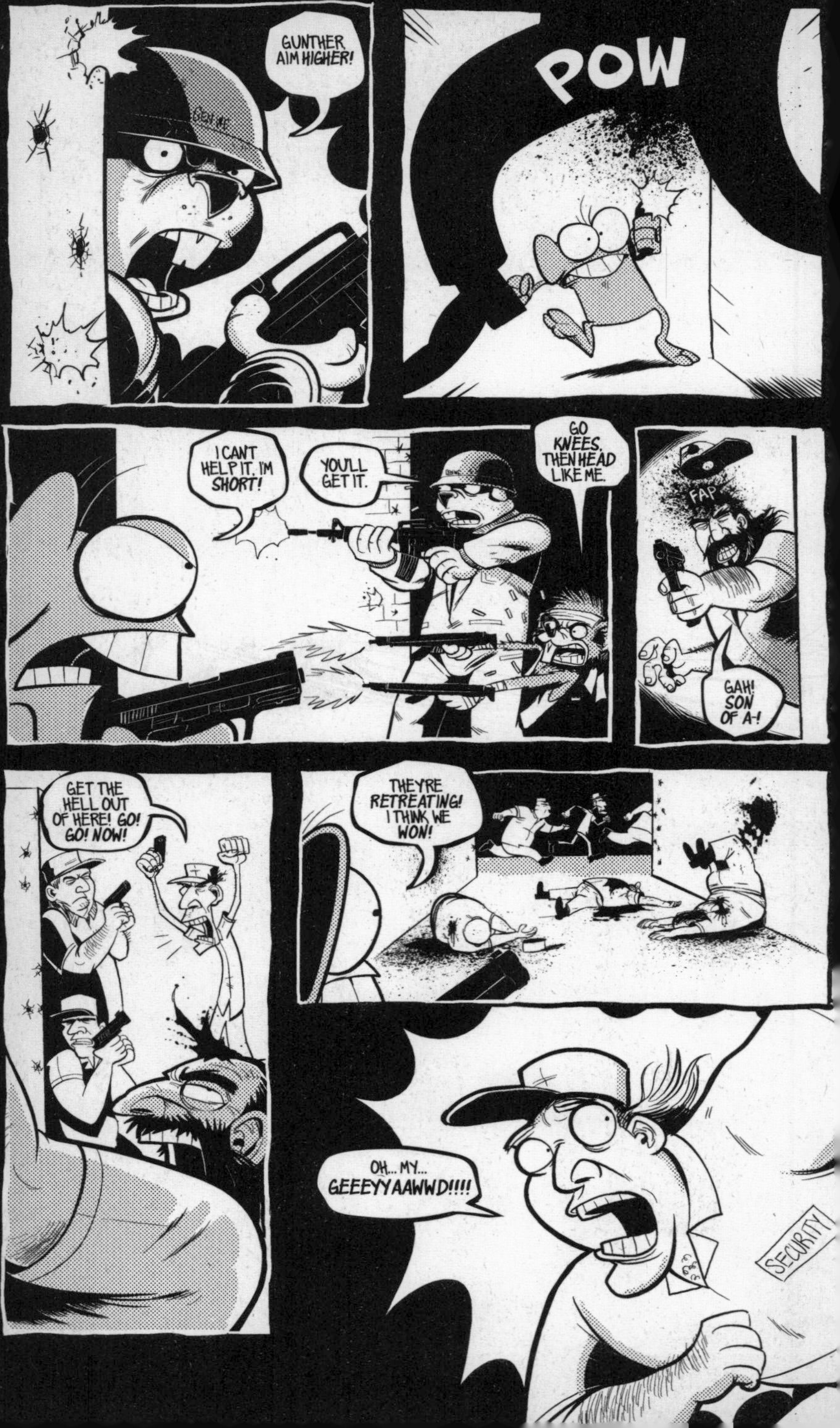
GUNTHER AIM HIGHER!
POW
I CAN'T HELP IT, I'M SHORT!
YOU'LL GET IT.
GO KNEES, THEN HEAD LIKE ME.
FAP
GAH! SON OF A-!
GET THE HELL OUT OF HERE! GO! GO! NOW!
THEY'RE RETREATING! I THINK WE WON!
OH... MY... GEEEYYAAWWD!!!!
SECURITY

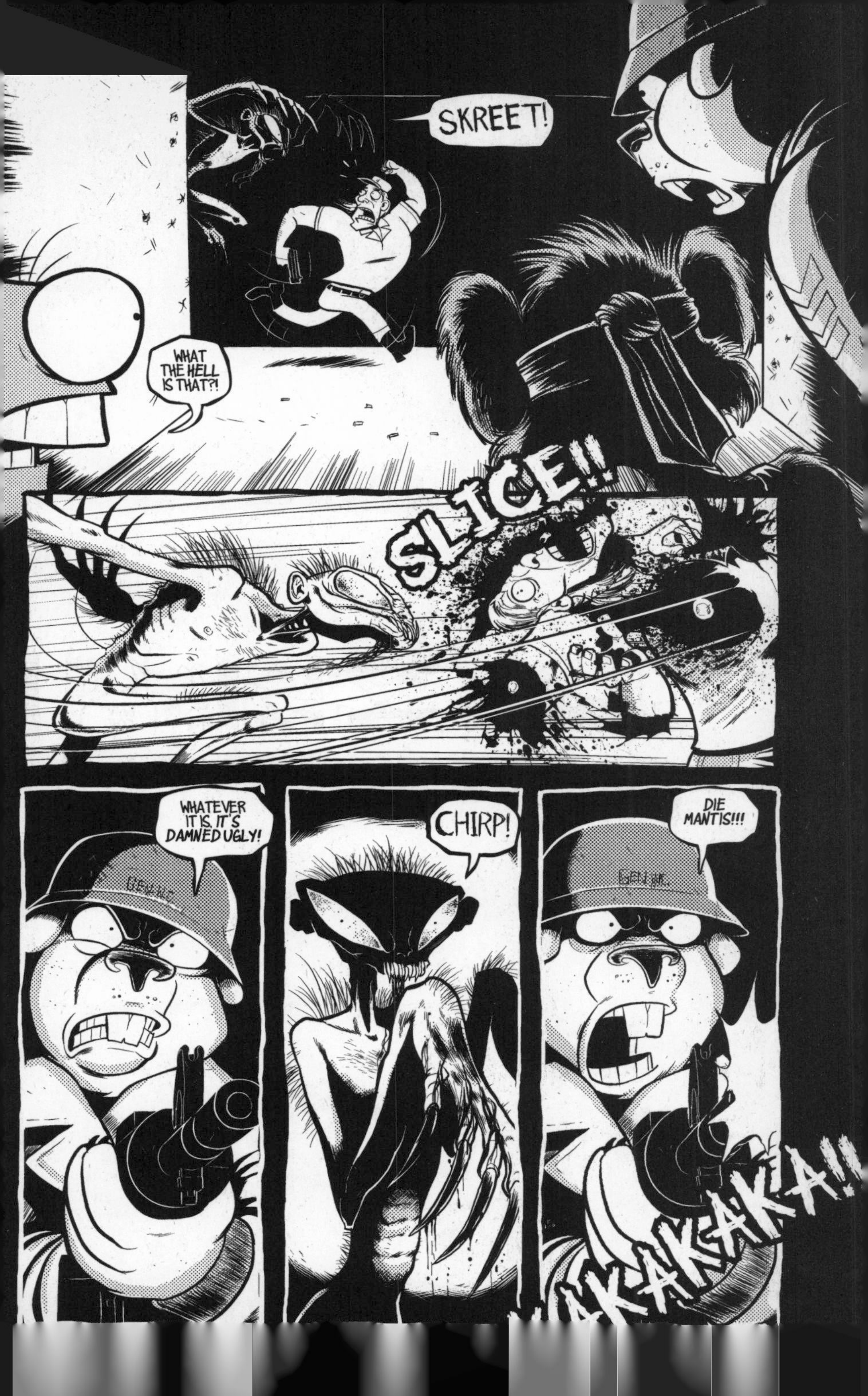
SKREET!
WHAT THE HELL IS THAT?!
SLICE!!
WHATEVER IT IS, IT'S DAMNED UGLY!
CHIRP!
DIE MANTIS!!!
KAKAKAKAKA!!

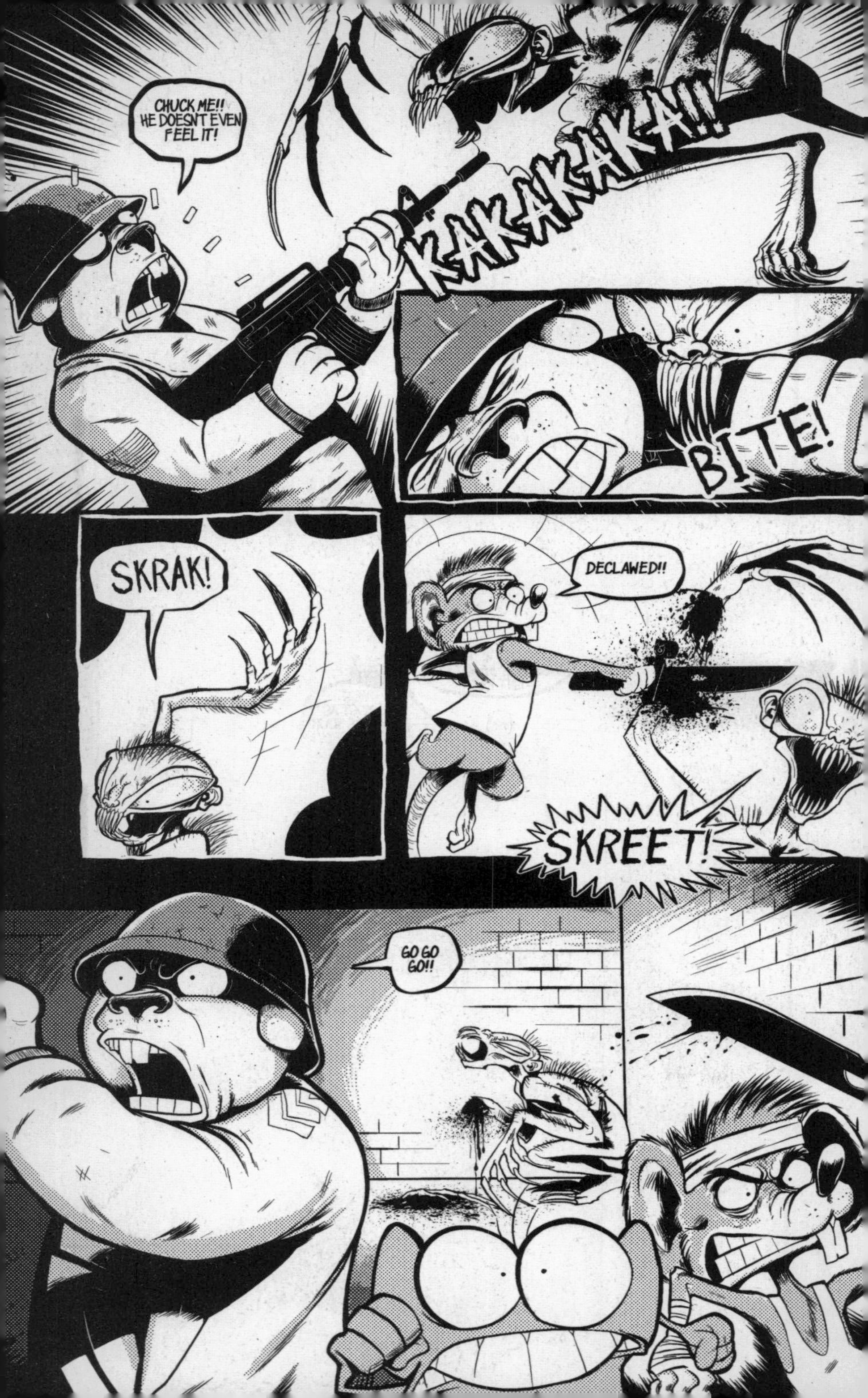

CHUCK ME!! HE DOESN'T EVEN FEEL IT!
KAKAKAKAKA!!
BITE!
SKRAK!
DECLAWED!!
SKREET!
GO GO GO!!

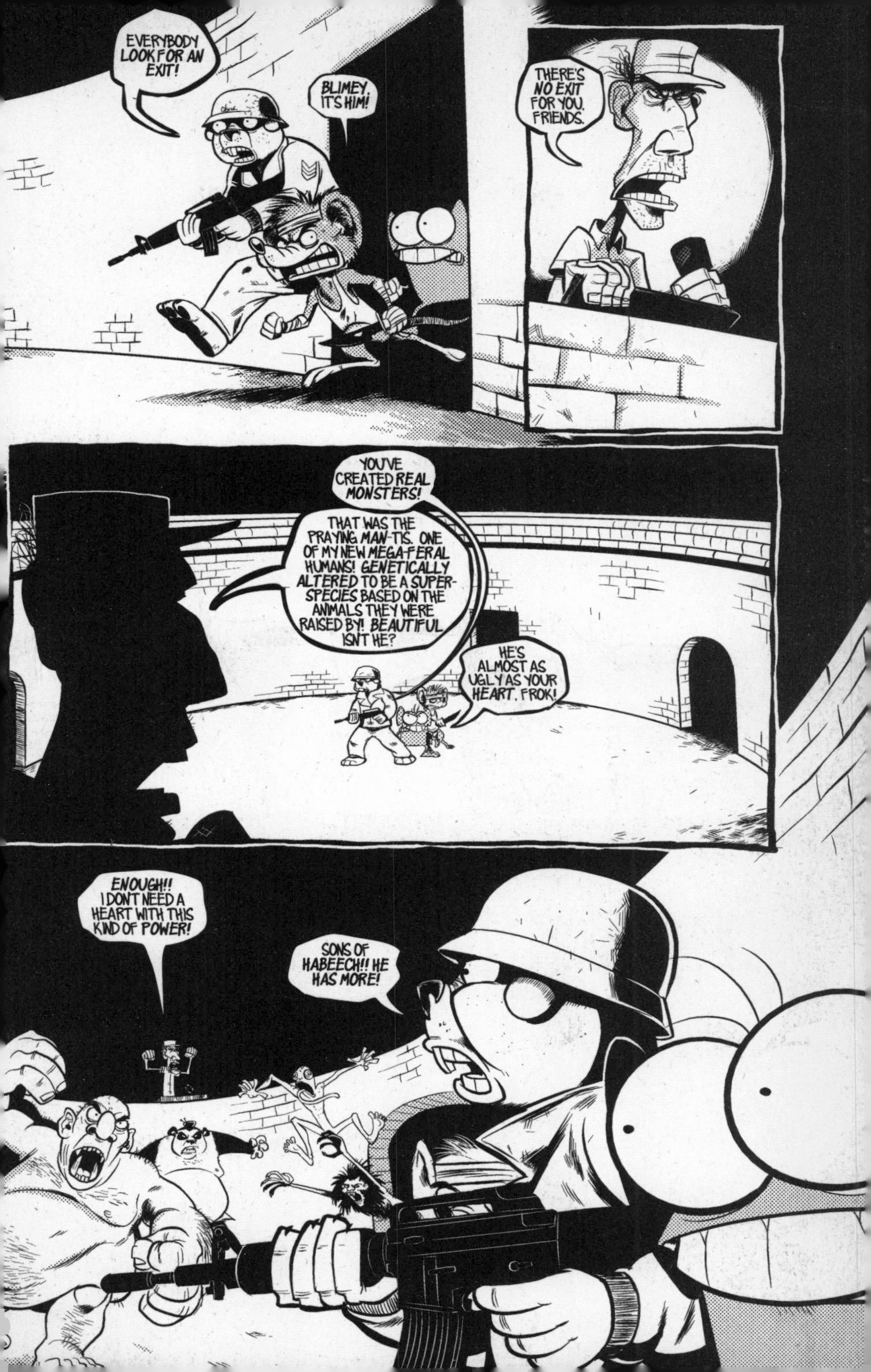
EVERYBODY LOOK FOR AN EXIT!
BLIMEY, IT'S HIM!
THERE'S NO EXIT FOR YOU, FRIENDS.
YOU'VE CREATED REAL MONSTERS!
THAT WAS THE PRAYING MAN-TIS. ONE OF MY NEW MEGA-FERAL HUMANS! GENETICALLY ALTERED TO BE A SUPER-SPECIES BASED ON THE ANIMALS THEY WERE RAISED BY! BEAUTIFUL ISN'T HE?
HE'S ALMOST AS UGLY AS YOUR HEART, FROK!
ENOUGH!! I DONT NEED A HEART WITH THIS KIND OF POWER!
SONS OF HABEECH!! HE HAS MORE!

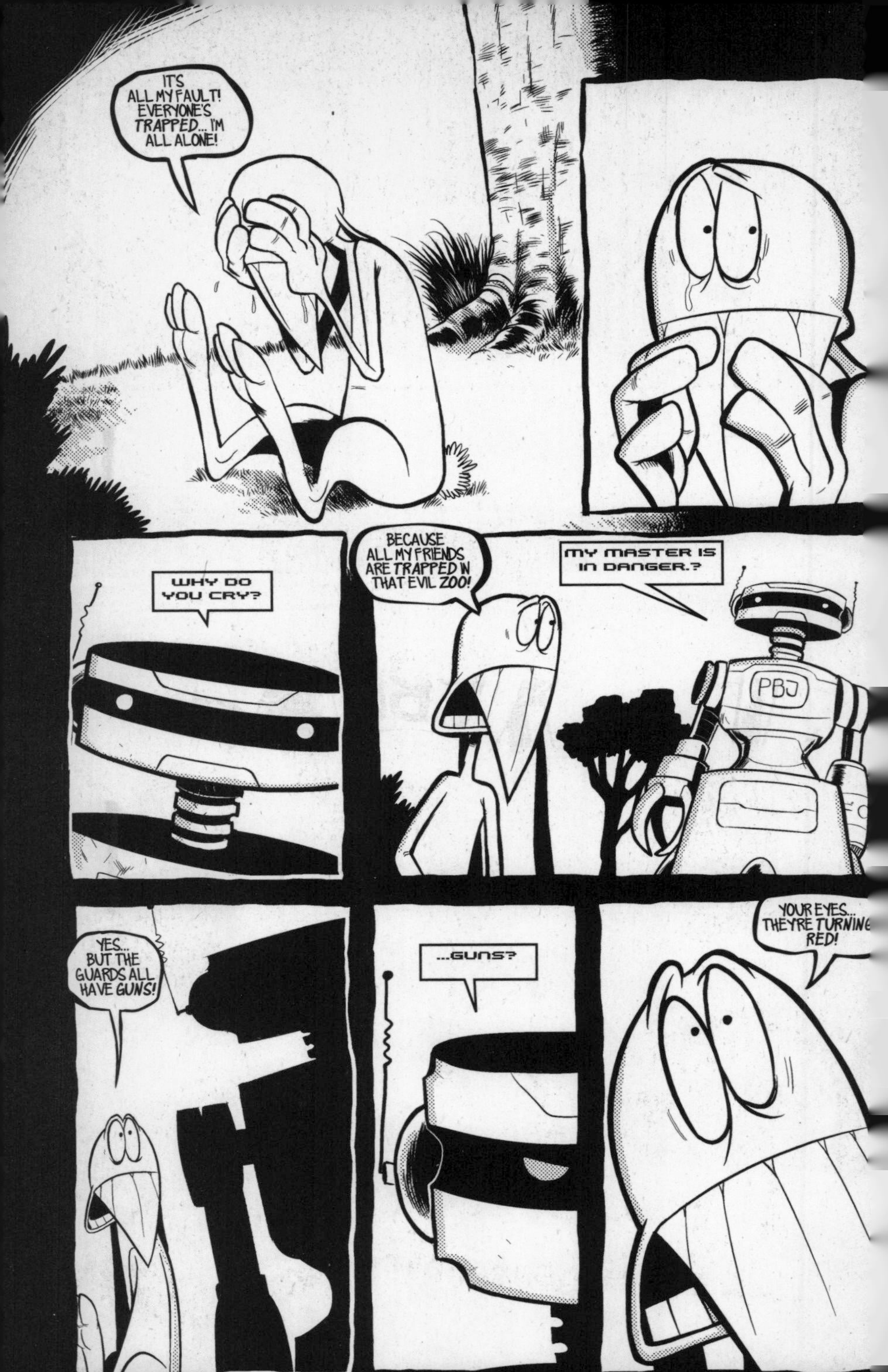

ITS ALL MY FAULT! EVERYONE'S TRAPPED... I'M ALL ALONE!
WHY DO YOU CRY?
BECAUSE ALL MY FRIENDS ARE TRAPPED IN THAT EVIL ZOO!
MY MASTER IS IN DANGER.?
PBJ
YES... BUT THE GUARDS ALL HAVE GUNS!
...GUNS?
YOUR EYES... THEY'RE TURNING RED!

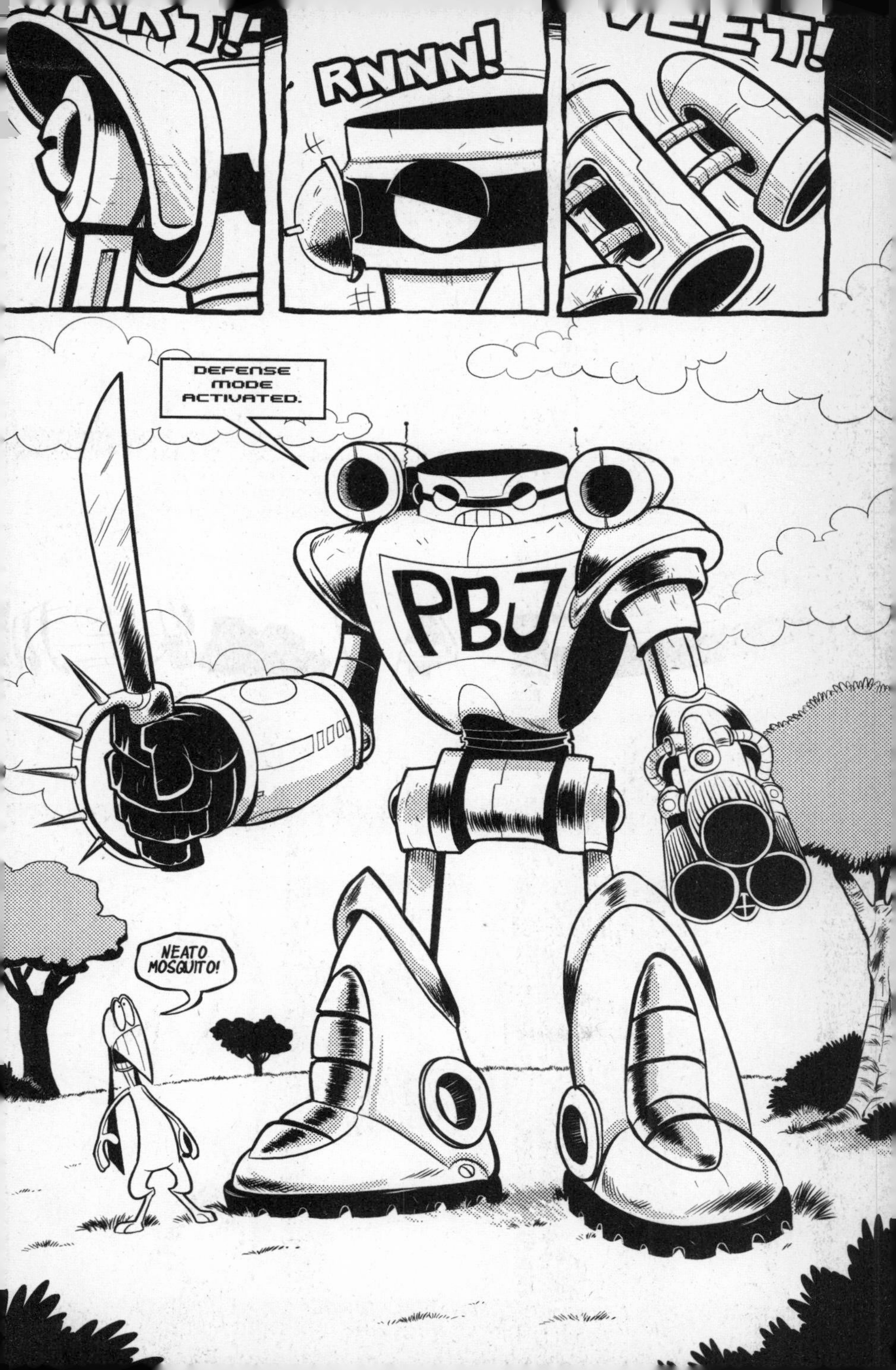
RNNN!
DEFENSE MODE ACTIVATED.
PBJ
NEATO MOSQUITO!

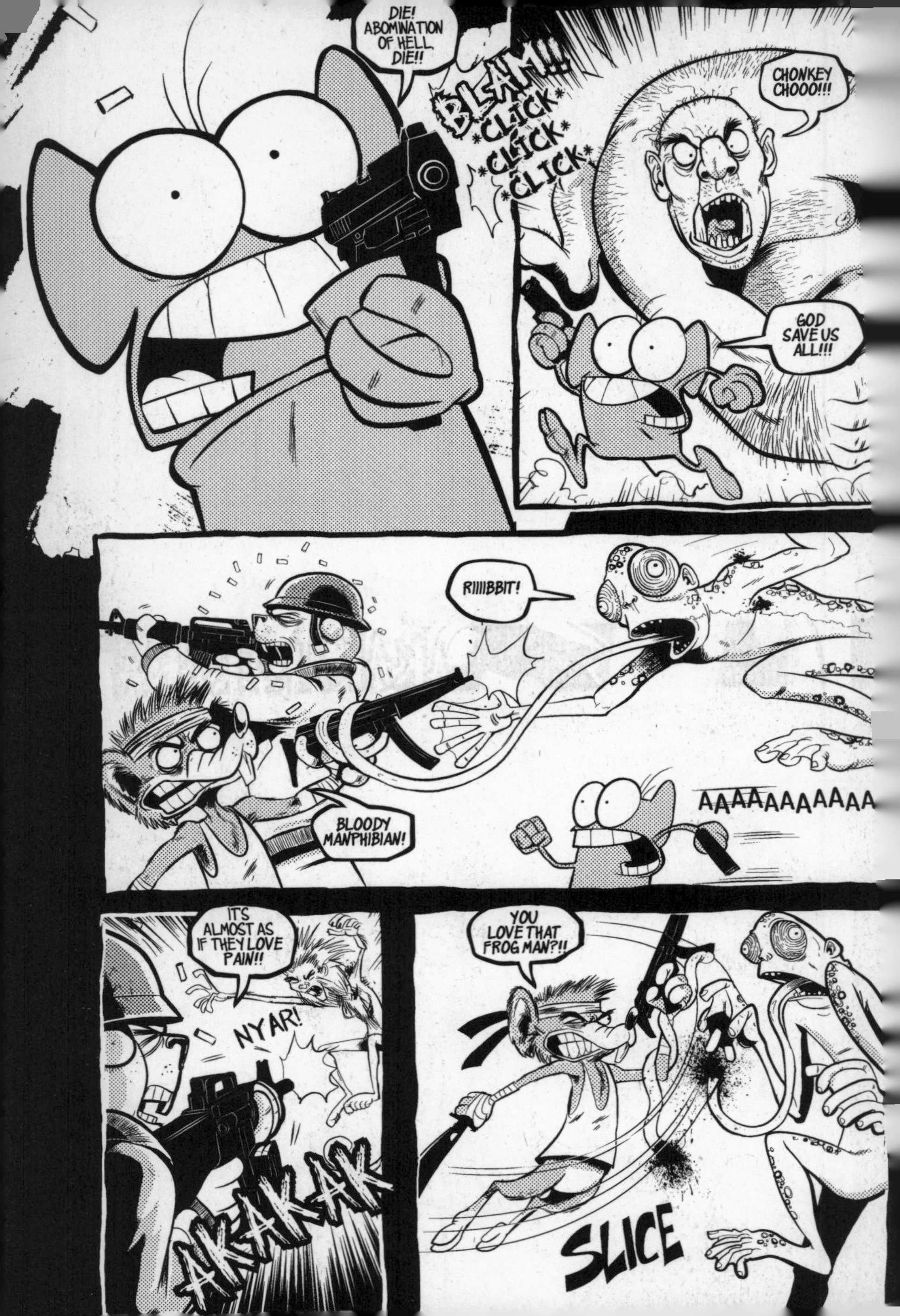
DIE! ABOMINATION OF HELL DIE!!
BLAM!!
CLICK *CLICK* *CLICK*
CHONKEY CHOOO!!!
GOD SAVE US ALL!!!
RIIIIBBIT!
BLOODY MANPHIBIAN!
AAAAAAAAAAA
ITS ALMOST AS IF THEY LOVE PAIN!!
NYAR!
AKAKAKAK
YOU LOVE THAT FROG MAN?!!
SLICE

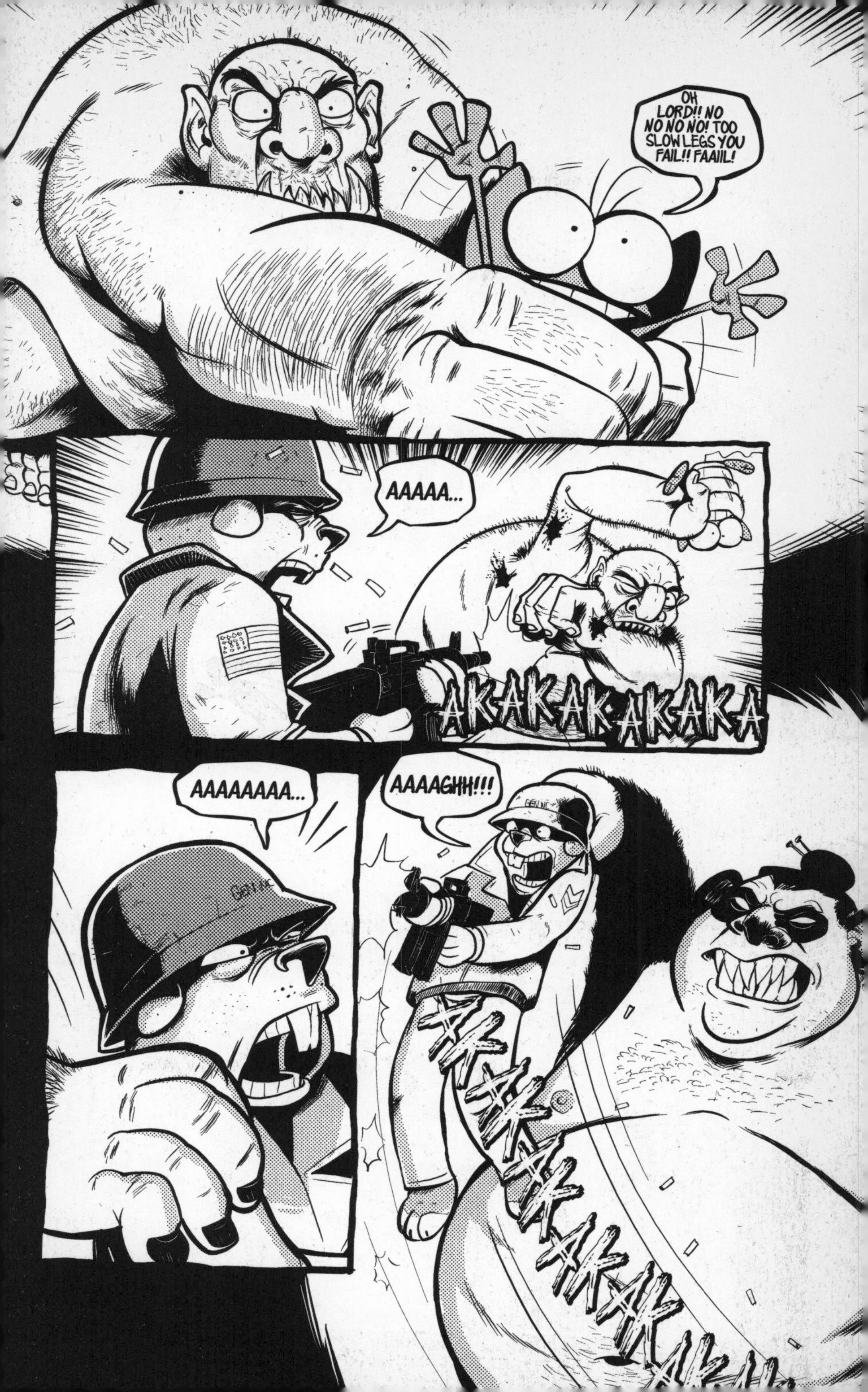
OH LORD!! NO NO NO NO! TOO SLOW LEGS YOU FAIL!! FAAIIL!
AAAAA...
AKAKAKAKAKAKA
AAAAAAAA...
AAAAGHH!!!

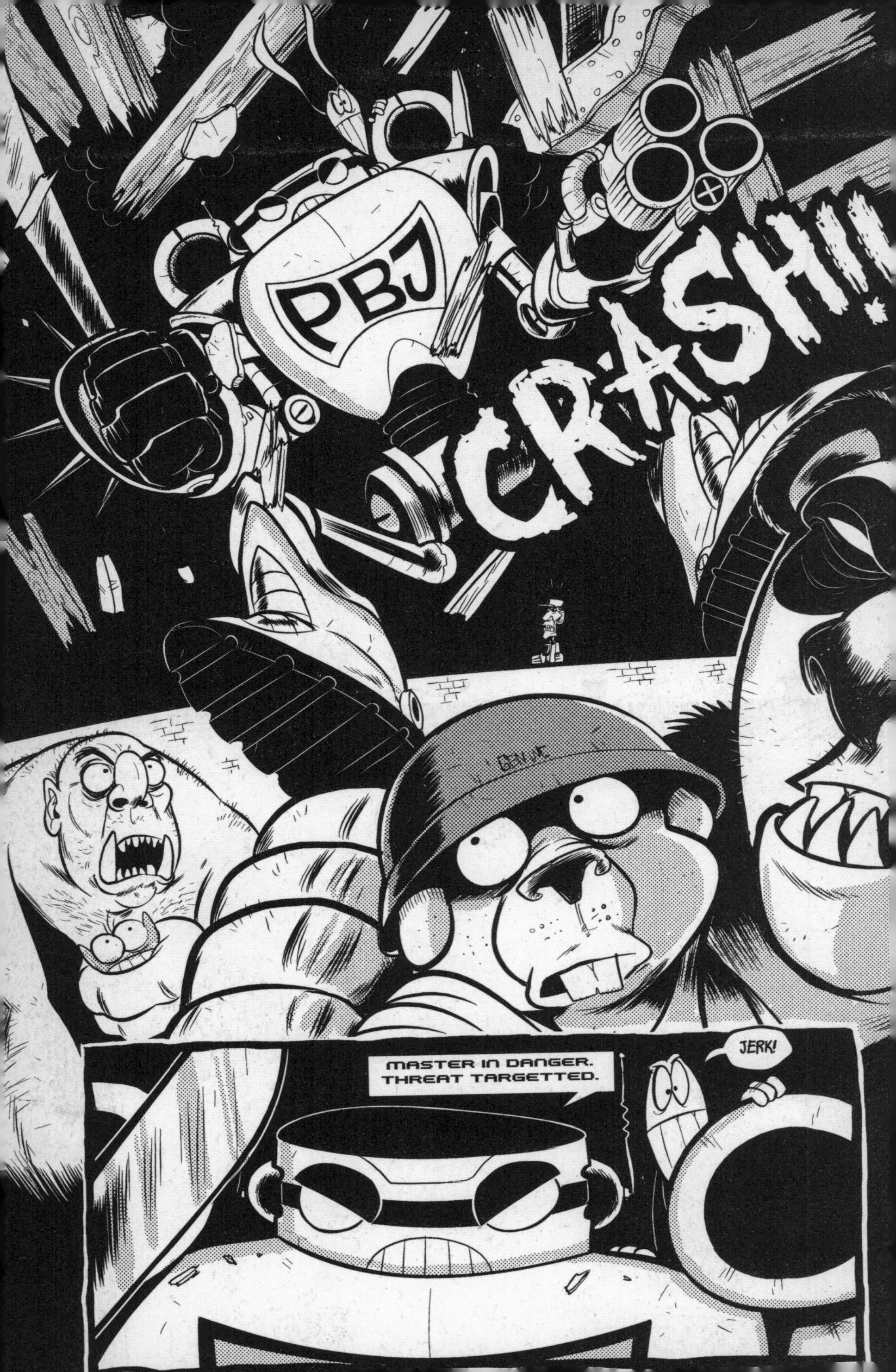
PBJ
CRASH!!
MASTER IN DANGER.
THREAT TARGETTED.
JERK!

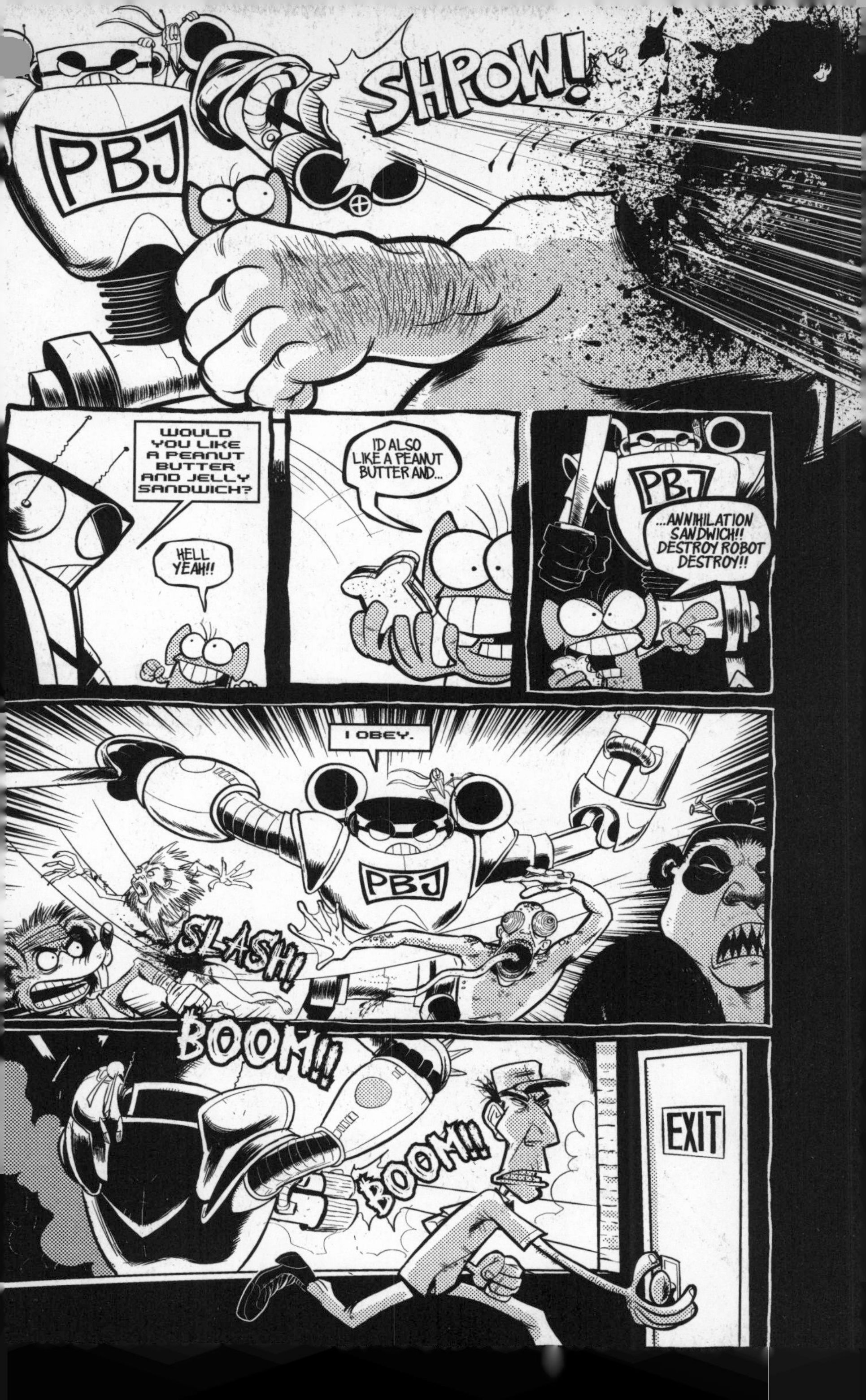
SHPOW!
WOULD YOU LIKE A PEANUT BUTTER AND JELLY SANDWICH?
HELL YEAH!!
I'D ALSO LIKE A PEANUT BUTTER AND...
...ANNIHILATION SANDWICH!! DESTROY ROBOT DESTROY!!
PBJ
I OBEY.
PBJ
SLASH!
BOOM!!
BOOM!!
EXIT

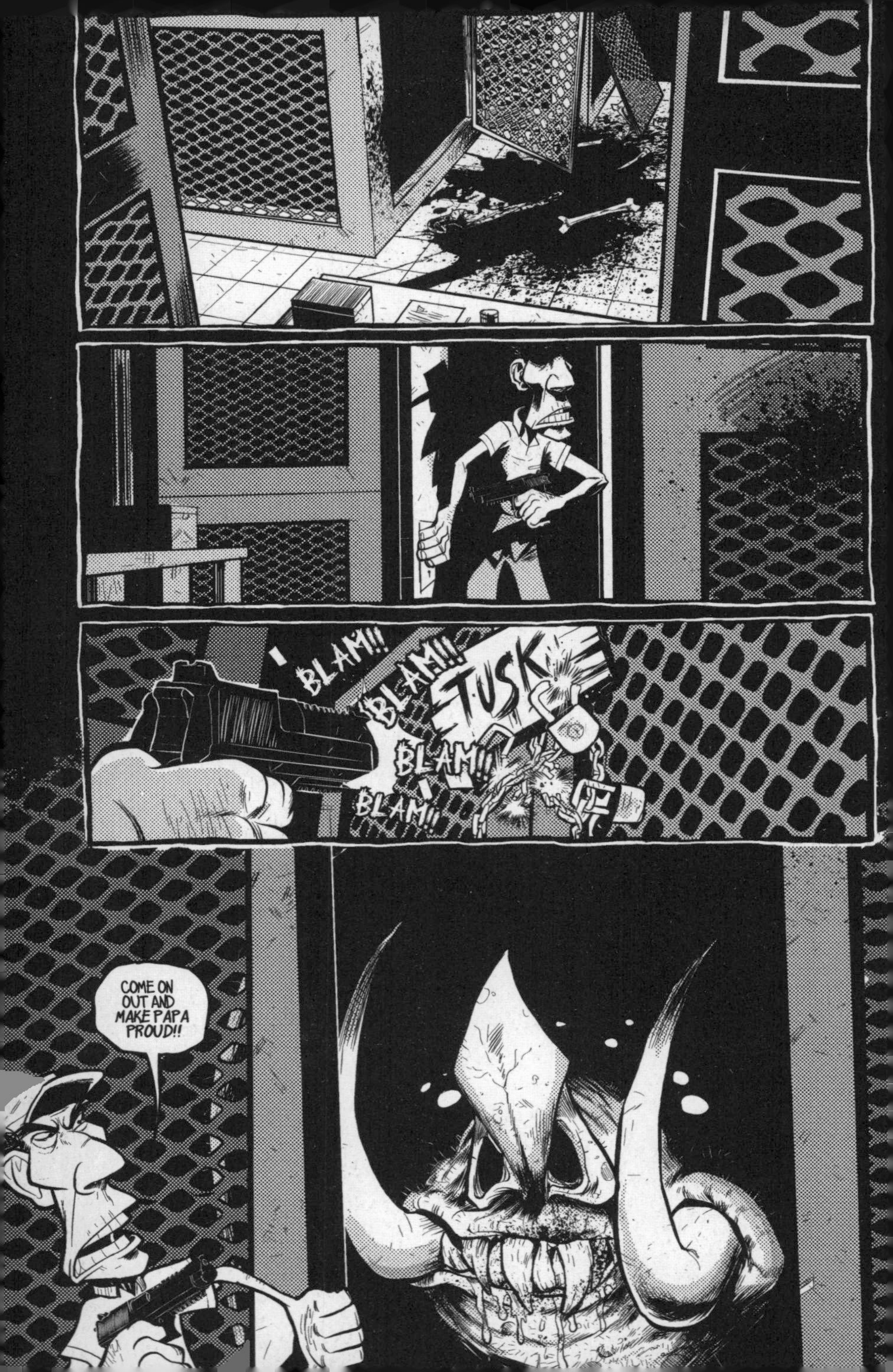

BLAM!!
BLAM!!
TUSK
BLAM!!
BLAM!!
COME ON OUT AND MAKE PAPA PROUD!!

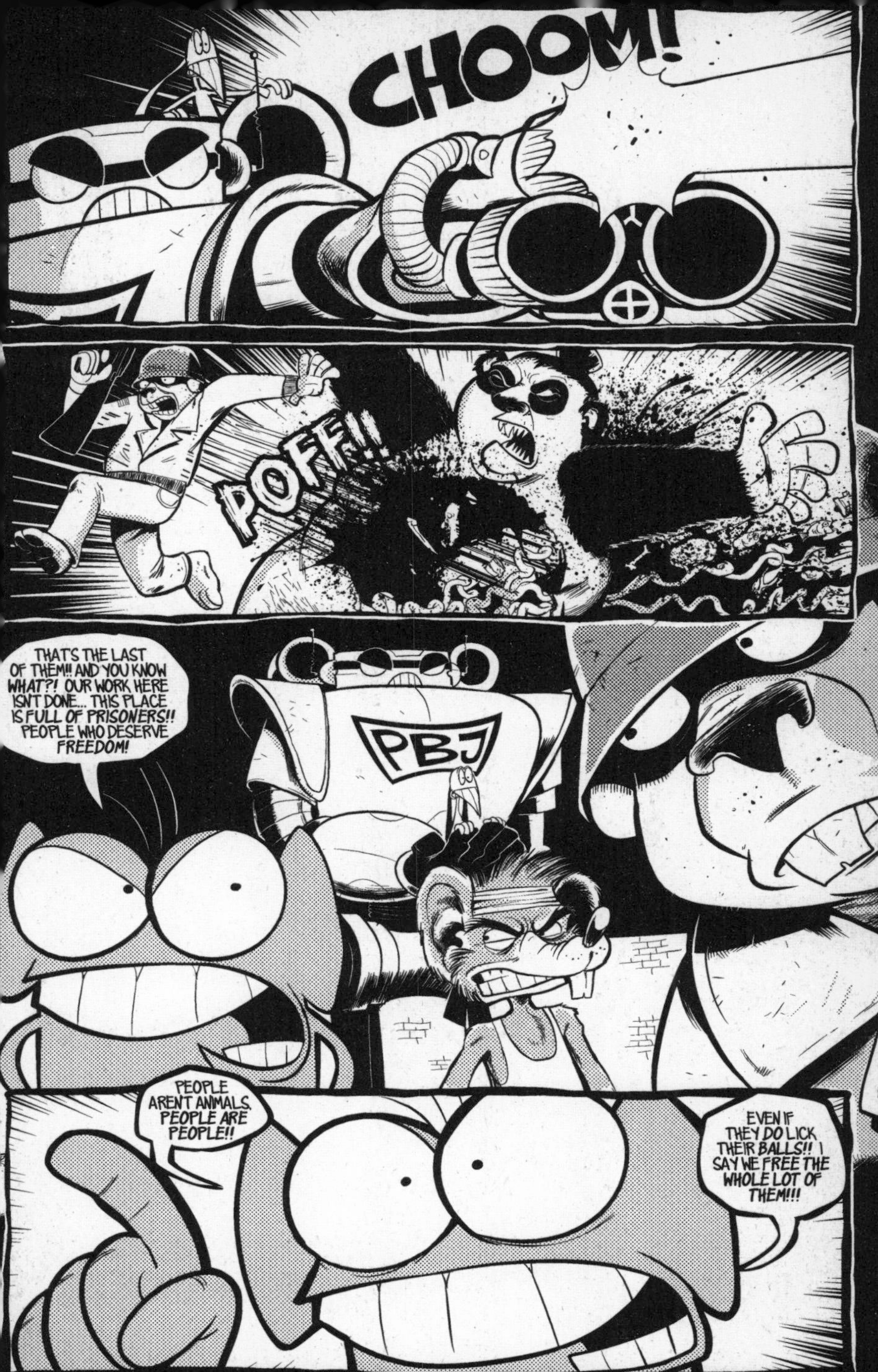
CHOOM!
POFF!!!
THAT'S THE LAST OF THEM!! AND YOU KNOW WHAT?! OUR WORK HERE ISN'T DONE... THIS PLACE IS FULL OF PRISONERS!! PEOPLE WHO DESERVE FREEDOM!
PBJ
PEOPLE AREN'T ANIMALS, PEOPLE ARE PEOPLE!!
EVEN IF THEY DO LICK THEIR BALLS!! I SAY WE FREE THE WHOLE LOT OF THEM!!!

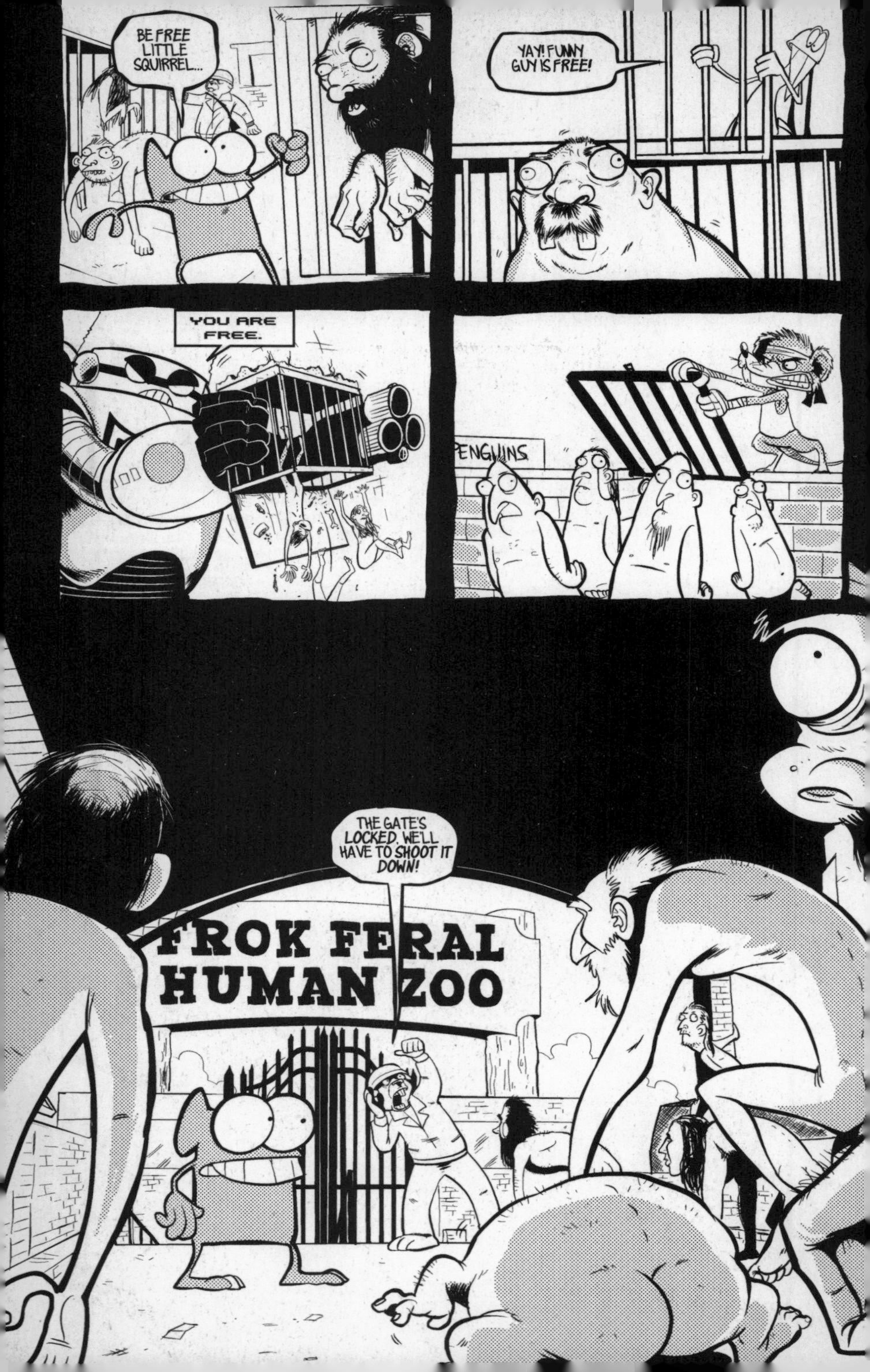
BE FREE LITTLE SQUIRREL...
YAY! FUNNY GUY IS FREE!
YOU ARE FREE.
PENGUINS
THE GATE'S LOCKED. WE'LL HAVE TO SHOOT IT DOWN!
FROK FERAL HUMAN ZOO

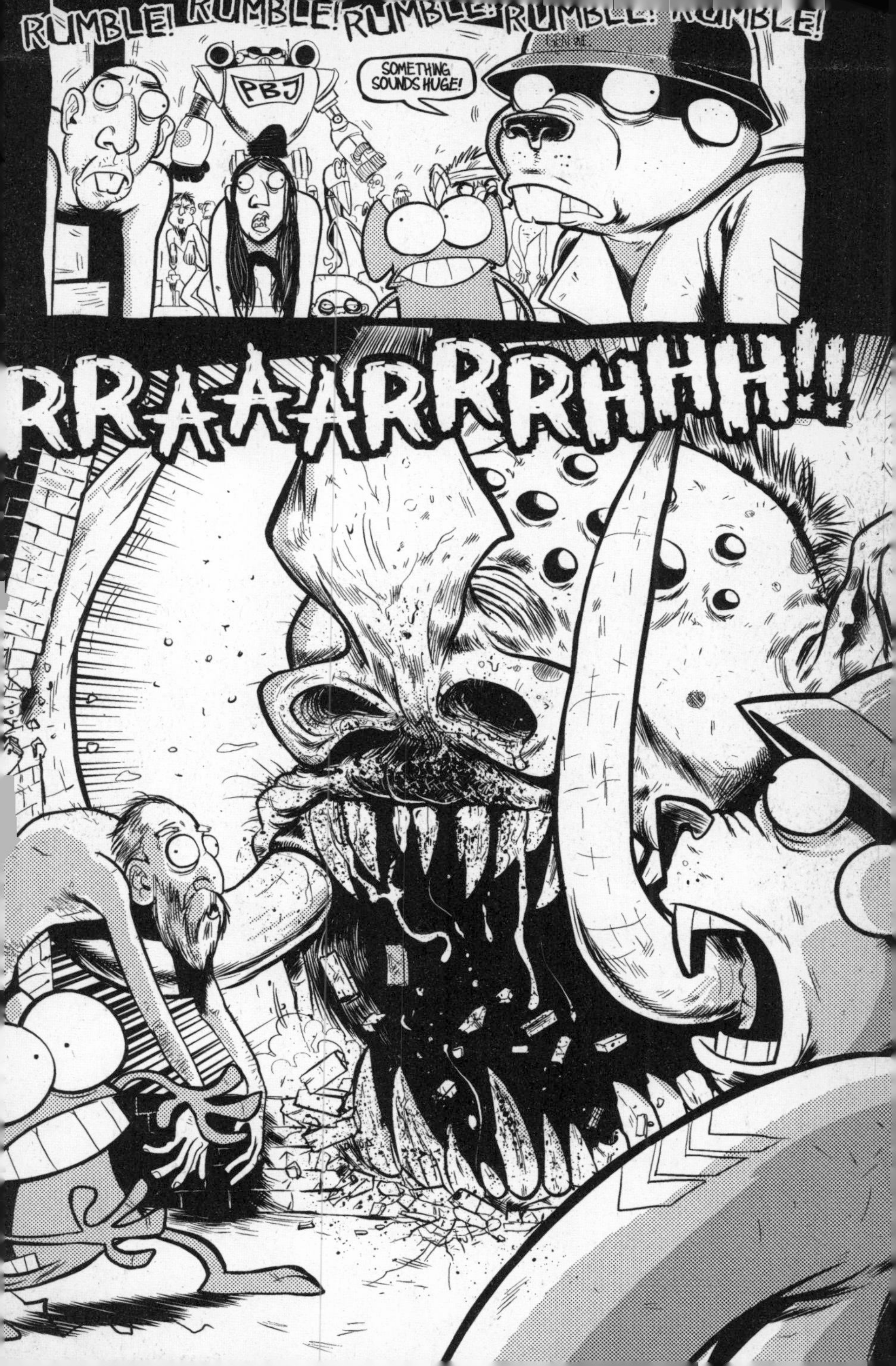
RUMBLE! RUMBLE! RUMBLE! RUMBLE! RUMBLE!
SOMETHING SOUNDS HUGE!
RRAAARRRRHHH!!

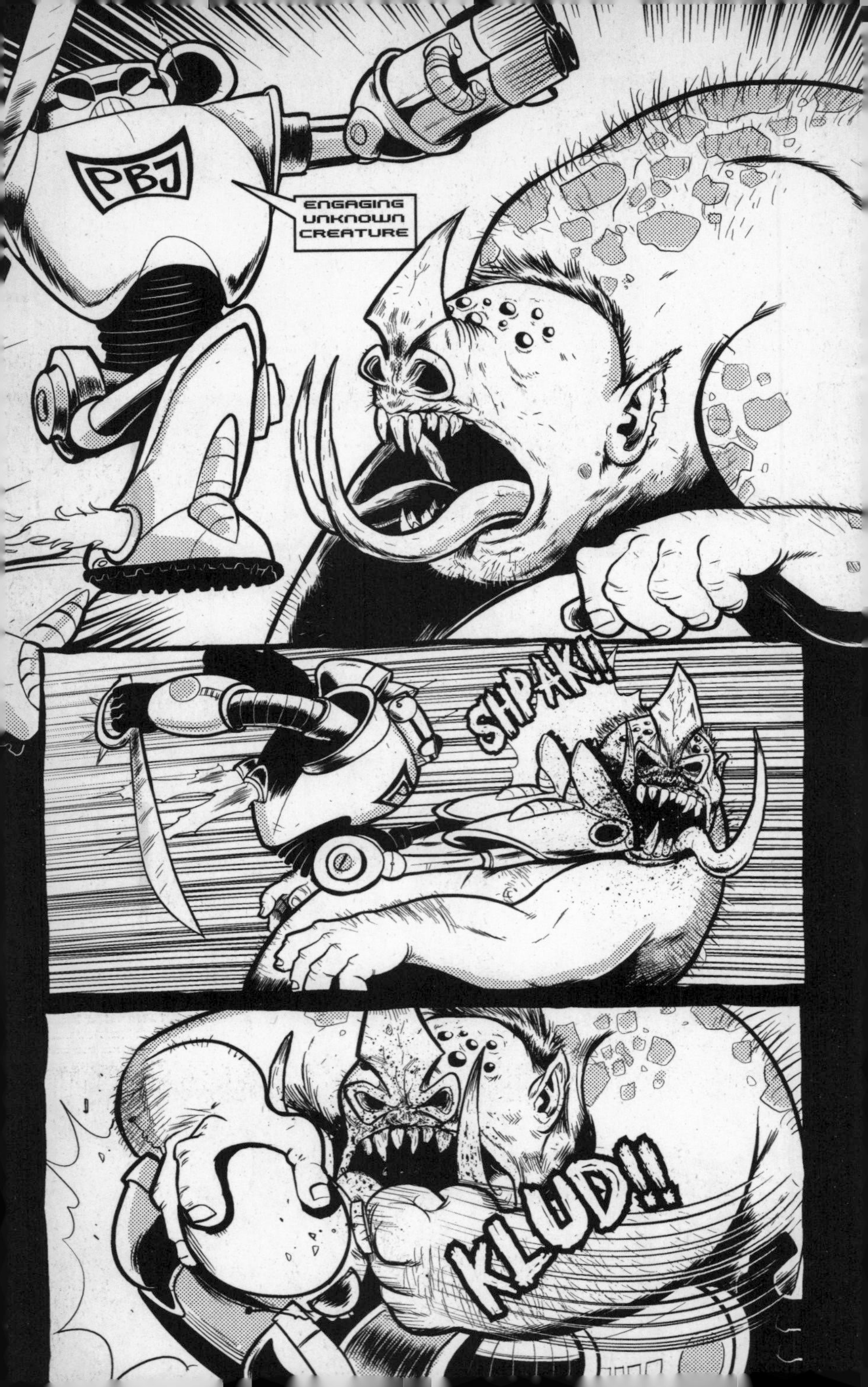

PBJ
ENGAGING UNKNOWN CREATURE
SHPAK!!
KLUD!!

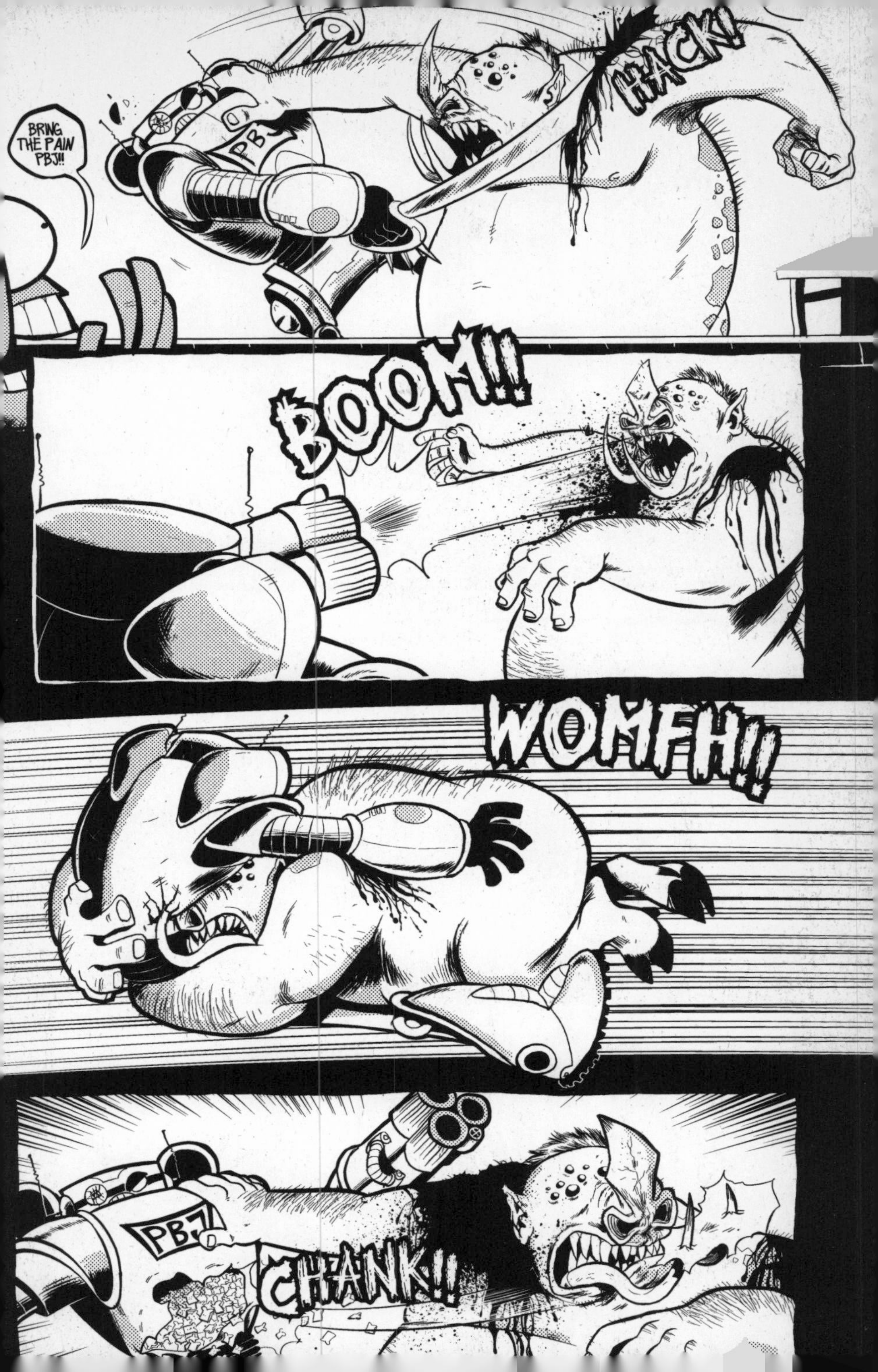
BRING THE PAIN PBJ!!
HACK!
PBJ
BOOM!!
WOMFH!!
PBJ
CHANK!!

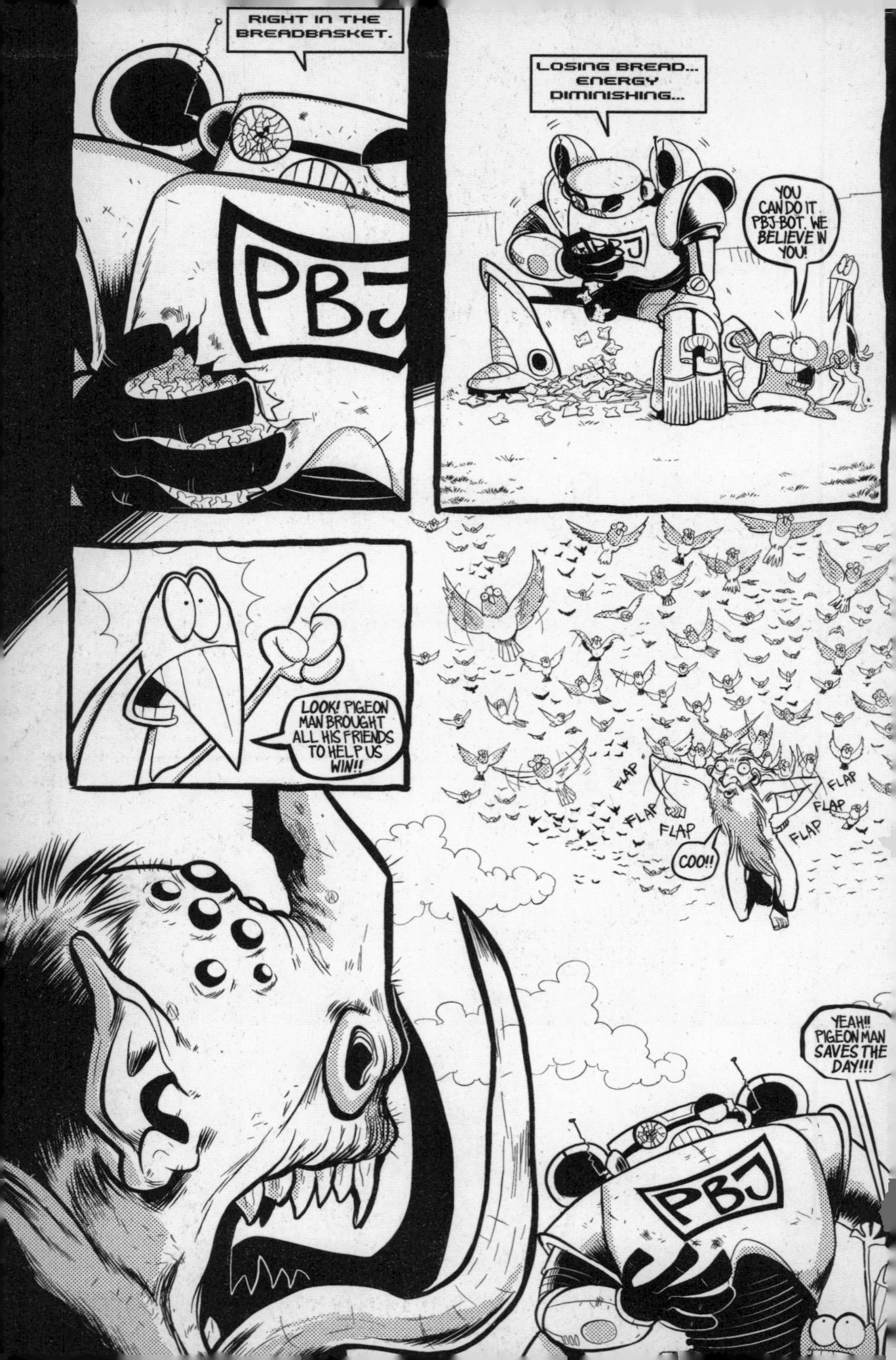
RIGHT IN THE BREADBASKET.
LOSING BREAD... ENERGY DIMINISHING...
YOU CAN DO IT, PBJ-BOT. WE BELIEVE IN YOU!
LOOK! PIGEON MAN BROUGHT ALL HIS FRIENDS TO HELP US WIN!!
FLAP
FLAP
FLAP
FLAP
FLAP
FLAP
COO!!
YEAH!! PIGEON MAN SAVES THE DAY!!!

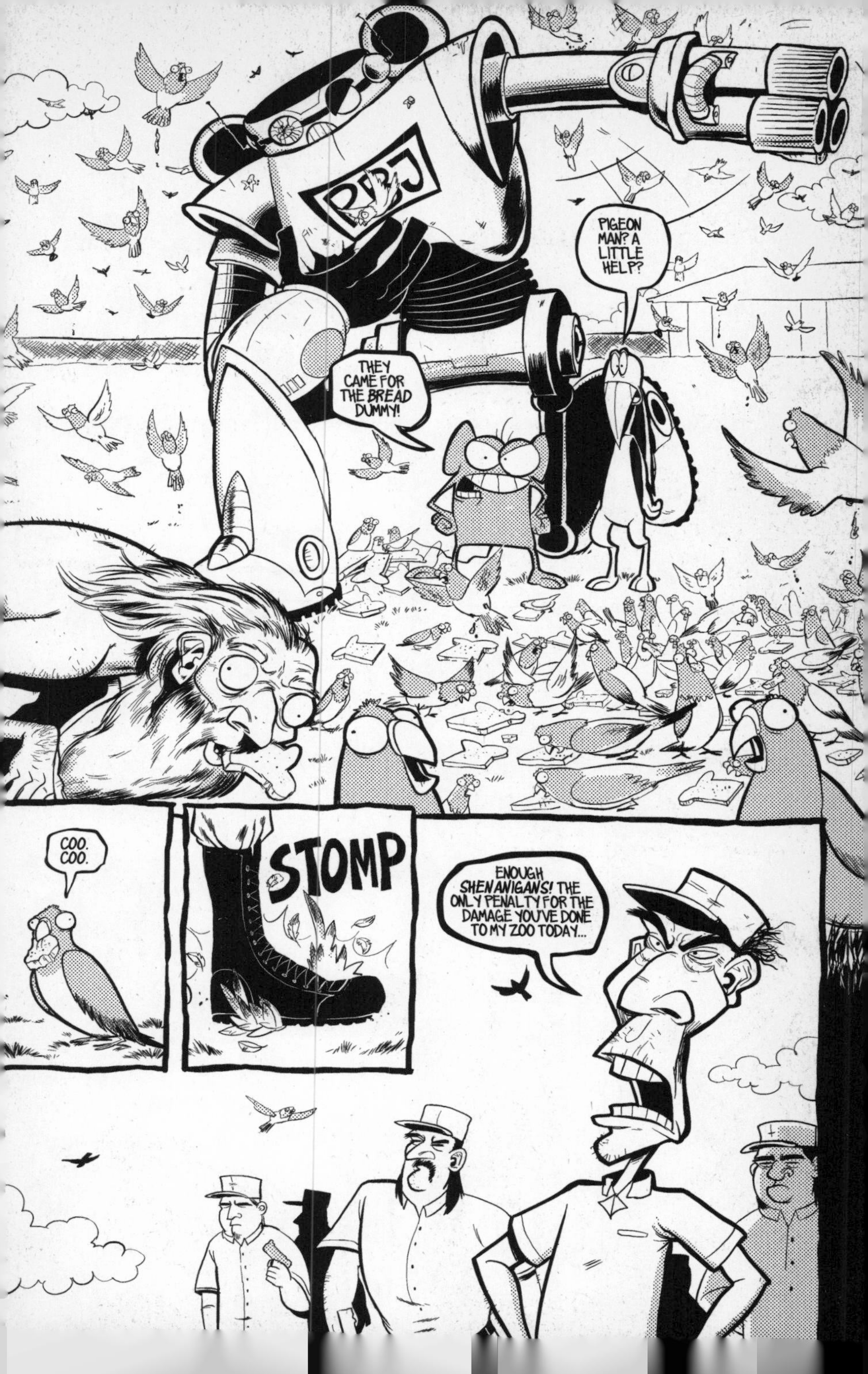
PIGEON MAN? A LITTLE HELP?
THEY CAME FOR THE BREAD DUMMY!
COO. COO.
STOMP
ENOUGH SHENANIGANS! THE ONLY PENALTY FOR THE DAMAGE YOU'VE DONE TO MY ZOO TODAY...

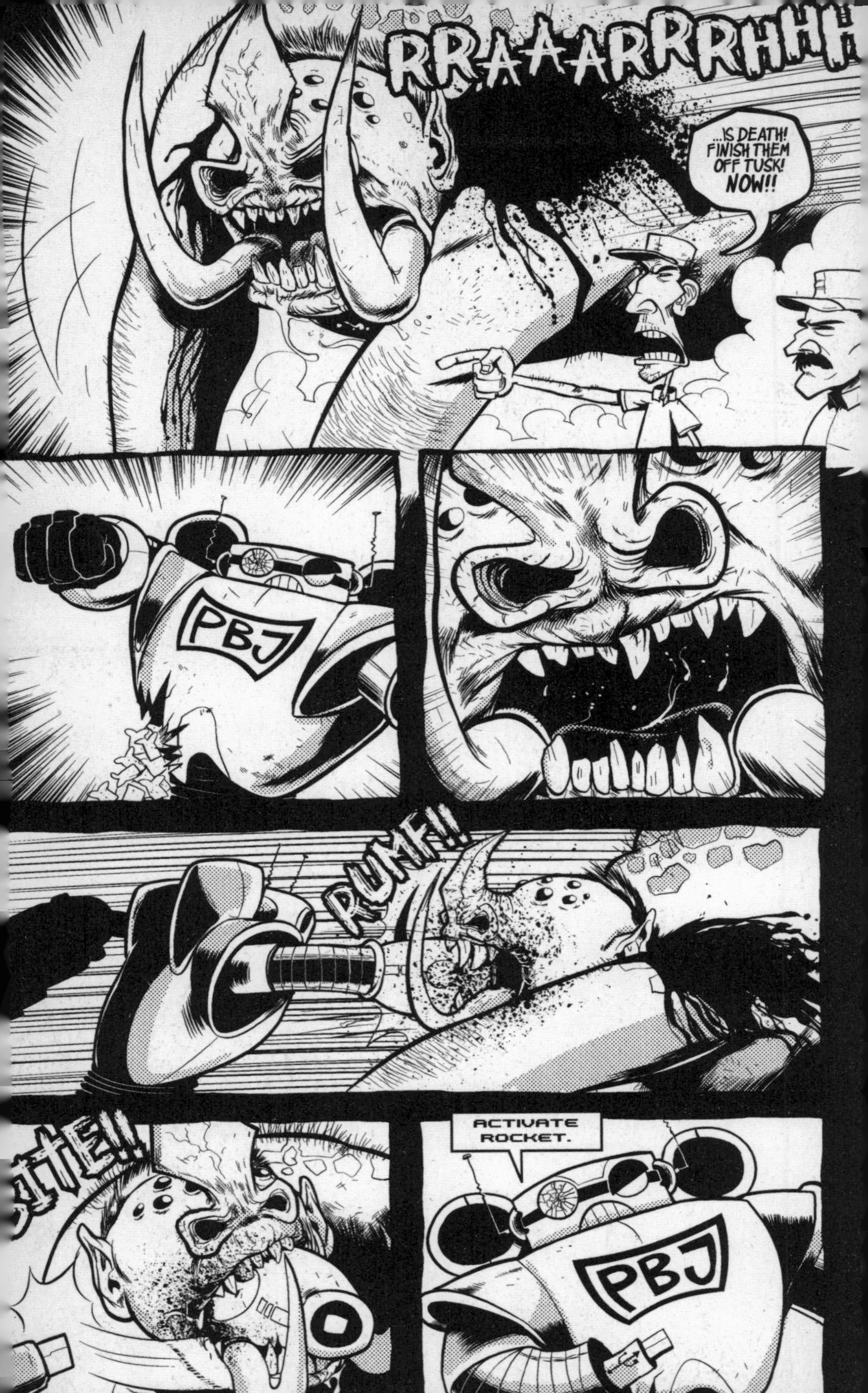
RRAAARRRHHH
...IS DEATH! FINISH THEM OFF TUSK! NOW!!
RUMF!!
ACTIVATE ROCKET.

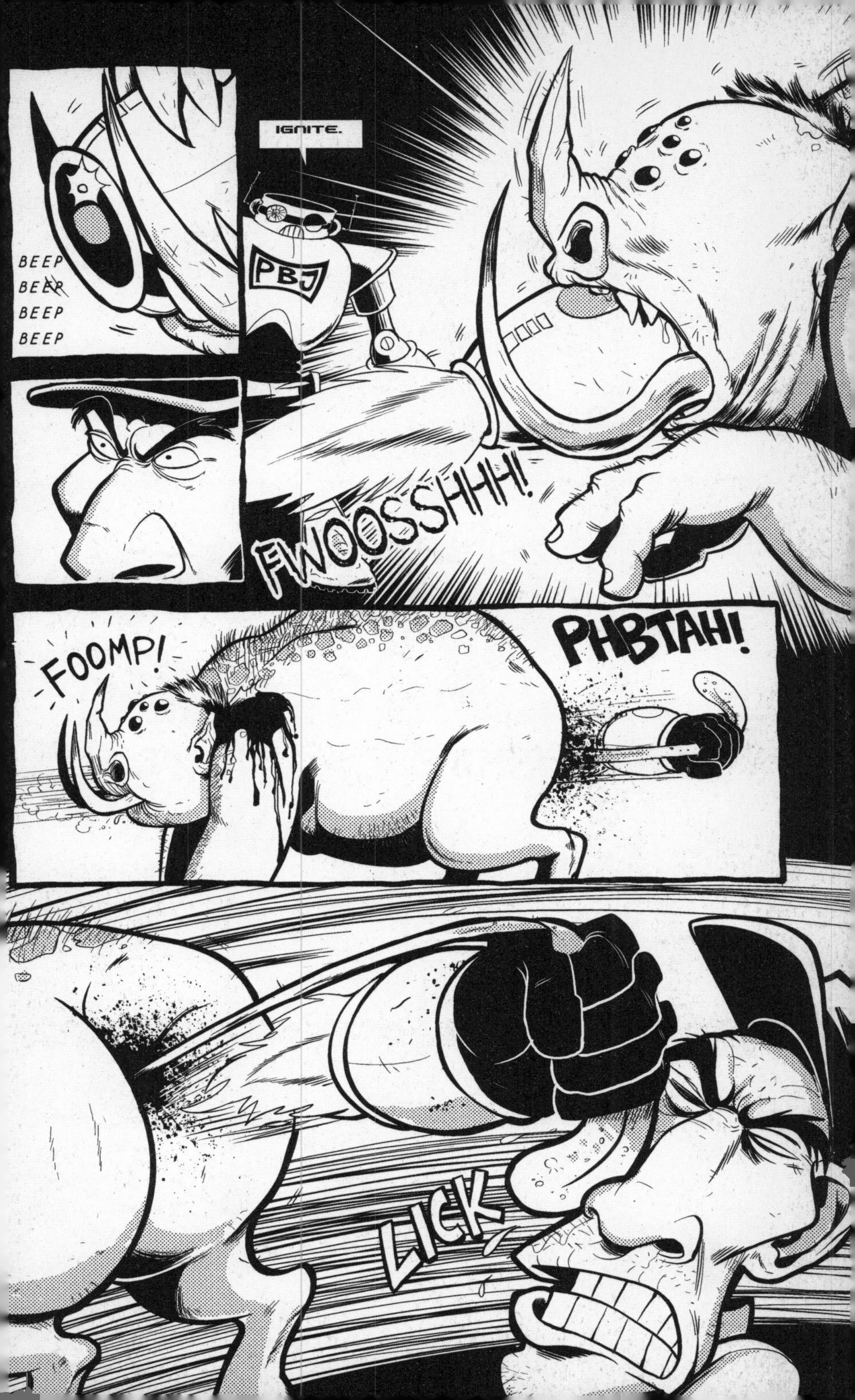
BEEP
BEEP
BEEP
BEEP
IGNITE.
PBJ
FWOOSSHHH!
FOOMP!
PHBTAH!
LICK

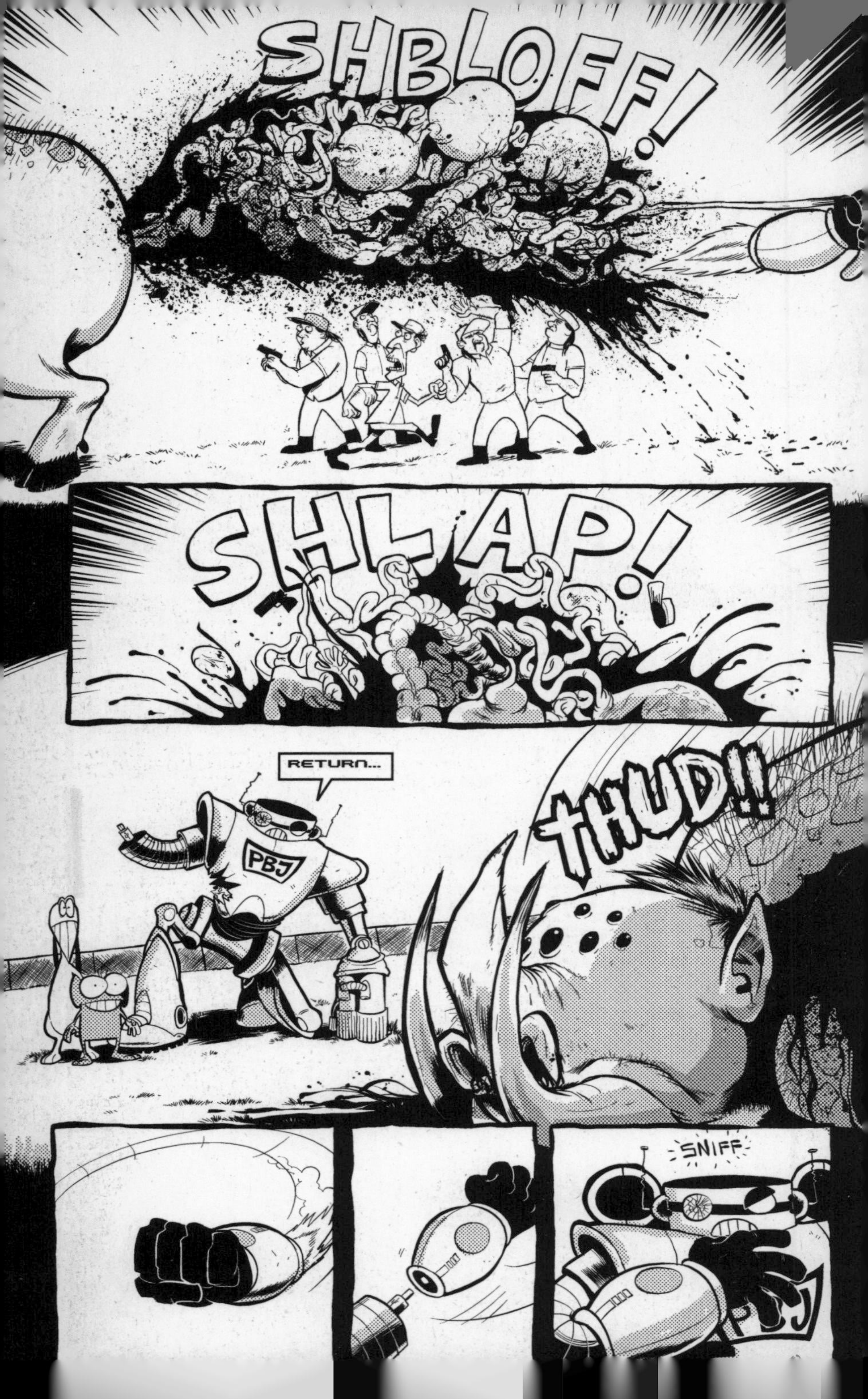
SHBLOFF!
SHLAP!
RETURN...
THUD!!
SNIFF

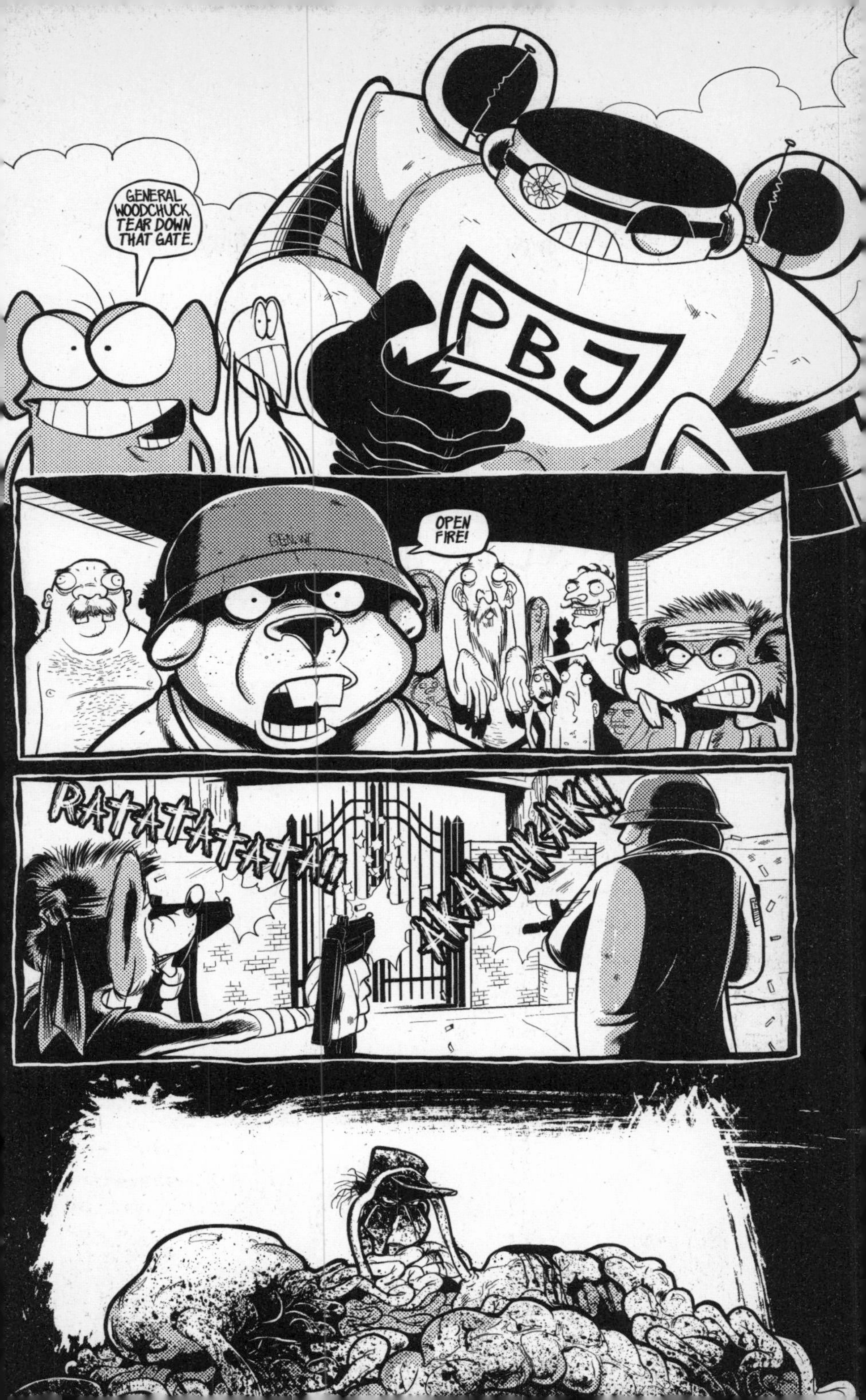

GENERAL WOODCHUCK. TEAR DOWN THAT GATE.
PBJ
OPEN FIRE!
RATATATATATA!!
AKAKAKAKAK!!

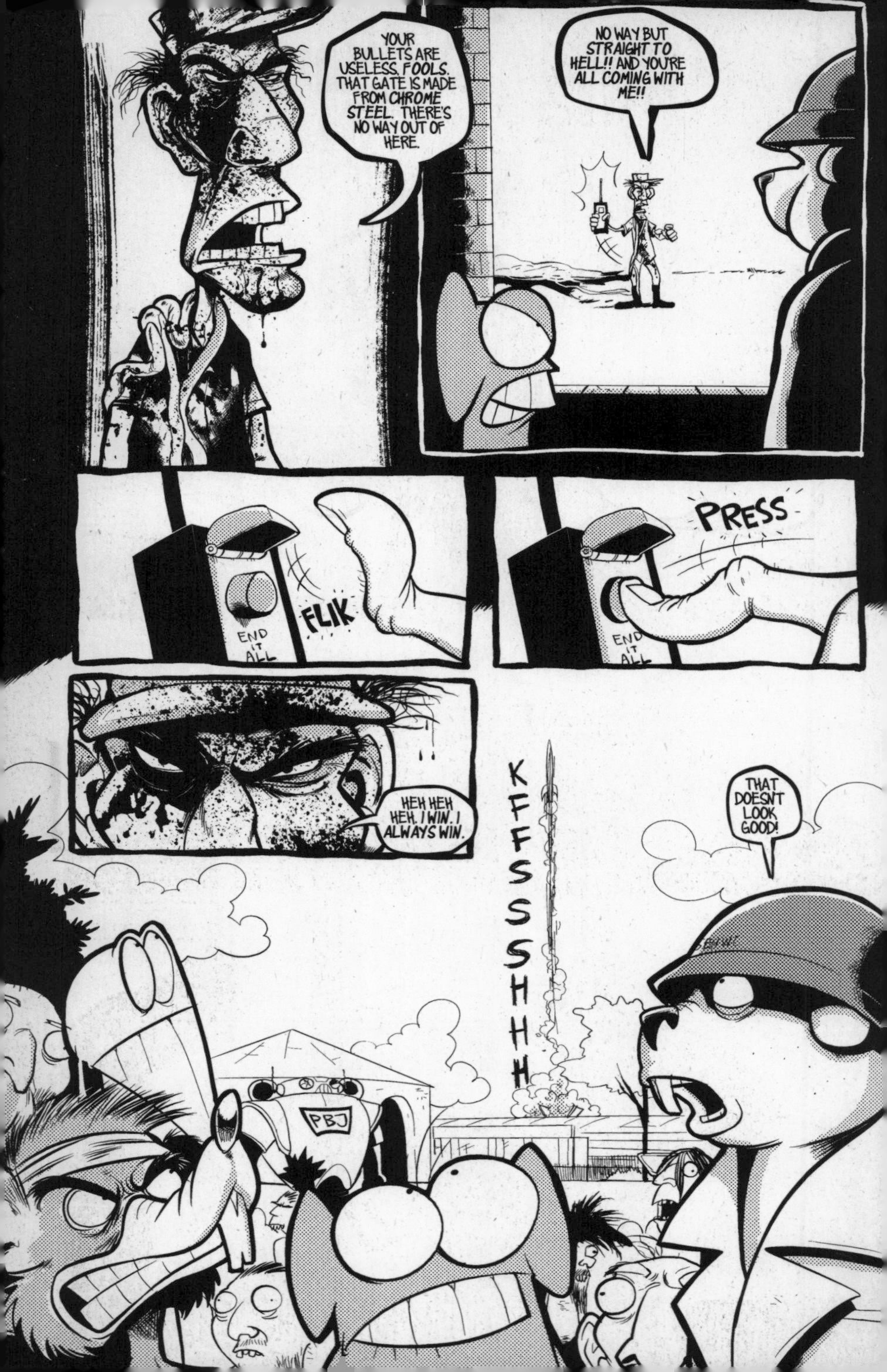
YOUR BULLETS ARE USELESS, FOOLS. THAT GATE IS MADE FROM CHROME STEEL. THERE'S NO WAY OUT OF HERE.
NO WAY BUT STRAIGHT TO HELL!! AND YOU'RE ALL COMING WITH ME!!
END IT ALL
FLIK
PRESS
END IT ALL
HEH HEH HEH. I WIN. I ALWAYS WIN.
KFFSSSHHH
THAT DOESN'T LOOK GOOD!
PBJ

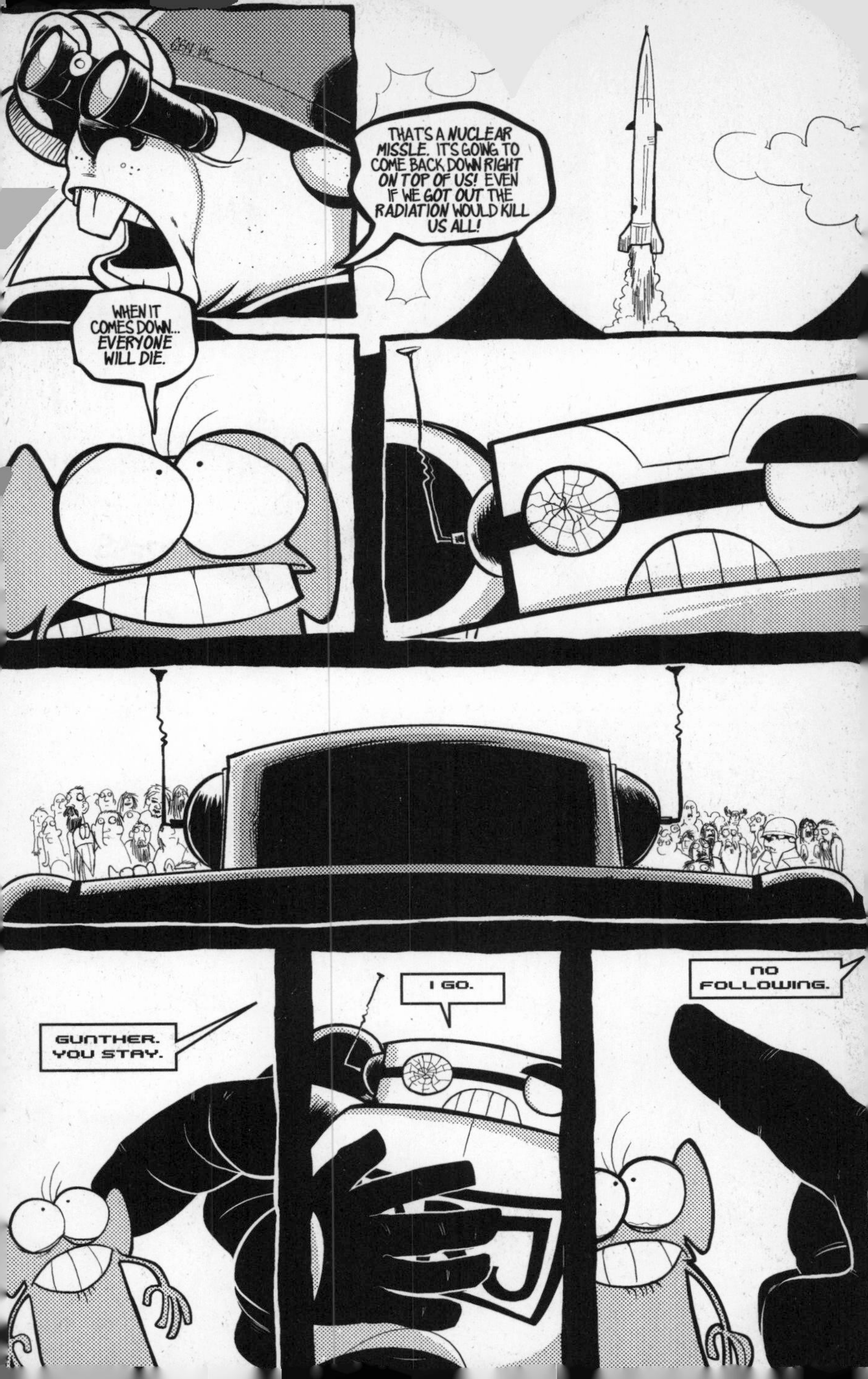
THAT'S A NUCLEAR MISSLE. IT'S GOING TO COME BACK DOWN RIGHT ON TOP OF US! EVEN IF WE GOT OUT THE RADIATION WOULD KILL US ALL!
WHEN IT COMES DOWN... EVERYONE WILL DIE.
GUNTHER. YOU STAY.
I GO.
NO FOLLOWING.

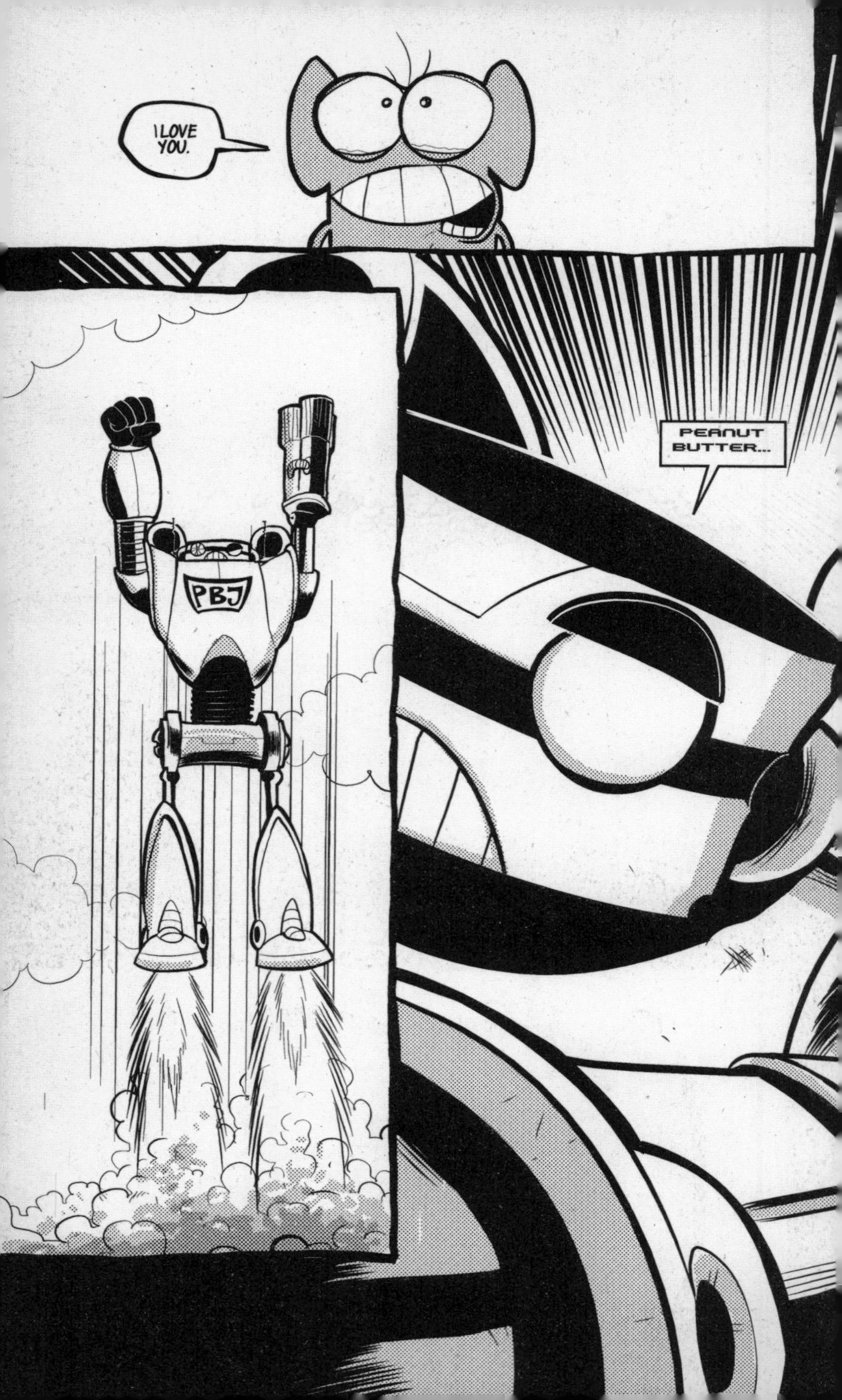
I LOVE YOU.
PEANUT BUTTER...
PBJ

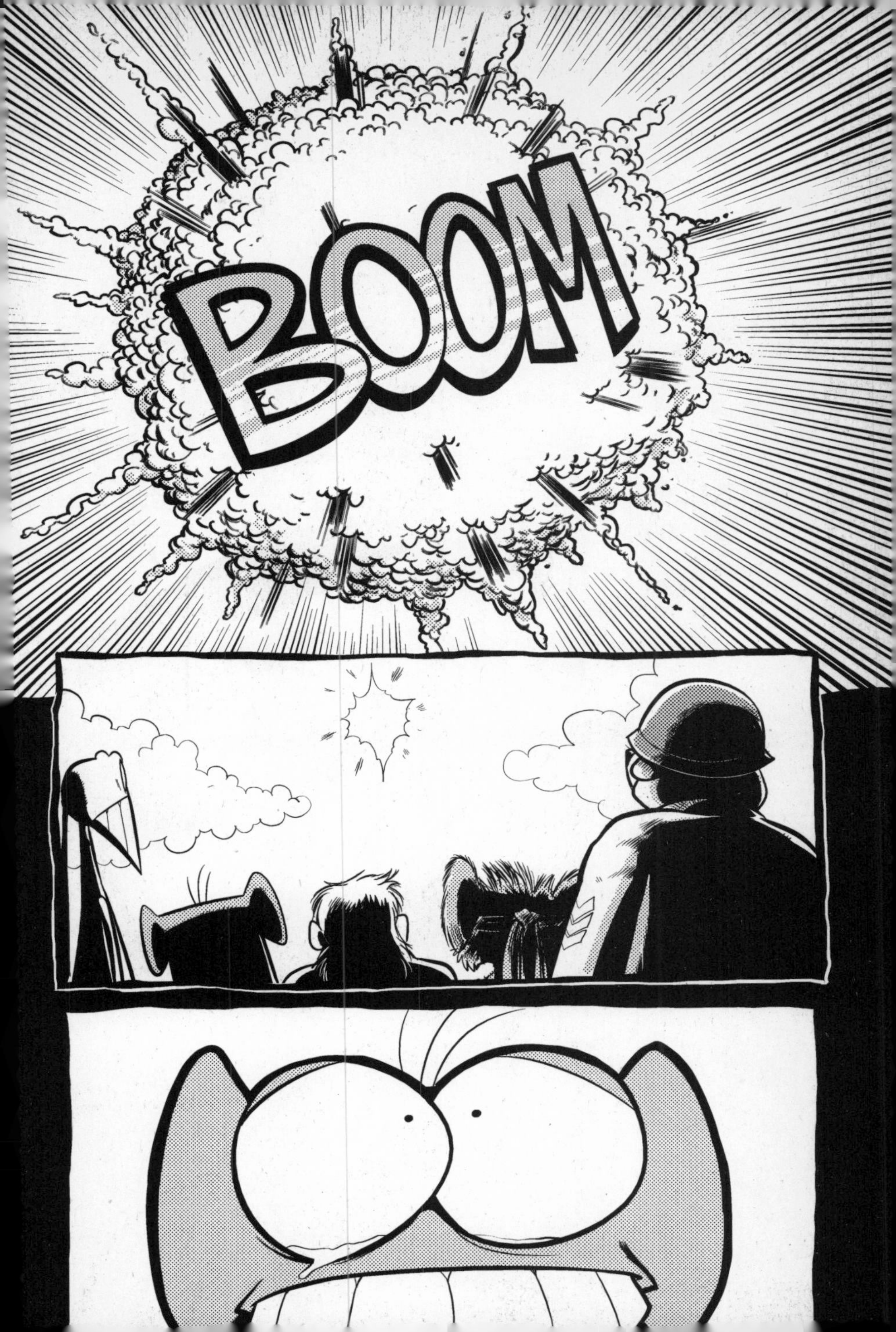
BOOM

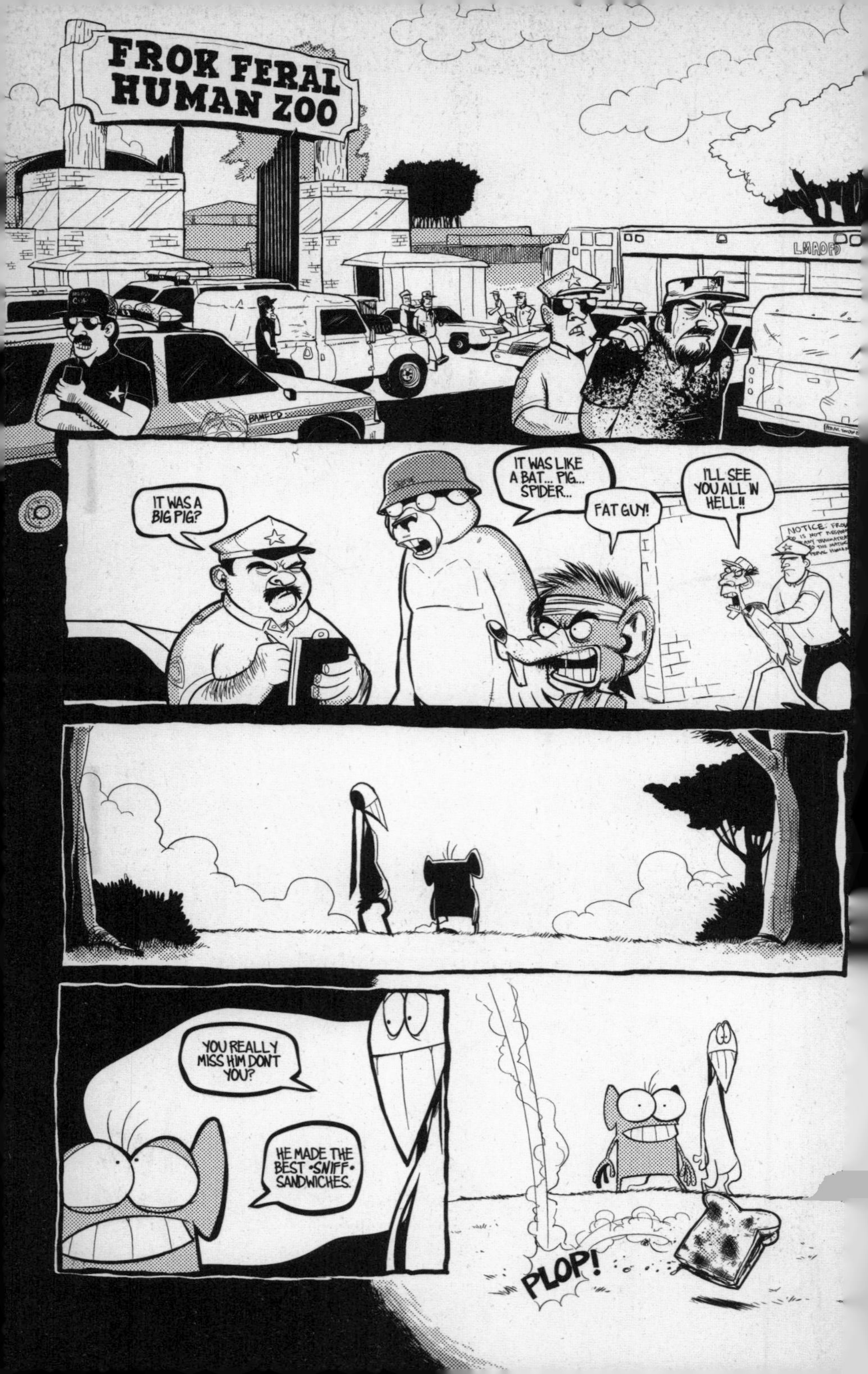
FROK FERAL HUMAN ZOO
LMAOFD
BAMFPD
IT WAS A BIG PIG?
IT WAS LIKE A BAT... PIG... SPIDER...
FAT GUY!
I'LL SEE YOU ALL IN HELL!!
YOU REALLY MISS HIM DON'T YOU?
HE MADE THE BEST •SNIFF• SANDWICHES.
PLOP!

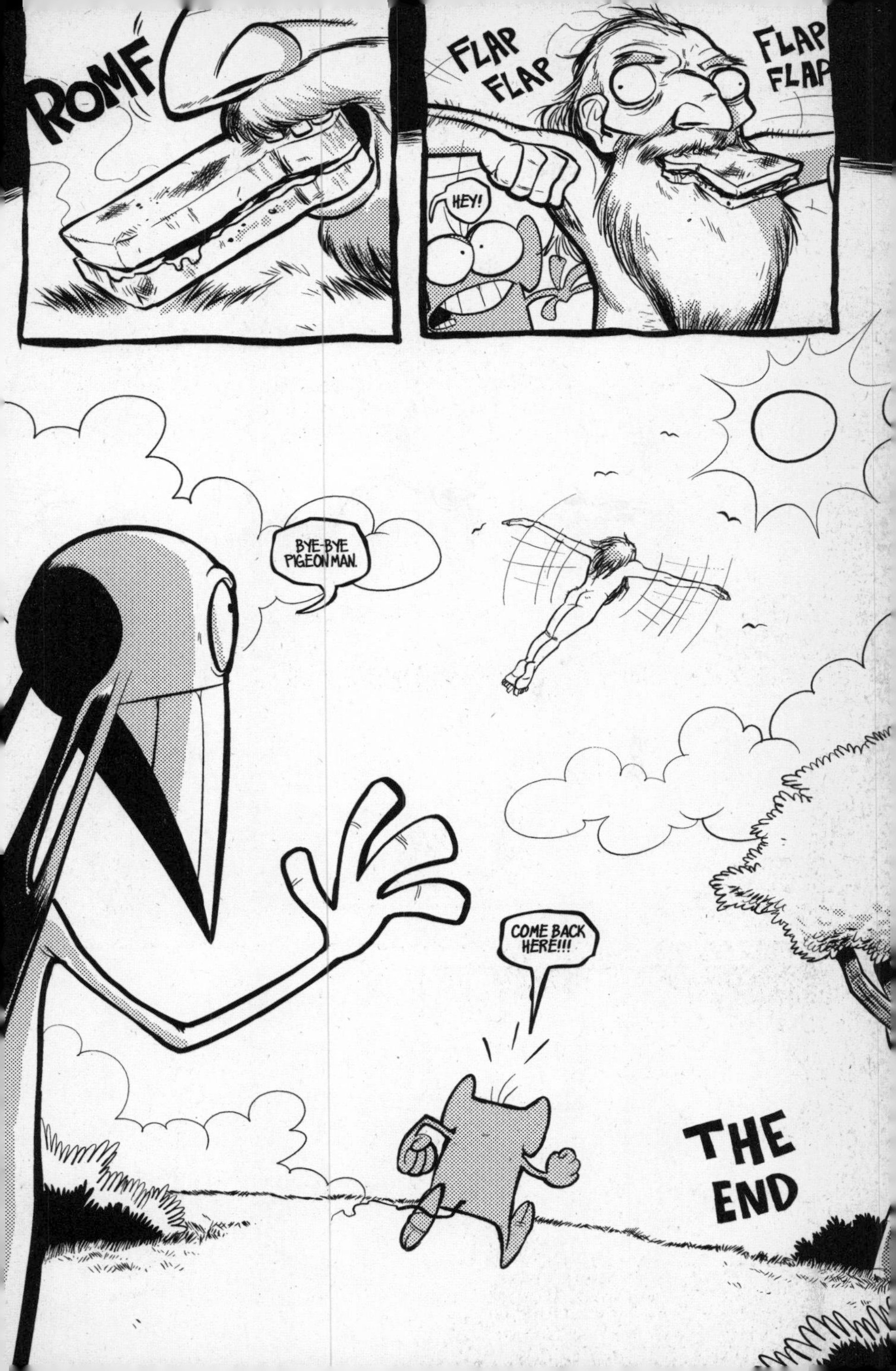
ROMF
FLAP FLAP
FLAP FLAP
HEY!
BYE-BYE PIGEON MAN.
COME BACK HERE!!!
THE END

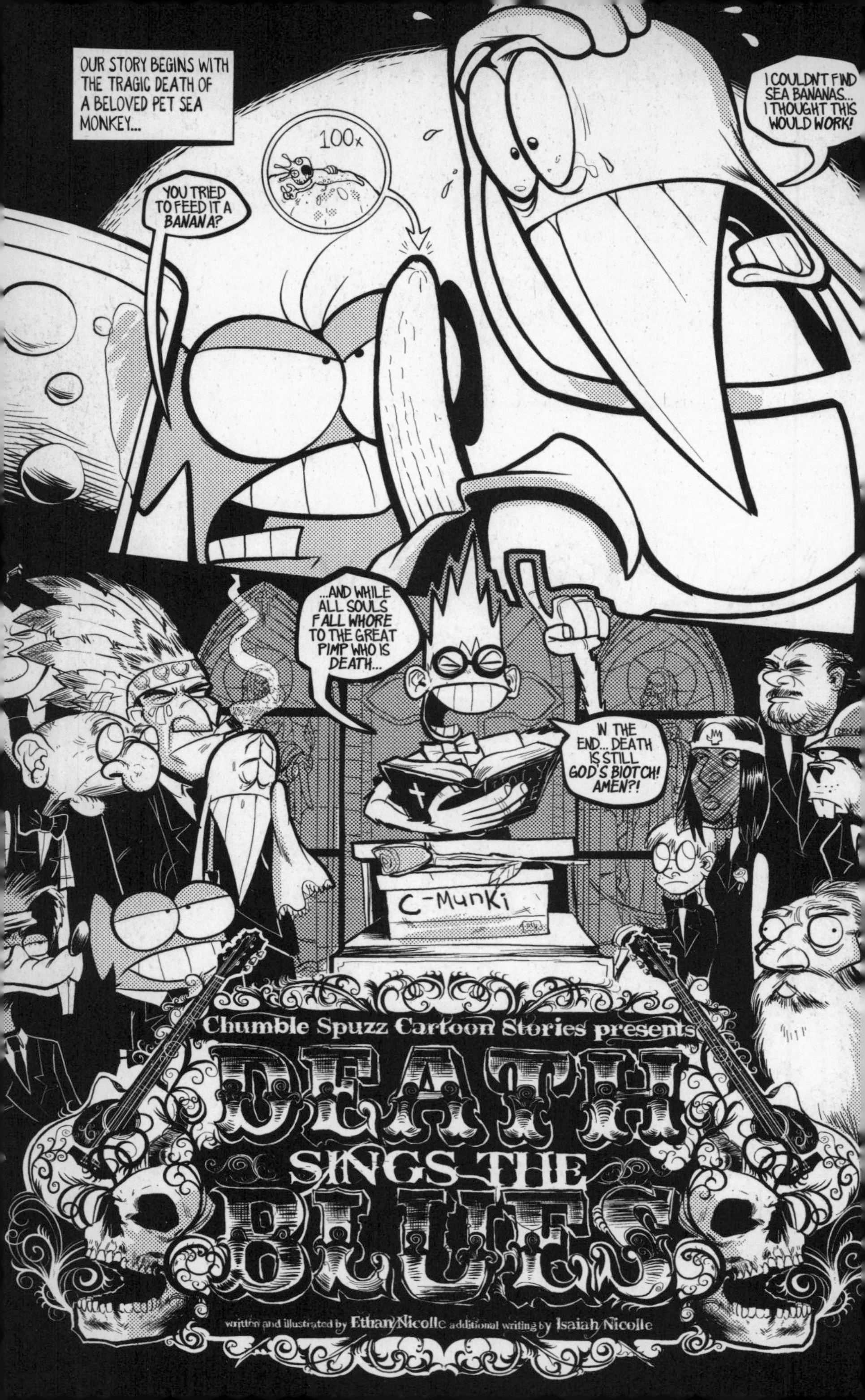

OUR STORY BEGINS WITH THE TRAGIC DEATH OF A BELOVED PET SEA MONKEY...
100x
YOU TRIED TO FEED IT A BANANA?
I COULDN'T FIND SEA BANANAS... I THOUGHT THIS WOULD WORK!
...AND WHILE ALL SOULS FALL WHORE TO THE GREAT PIMP WHO IS DEATH...
IN THE END... DEATH IS STILL GOD'S BIOTCH! AMEN?!
C-MunKi
Chumble Spuzz Cartoon Stories presents
DEATH SINGS THE BLUES
written and illustrated by Ethan Nicolle additional writing by Isaiah Nicolle

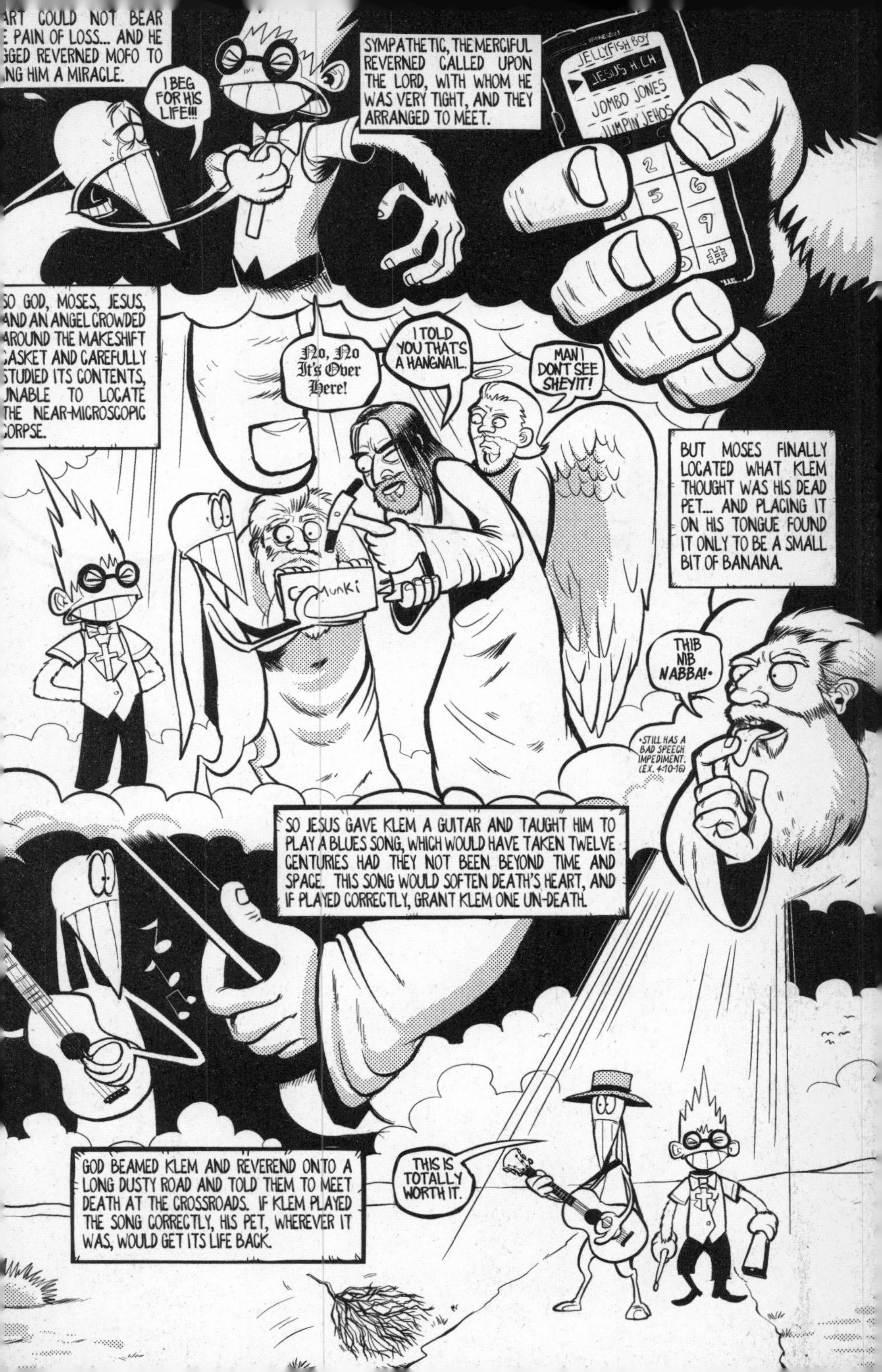
ART COULD NOT BEAR
E PAIN OF LOSS... AND HE
GGED REVERNED MOFO TO
NG HIM A MIRACLE.
I BEG FOR HIS LIFE!!!
SYMPATHETIC, THE MERCIFUL REVERNED CALLED UPON THE LORD, WITH WHOM HE WAS VERY TIGHT, AND THEY ARRANGED TO MEET.
JELLYFISH BOY
JESUS H. CH.
JOMBO JONES
JUMPIN' JEHOS
SO GOD, MOSES, JESUS, AND AN ANGEL CROWDED AROUND THE MAKESHIFT CASKET AND CAREFULLY STUDIED ITS CONTENTS, UNABLE TO LOCATE THE NEAR-MICROSCOPIC CORPSE.
No, No It's Over Here!
I TOLD YOU THAT'S A HANGNAIL.
MAN! I DON'T SEE SHEYIT!
Munki
BUT MOSES FINALLY LOCATED WHAT KLEM THOUGHT WAS HIS DEAD PET... AND PLACING IT ON HIS TONGUE FOUND IT ONLY TO BE A SMALL BIT OF BANANA.
THIB NIB NABBA!*
*STILL HAS A BAD SPEECH IMPEDIMENT. (EX. 4:10-16)
SO JESUS GAVE KLEM A GUITAR AND TAUGHT HIM TO PLAY A BLUES SONG, WHICH WOULD HAVE TAKEN TWELVE CENTURIES HAD THEY NOT BEEN BEYOND TIME AND SPACE. THIS SONG WOULD SOFTEN DEATH'S HEART, AND IF PLAYED CORRECTLY, GRANT KLEM ONE UN-DEATH.
GOD BEAMED KLEM AND REVEREND ONTO A LONG DUSTY ROAD AND TOLD THEM TO MEET DEATH AT THE CROSSROADS. IF KLEM PLAYED THE SONG CORRECTLY, HIS PET, WHEREVER IT WAS, WOULD GET ITS LIFE BACK.
THIS IS TOTALLY WORTH IT.

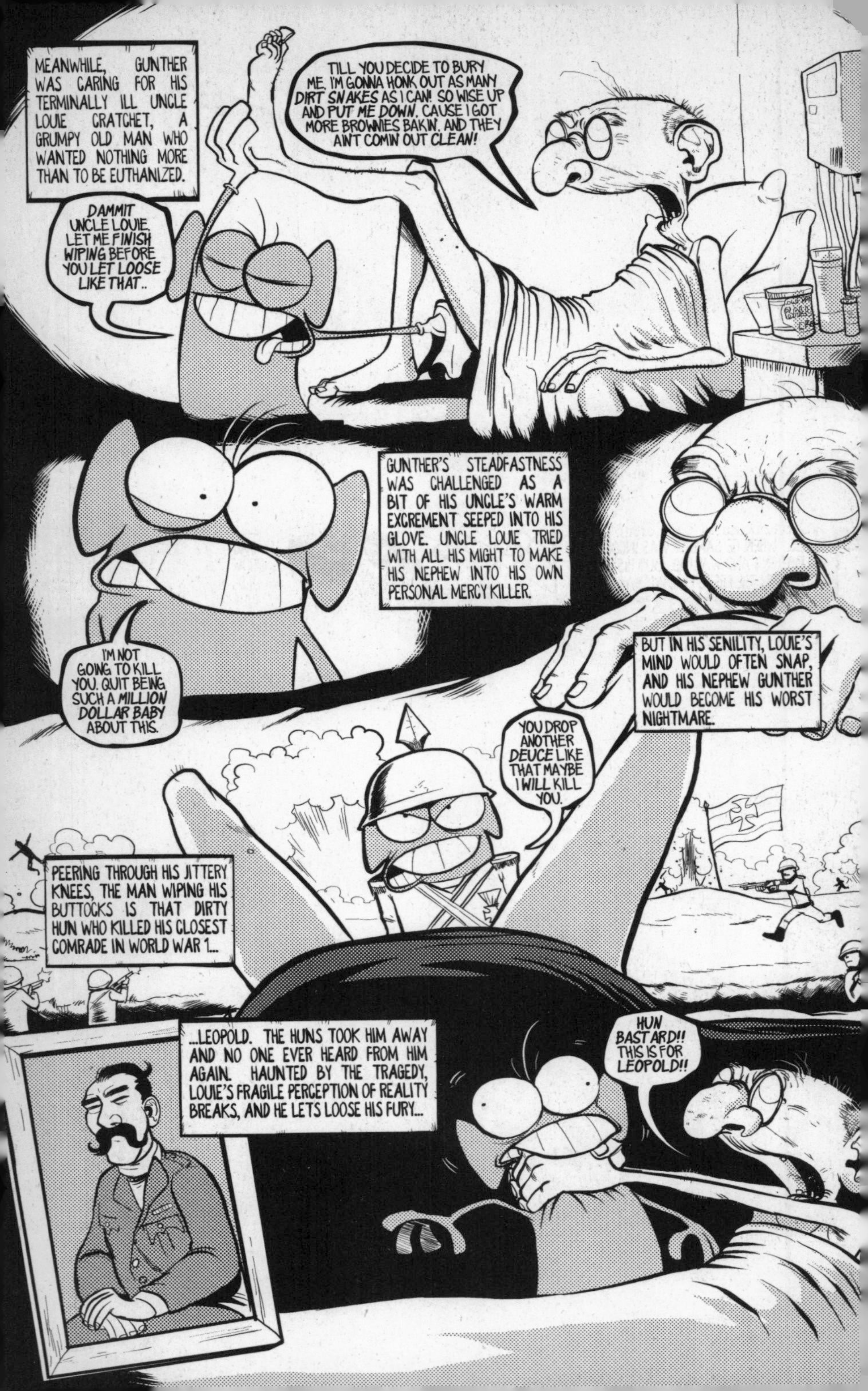

MEANWHILE, GUNTHER WAS CARING FOR HIS TERMINALLY ILL UNCLE LOUIE CRATCHET, A GRUMPY OLD MAN WHO WANTED NOTHING MORE THAN TO BE EUTHANIZED.
TILL YOU DECIDE TO BURY ME, I'M GONNA HONK OUT AS MANY DIRT SNAKES AS I CAN! SO WISE UP AND PUT ME DOWN, CAUSE I GOT MORE BROWNIES BAKIN, AND THEY AIN'T COMIN OUT CLEAN!
DAMMIT UNCLE LOUIE, LET ME FINISH WIPING BEFORE YOU LET LOOSE LIKE THAT..
GUNTHER'S STEADFASTNESS WAS CHALLENGED AS A BIT OF HIS UNCLE'S WARM EXCREMENT SEEPED INTO HIS GLOVE. UNCLE LOUIE TRIED WITH ALL HIS MIGHT TO MAKE HIS NEPHEW INTO HIS OWN PERSONAL MERCY KILLER.
I'M NOT GOING TO KILL YOU. QUIT BEING SUCH A MILLION DOLLAR BABY ABOUT THIS.
YOU DROP ANOTHER DEUCE LIKE THAT MAYBE I WILL KILL YOU.
BUT IN HIS SENILITY, LOUIE'S MIND WOULD OFTEN SNAP, AND HIS NEPHEW GUNTHER WOULD BECOME HIS WORST NIGHTMARE.
PEERING THROUGH HIS JITTERY KNEES, THE MAN WIPING HIS BUTTOCKS IS THAT DIRTY HUN WHO KILLED HIS CLOSEST COMRADE IN WORLD WAR 1...
...LEOPOLD. THE HUNS TOOK HIM AWAY AND NO ONE EVER HEARD FROM HIM AGAIN. HAUNTED BY THE TRAGEDY, LOUIE'S FRAGILE PERCEPTION OF REALITY BREAKS, AND HE LETS LOOSE HIS FURY...
HUN BASTARD!! THIS IS FOR LEOPOLD!!

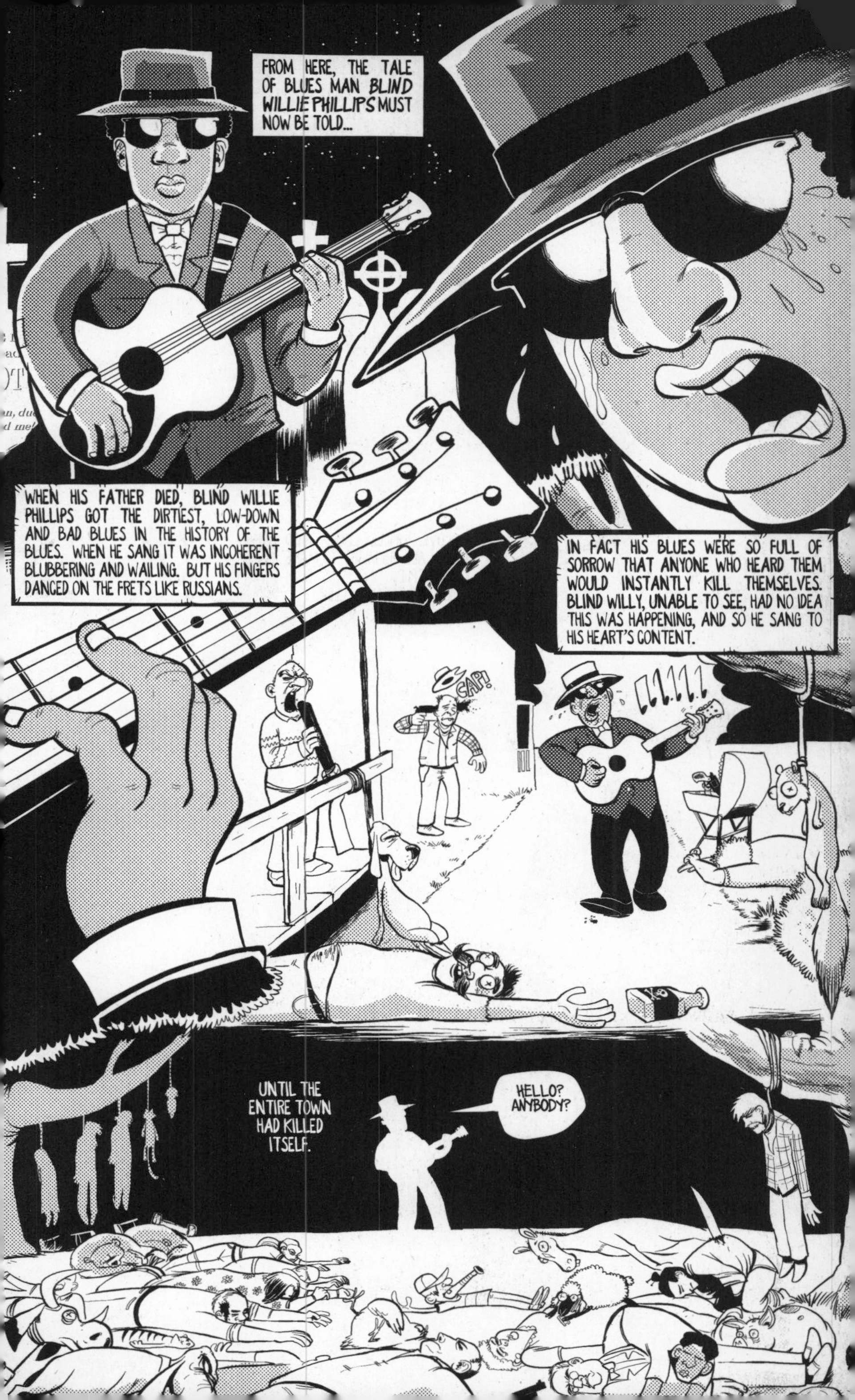
FROM HERE, THE TALE OF BLUES MAN BLIND WILLIE PHILLIPS MUST NOW BE TOLD...
WHEN HIS FATHER DIED, BLIND WILLIE PHILLIPS GOT THE DIRTIEST, LOW-DOWN AND BAD BLUES IN THE HISTORY OF THE BLUES. WHEN HE SANG IT WAS INCOHERENT BLUBBERING AND WAILING. BUT HIS FINGERS DANCED ON THE FRETS LIKE RUSSIANS.
IN FACT HIS BLUES WERE SO FULL OF SORROW THAT ANYONE WHO HEARD THEM WOULD INSTANTLY KILL THEMSELVES. BLIND WILLY, UNABLE TO SEE, HAD NO IDEA THIS WAS HAPPENING, AND SO HE SANG TO HIS HEART'S CONTENT.
CAP!
UNTIL THE ENTIRE TOWN HAD KILLED ITSELF.
HELLO? ANYBODY?

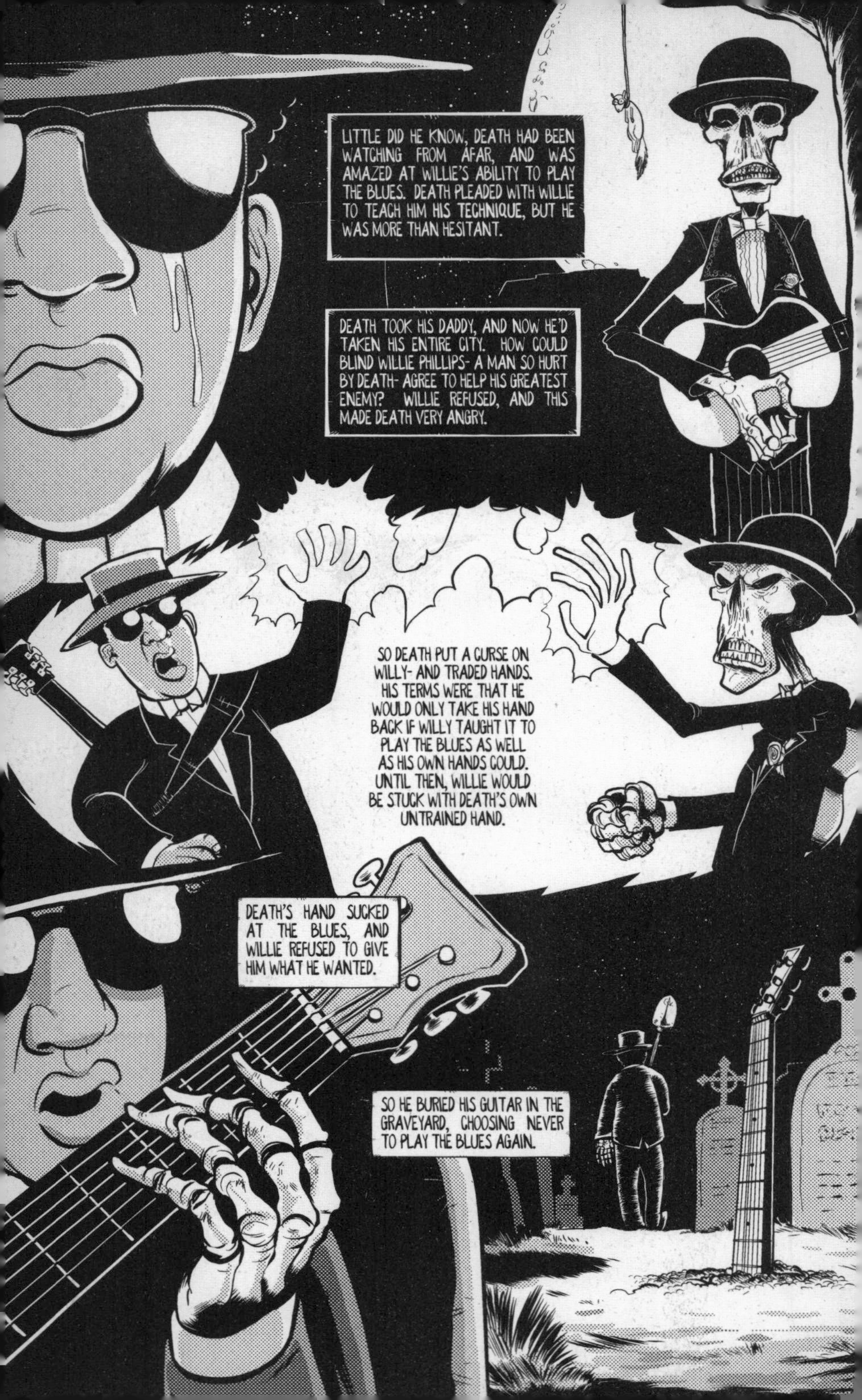
LITTLE DID HE KNOW, DEATH HAD BEEN WATCHING FROM AFAR, AND WAS AMAZED AT WILLIE'S ABILITY TO PLAY THE BLUES. DEATH PLEADED WITH WILLIE TO TEACH HIM HIS TECHNIQUE, BUT HE WAS MORE THAN HESITANT.
DEATH TOOK HIS DADDY, AND NOW HE'D TAKEN HIS ENTIRE CITY. HOW COULD BLIND WILLIE PHILLIPS- A MAN SO HURT BY DEATH- AGREE TO HELP HIS GREATEST ENEMY? WILLIE REFUSED, AND THIS MADE DEATH VERY ANGRY.
SO DEATH PUT A CURSE ON WILLY- AND TRADED HANDS. HIS TERMS WERE THAT HE WOULD ONLY TAKE HIS HAND BACK IF WILLY TAUGHT IT TO PLAY THE BLUES AS WELL AS HIS OWN HANDS COULD. UNTIL THEN, WILLIE WOULD BE STUCK WITH DEATH'S OWN UNTRAINED HAND.
DEATH'S HAND SUCKED AT THE BLUES, AND WILLIE REFUSED TO GIVE HIM WHAT HE WANTED.
SO HE BURIED HIS GUITAR IN THE GRAVEYARD, CHOOSING NEVER TO PLAY THE BLUES AGAIN.

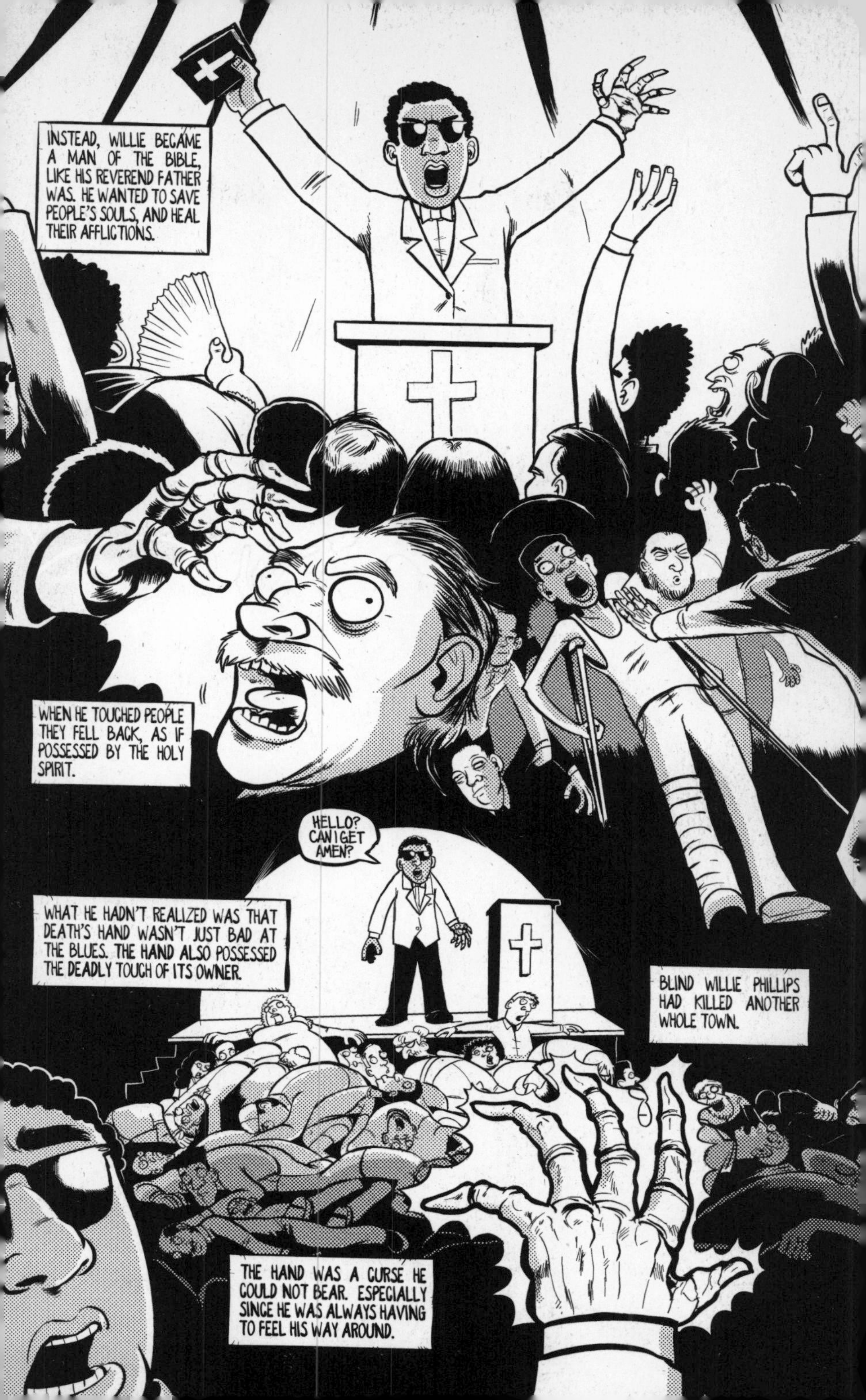
INSTEAD, WILLIE BECAME A MAN OF THE BIBLE, LIKE HIS REVEREND FATHER WAS. HE WANTED TO SAVE PEOPLE'S SOULS, AND HEAL THEIR AFFLICTIONS.
WHEN HE TOUCHED PEOPLE THEY FELL BACK, AS IF POSSESSED BY THE HOLY SPIRIT.
HELLO? CAN I GET AMEN?
WHAT HE HADN'T REALIZED WAS THAT DEATH'S HAND WASN'T JUST BAD AT THE BLUES. THE HAND ALSO POSSESSED THE DEADLY TOUCH OF ITS OWNER.
BLIND WILLIE PHILLIPS HAD KILLED ANOTHER WHOLE TOWN.
THE HAND WAS A CURSE HE COULD NOT BEAR. ESPECIALLY SINCE HE WAS ALWAYS HAVING TO FEEL HIS WAY AROUND.

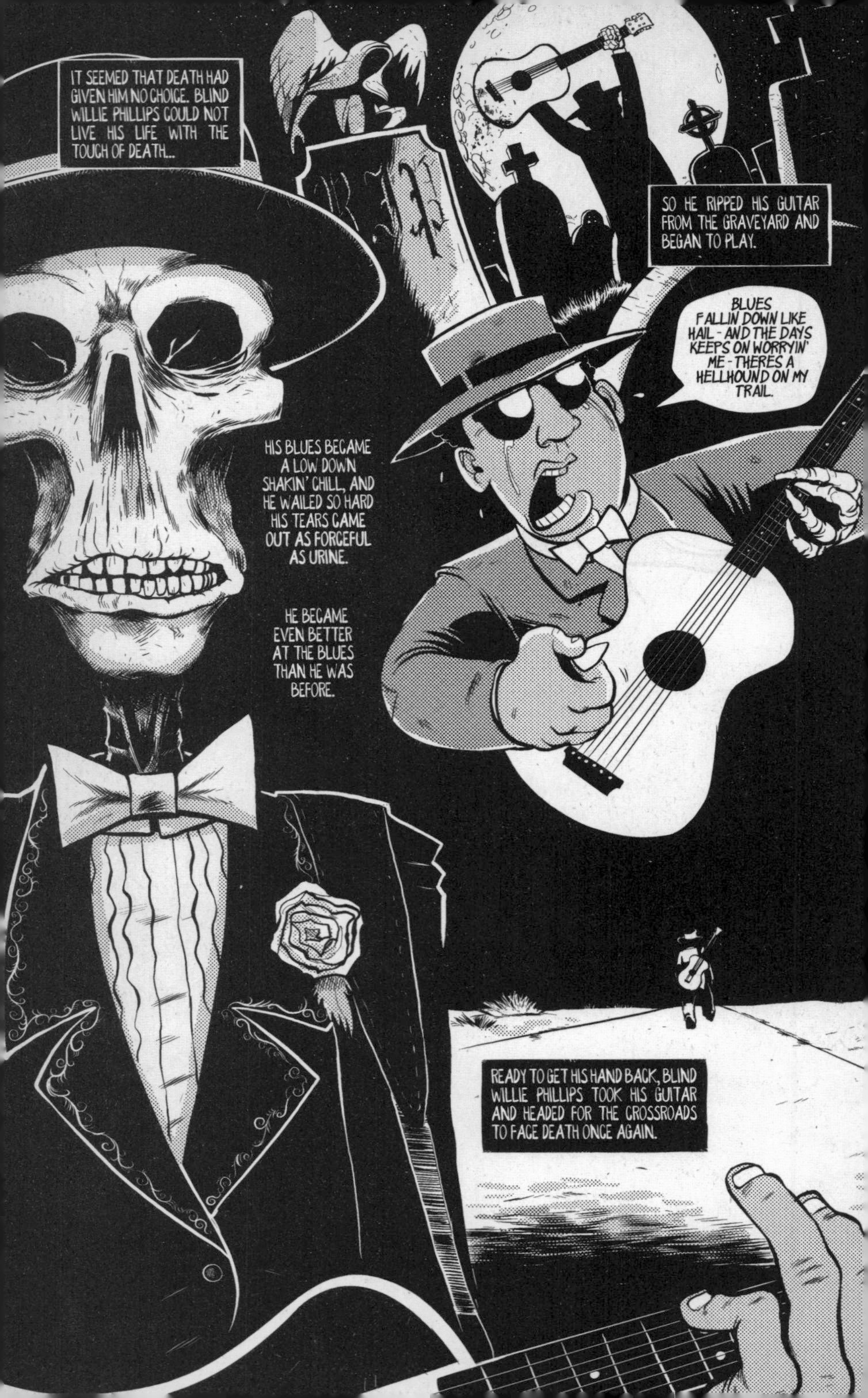
IT SEEMED THAT DEATH HAD GIVEN HIM NO CHOICE. BLIND WILLIE PHILLIPS COULD NOT LIVE HIS LIFE WITH THE TOUCH OF DEATH...
SO HE RIPPED HIS GUITAR FROM THE GRAVEYARD AND BEGAN TO PLAY.
BLUES FALLIN DOWN LIKE HAIL - AND THE DAYS KEEPS ON WORRYIN' ME - THERES A HELLHOUND ON MY TRAIL.
HIS BLUES BECAME A LOW DOWN SHAKIN' CHILL, AND HE WAILED SO HARD HIS TEARS CAME OUT AS FORCEFUL AS URINE.
HE BECAME EVEN BETTER AT THE BLUES THAN HE WAS BEFORE.
READY TO GET HIS HAND BACK, BLIND WILLIE PHILLIPS TOOK HIS GUITAR AND HEADED FOR THE CROSSROADS TO FACE DEATH ONCE AGAIN.

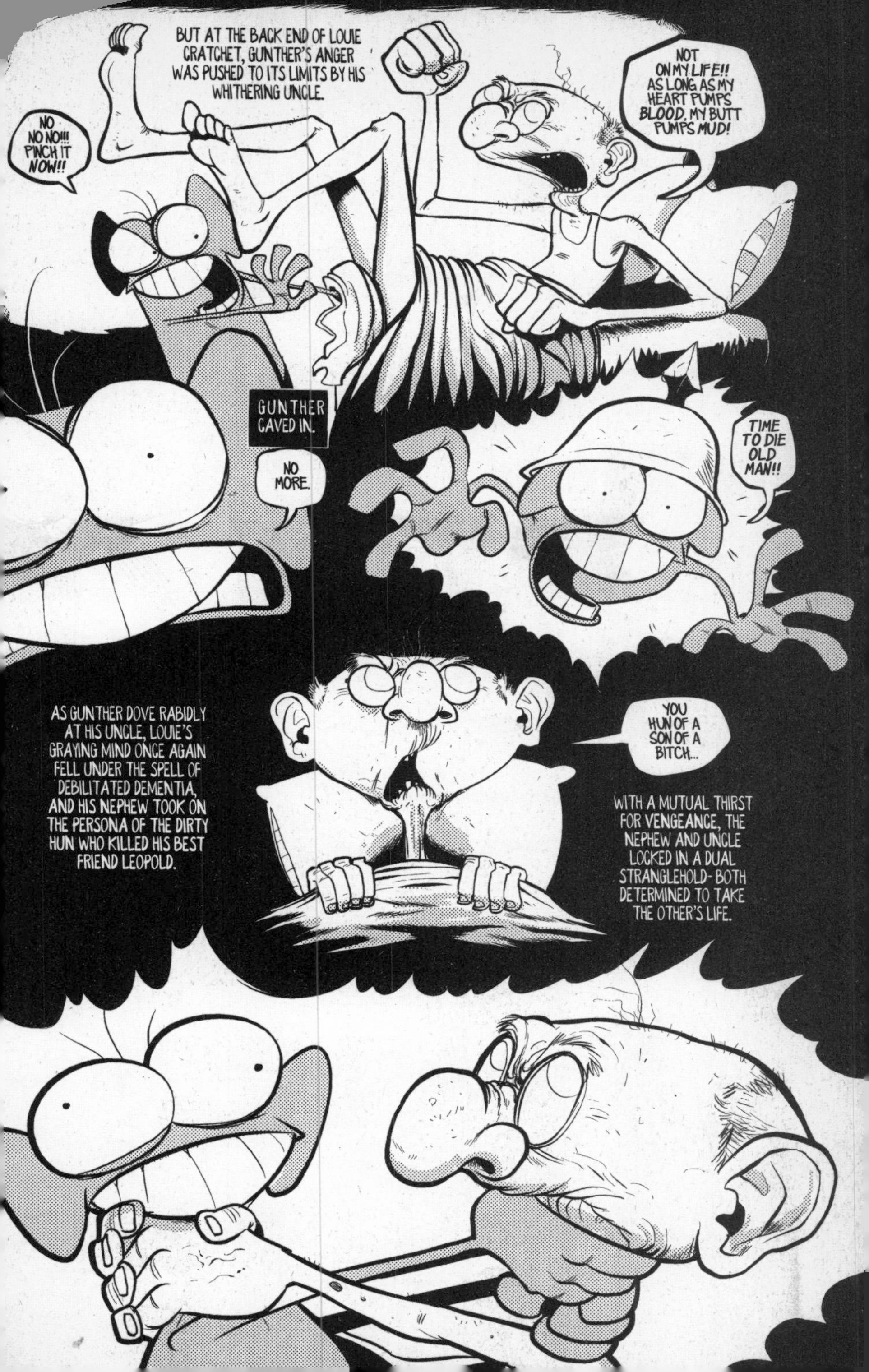

BUT AT THE BACK END OF LOUIE CRATCHET, GUNTHER'S ANGER WAS PUSHED TO ITS LIMITS BY HIS WHITHERING UNCLE.
NO NO NO!!! PINCH IT NOW!!
NOT ON MY LIFE!! AS LONG AS MY HEART PUMPS BLOOD, MY BUTT PUMPS MUD!
GUNTHER CAVED IN.
NO MORE.
TIME TO DIE OLD MAN!!
AS GUNTHER DOVE RABIDLY AT HIS UNCLE, LOUIE'S GRAYING MIND ONCE AGAIN FELL UNDER THE SPELL OF DEBILITATED DEMENTIA, AND HIS NEPHEW TOOK ON THE PERSONA OF THE DIRTY HUN WHO KILLED HIS BEST FRIEND LEOPOLD.
YOU HUN OF A SON OF A BITCH...
WITH A MUTUAL THIRST FOR VENGEANCE, THE NEPHEW AND UNCLE LOCKED IN A DUAL STRANGLEHOLD- BOTH DETERMINED TO TAKE THE OTHER'S LIFE.

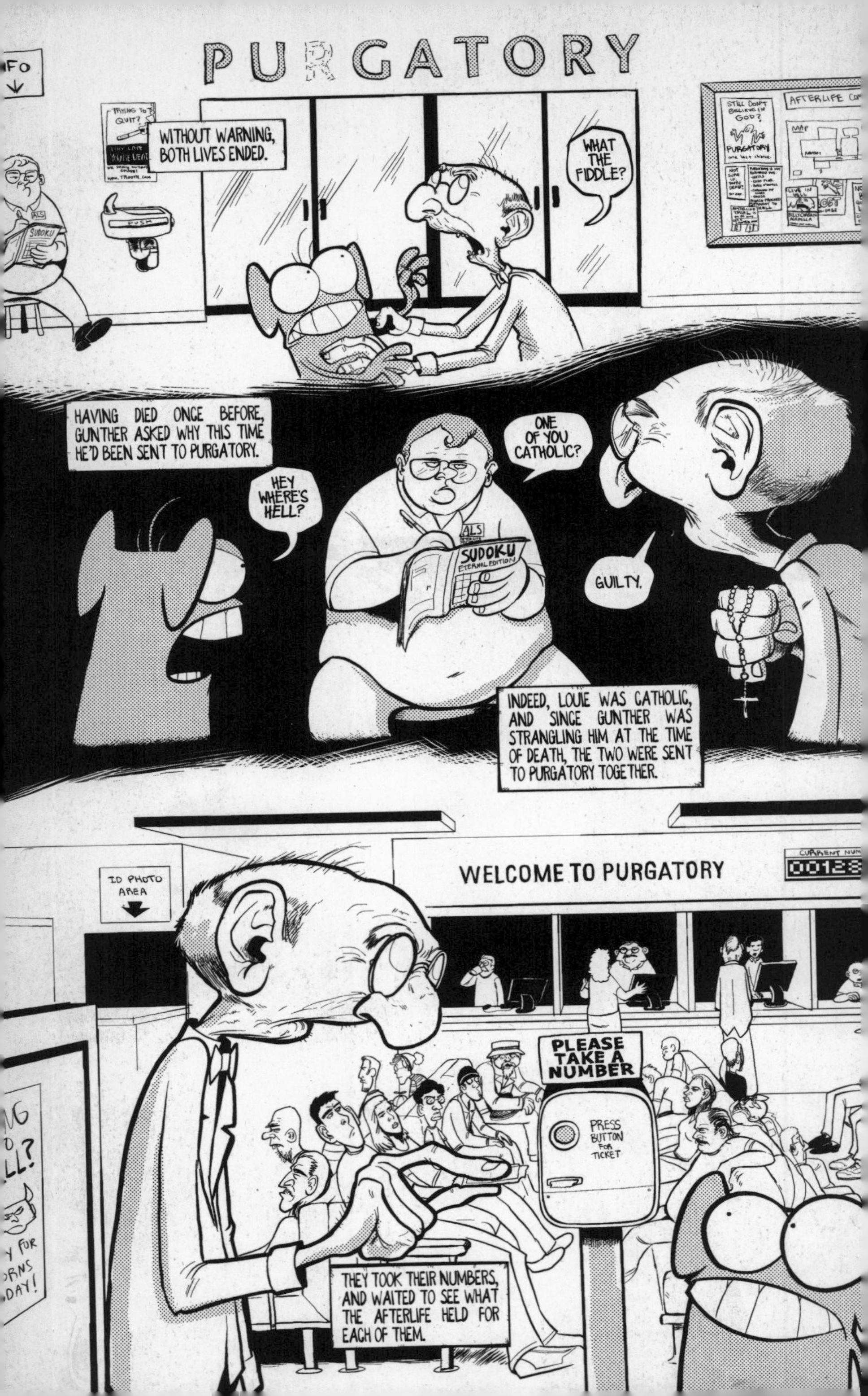
PURGATORY
WITHOUT WARNING, BOTH LIVES ENDED.
WHAT THE FIDDLE?
HAVING DIED ONCE BEFORE, GUNTHER ASKED WHY THIS TIME HE'D BEEN SENT TO PURGATORY.
HEY WHERE'S HELL?
ONE OF YOU CATHOLIC?
GUILTY.
SUDOKU ETERNAL EDITION
INDEED, LOUIE WAS CATHOLIC, AND SINCE GUNTHER WAS STRANGLING HIM AT THE TIME OF DEATH, THE TWO WERE SENT TO PURGATORY TOGETHER.
ID PHOTO AREA
WELCOME TO PURGATORY
PLEASE TAKE A NUMBER
PRESS BUTTON FOR TICKET
THEY TOOK THEIR NUMBERS, AND WAITED TO SEE WHAT THE AFTERLIFE HELD FOR EACH OF THEM.

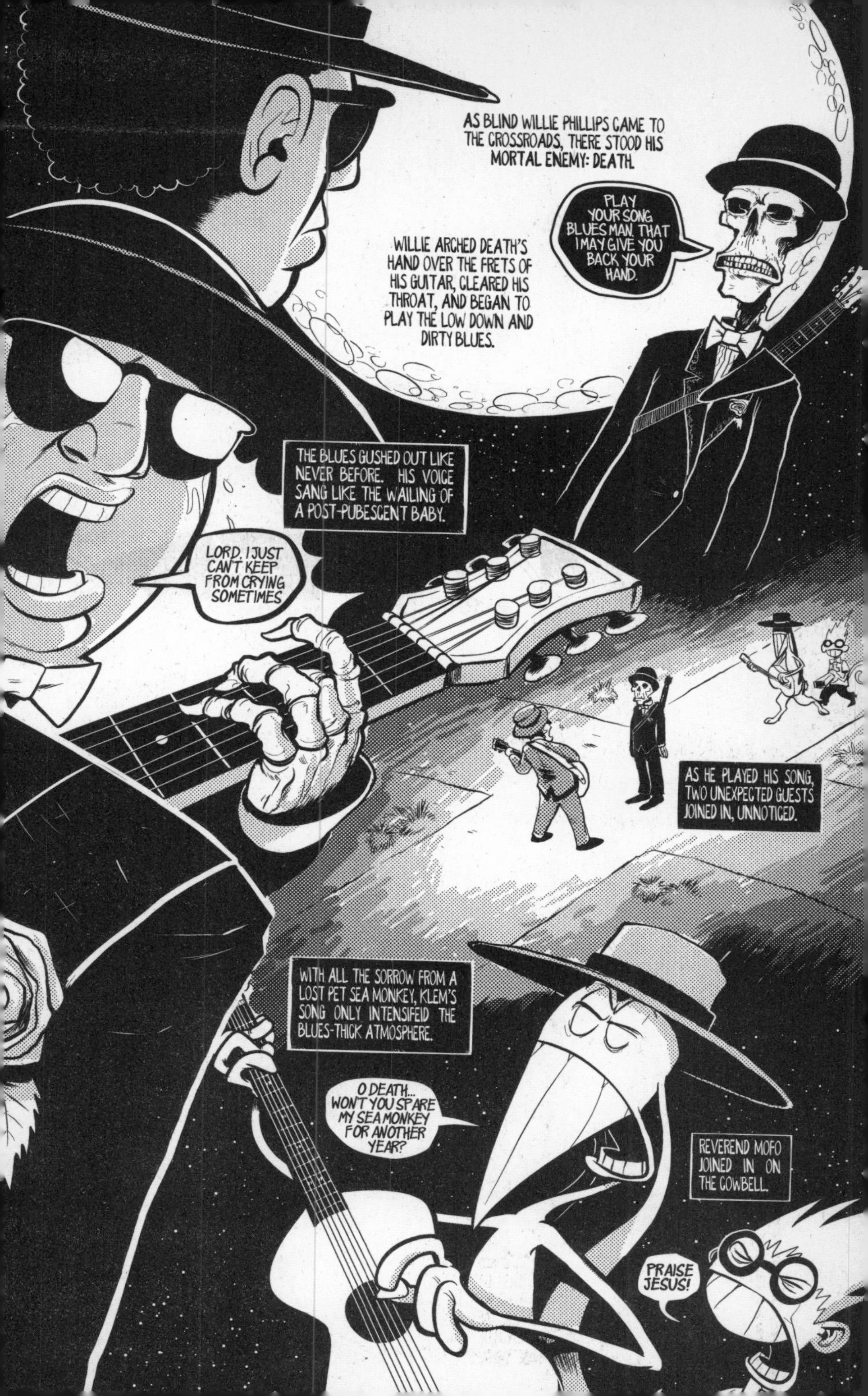
AS BLIND WILLIE PHILLIPS CAME TO THE CROSSROADS, THERE STOOD HIS MORTAL ENEMY: DEATH.
PLAY YOUR SONG BLUES MAN. THAT I MAY GIVE YOU BACK YOUR HAND.
WILLIE ARCHED DEATH'S HAND OVER THE FRETS OF HIS GUITAR, CLEARED HIS THROAT, AND BEGAN TO PLAY THE LOW DOWN AND DIRTY BLUES.
THE BLUES GUSHED OUT LIKE NEVER BEFORE. HIS VOICE SANG LIKE THE WAILING OF A POST-PUBESCENT BABY.
LORD. I JUST CAN'T KEEP FROM CRYING SOMETIMES
AS HE PLAYED HIS SONG, TWO UNEXPECTED GUESTS JOINED IN, UNNOTICED.
WITH ALL THE SORROW FROM A LOST PET SEA MONKEY, KLEM'S SONG ONLY INTENSIFEID THE BLUES-THICK ATMOSPHERE.
O DEATH... WON'T YOU SPARE MY SEA MONKEY FOR ANOTHER YEAR?
REVEREND MOFO JOINED IN ON THE COWBELL.
PRAISE JESUS!

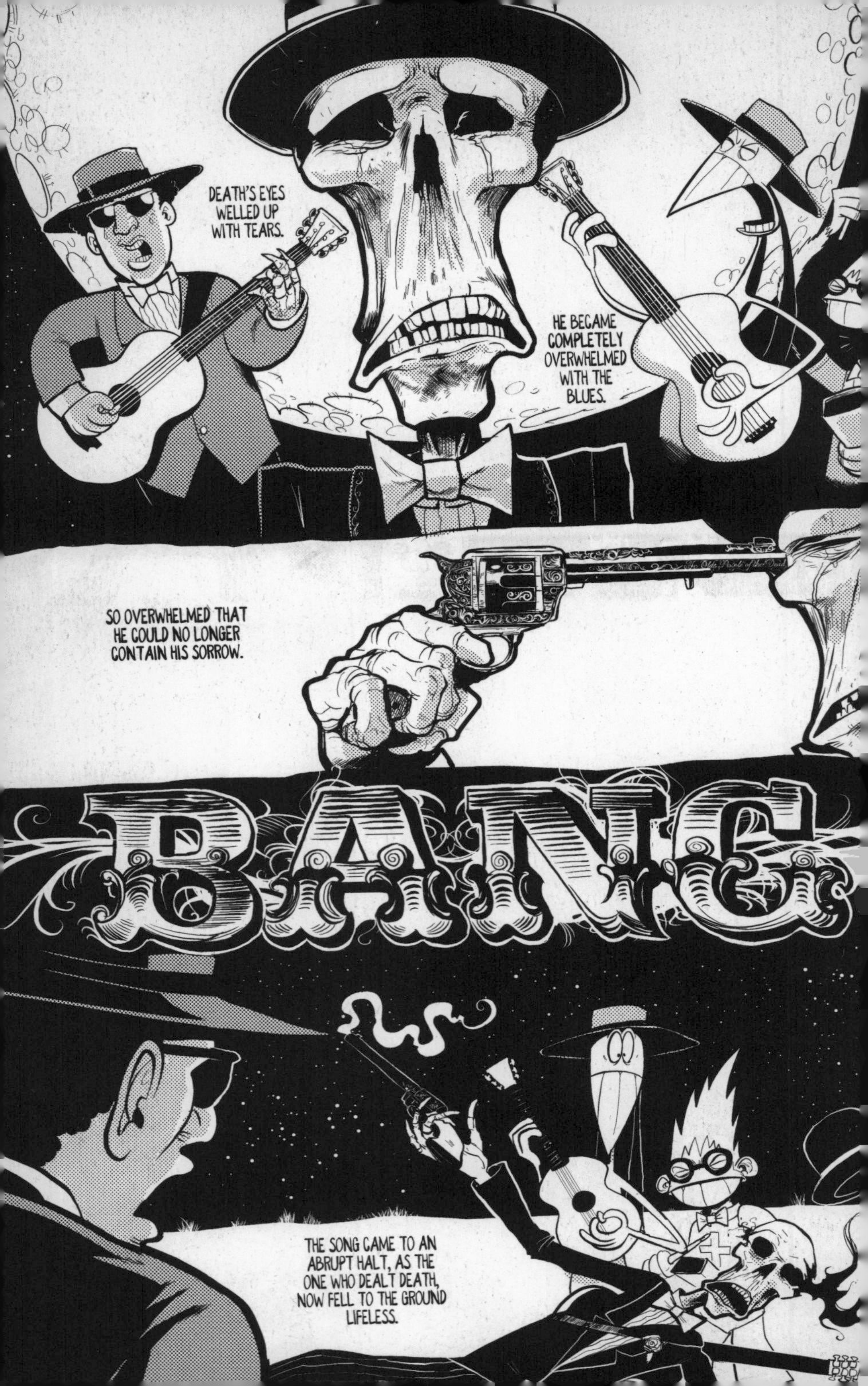
DEATH'S EYES WELLED UP WITH TEARS.
HE BECAME COMPLETELY OVERWHELMED WITH THE BLUES.
SO OVERWHELMED THAT HE COULD NO LONGER CONTAIN HIS SORROW.
BANG
THE SONG CAME TO AN ABRUPT HALT, AS THE ONE WHO DEALT DEATH, NOW FELL TO THE GROUND LIFELESS.

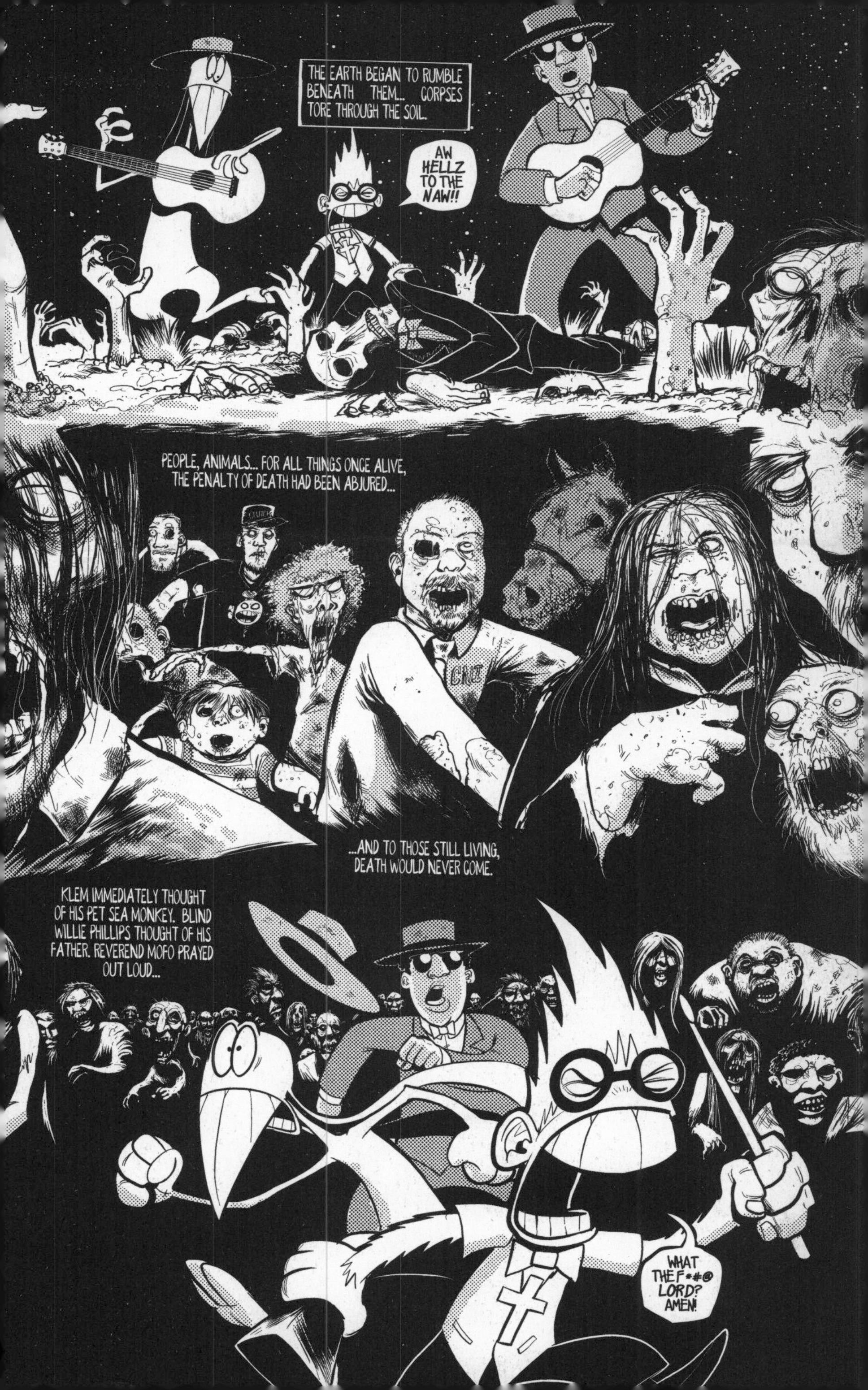
THE EARTH BEGAN TO RUMBLE BENEATH THEM... CORPSES TORE THROUGH THE SOIL.
AW HELLZ TO THE NAW!!
PEOPLE, ANIMALS... FOR ALL THINGS ONCE ALIVE, THE PENALTY OF DEATH HAD BEEN ABJURED...
...AND TO THOSE STILL LIVING, DEATH WOULD NEVER COME.
KLEM IMMEDIATELY THOUGHT OF HIS PET SEA MONKEY. BLIND WILLIE PHILLIPS THOUGHT OF HIS FATHER. REVEREND MOFO PRAYED OUT LOUD...
WHAT THE F*#@ LORD? AMEN!

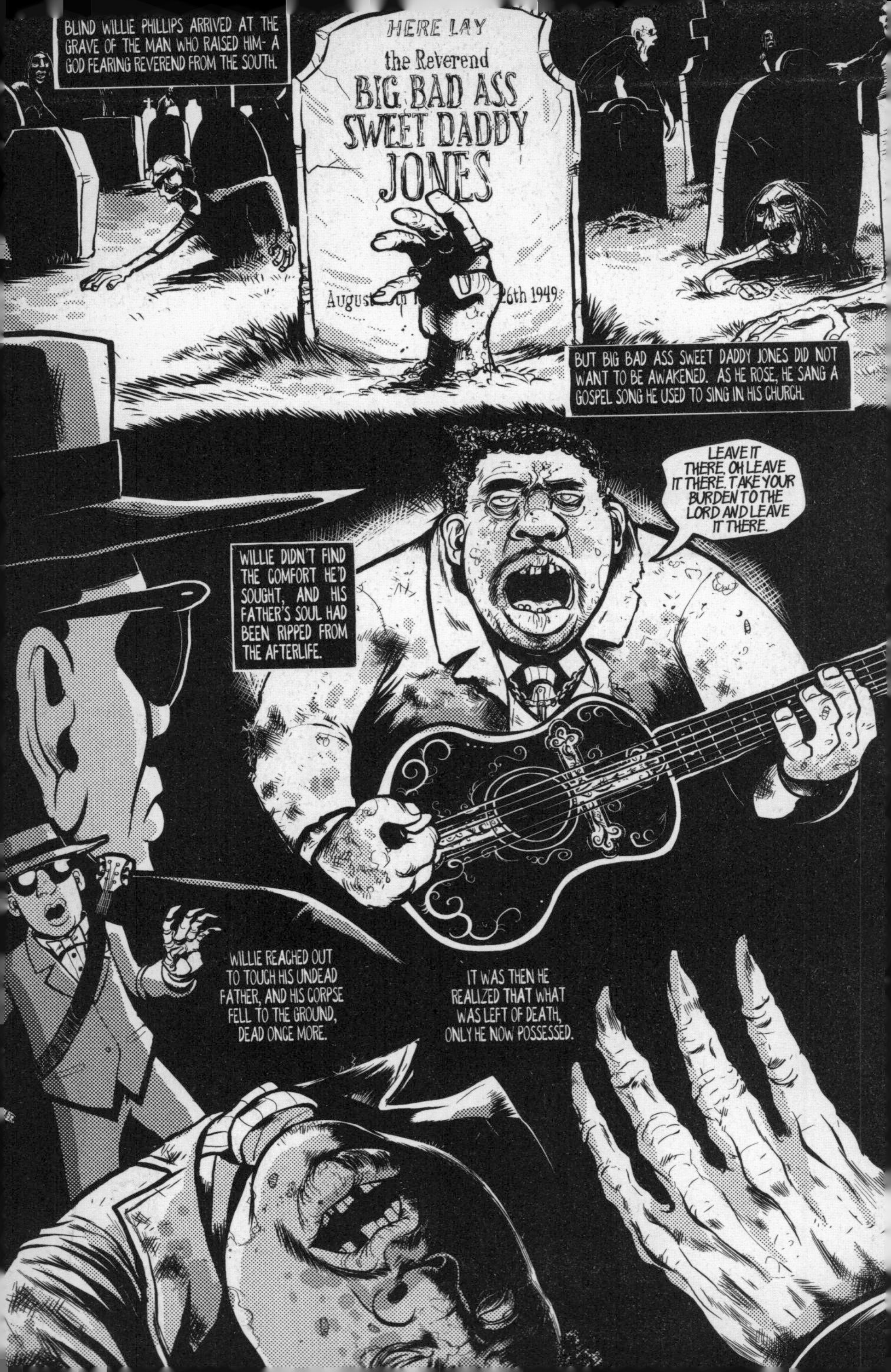
BLIND WILLIE PHILLIPS ARRIVED AT THE GRAVE OF THE MAN WHO RAISED HIM- A GOD FEARING REVEREND FROM THE SOUTH.
HERE LAY
the Reverend
BIG BAD ASS
SWEET DADDY
JONES
BUT BIG BAD ASS SWEET DADDY JONES DID NOT WANT TO BE AWAKENED. AS HE ROSE, HE SANG A GOSPEL SONG HE USED TO SING IN HIS CHURCH.
WILLIE DIDN'T FIND THE COMFORT HE'D SOUGHT, AND HIS FATHER'S SOUL HAD BEEN RIPPED FROM THE AFTERLIFE.
LEAVE IT THERE, OH LEAVE IT THERE. TAKE YOUR BURDEN TO THE LORD AND LEAVE IT THERE.
WILLIE REACHED OUT TO TOUCH HIS UNDEAD FATHER, AND HIS CORPSE FELL TO THE GROUND, DEAD ONCE MORE.
IT WAS THEN HE REALIZED THAT WHAT WAS LEFT OF DEATH, ONLY HE NOW POSSESSED.

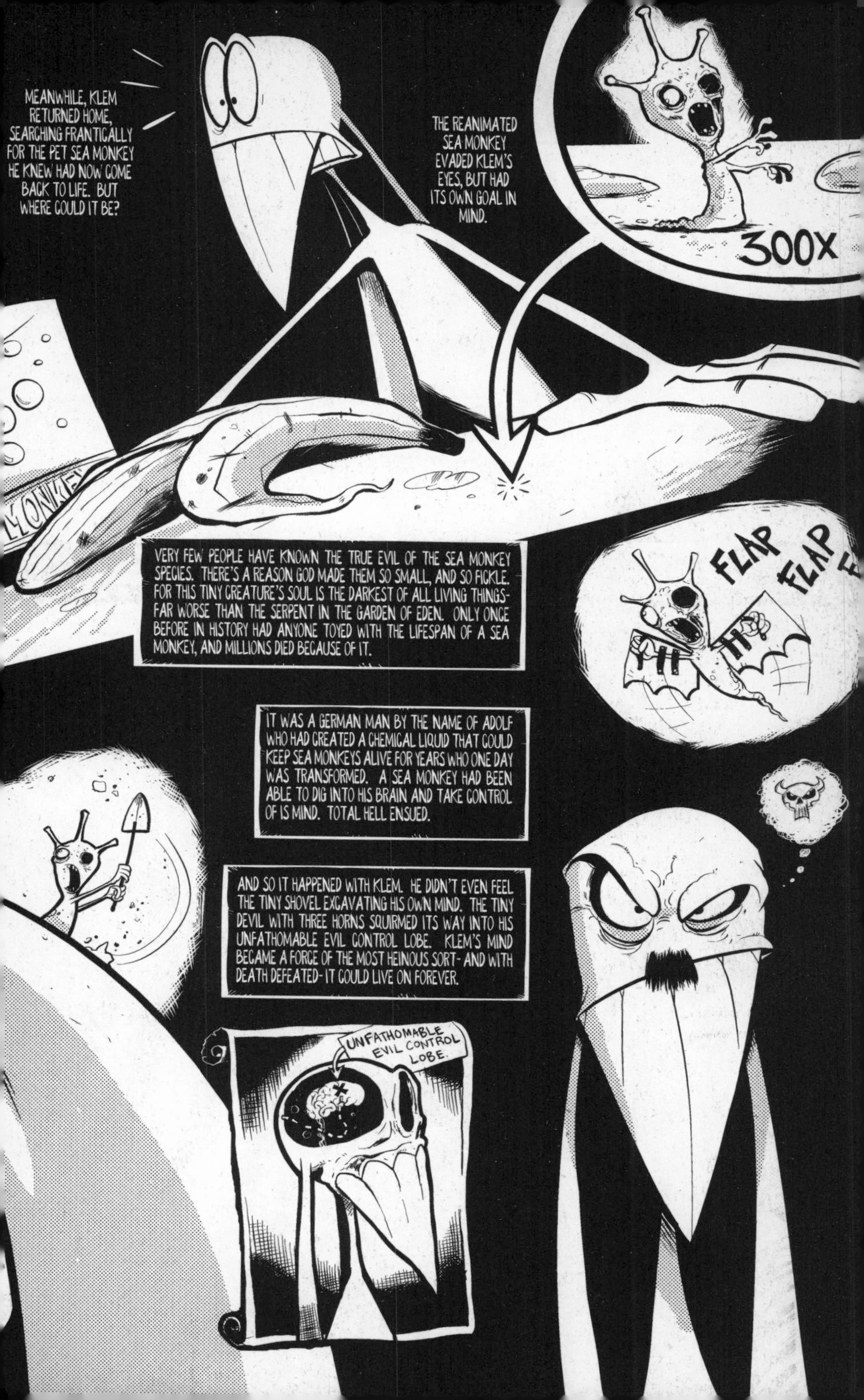

MEANWHILE, KLEM RETURNED HOME, SEARCHING FRANTICALLY FOR THE PET SEA MONKEY HE KNEW HAD NOW COME BACK TO LIFE. BUT WHERE COULD IT BE?
THE REANIMATED SEA MONKEY EVADED KLEM'S EYES, BUT HAD ITS OWN GOAL IN MIND.
300X
MONKEY
VERY FEW PEOPLE HAVE KNOWN THE TRUE EVIL OF THE SEA MONKEY SPECIES. THERE'S A REASON GOD MADE THEM SO SMALL, AND SO FICKLE. FOR THIS TINY CREATURE'S SOUL IS THE DARKEST OF ALL LIVING THINGS- FAR WORSE THAN THE SERPENT IN THE GARDEN OF EDEN. ONLY ONCE BEFORE IN HISTORY HAD ANYONE TOYED WITH THE LIFESPAN OF A SEA MONKEY, AND MILLIONS DIED BECAUSE OF IT.
FLAP FLAP
IT WAS A GERMAN MAN BY THE NAME OF ADOLF WHO HAD CREATED A CHEMICAL LIQUID THAT COULD KEEP SEA MONKEYS ALIVE FOR YEARS WHO ONE DAY WAS TRANSFORMED. A SEA MONKEY HAD BEEN ABLE TO DIG INTO HIS BRAIN AND TAKE CONTROL OF IS MIND. TOTAL HELL ENSUED.
AND SO IT HAPPENED WITH KLEM. HE DIDN'T EVEN FEEL THE TINY SHOVEL EXCAVATING HIS OWN MIND. THE TINY DEVIL WITH THREE HORNS SQUIRMED ITS WAY INTO HIS UNFATHOMABLE EVIL CONTROL LOBE. KLEM'S MIND BECAME A FORCE OF THE MOST HEINOUS SORT- AND WITH DEATH DEFEATED- IT COULD LIVE ON FOREVER.
UNFATHOMABLE EVIL CONTROL LOBE.

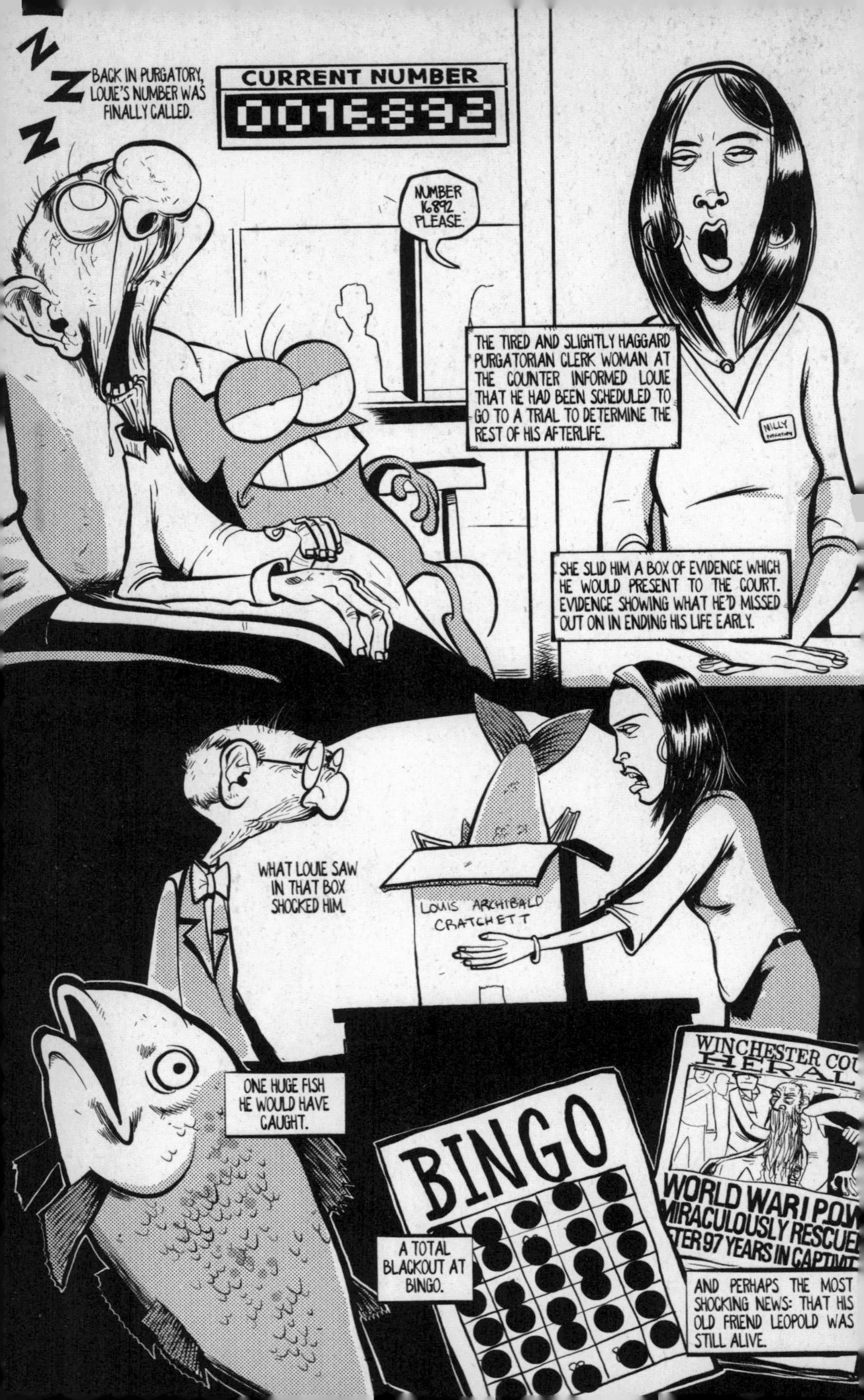
Z Z Z
BACK IN PURGATORY, LOUIE'S NUMBER WAS FINALLY CALLED.
CURRENT NUMBER
0016892
NUMBER 16892 PLEASE.
THE TIRED AND SLIGHTLY HAGGARD PURGATORIAN CLERK WOMAN AT THE COUNTER INFORMED LOUIE THAT HE HAD BEEN SCHEDULED TO GO TO A TRIAL TO DETERMINE THE REST OF HIS AFTERLIFE.
NILLY
SHE SLID HIM A BOX OF EVIDENCE WHICH HE WOULD PRESENT TO THE COURT. EVIDENCE SHOWING WHAT HE'D MISSED OUT ON IN ENDING HIS LIFE EARLY.
WHAT LOUIE SAW IN THAT BOX SHOCKED HIM.
LOUIS ARCHIBALD CRATCHETT
ONE HUGE FISH HE WOULD HAVE CAUGHT.
BINGO
A TOTAL BLACKOUT AT BINGO.
WINCHESTER COU
HERAL
WORLD WAR I P.O.W
MIRACULOUSLY RESCUE
TER 97 YEARS IN CAPTIVI
AND PERHAPS THE MOST SHOCKING NEWS: THAT HIS OLD FRIEND LEOPOLD WAS STILL ALIVE.

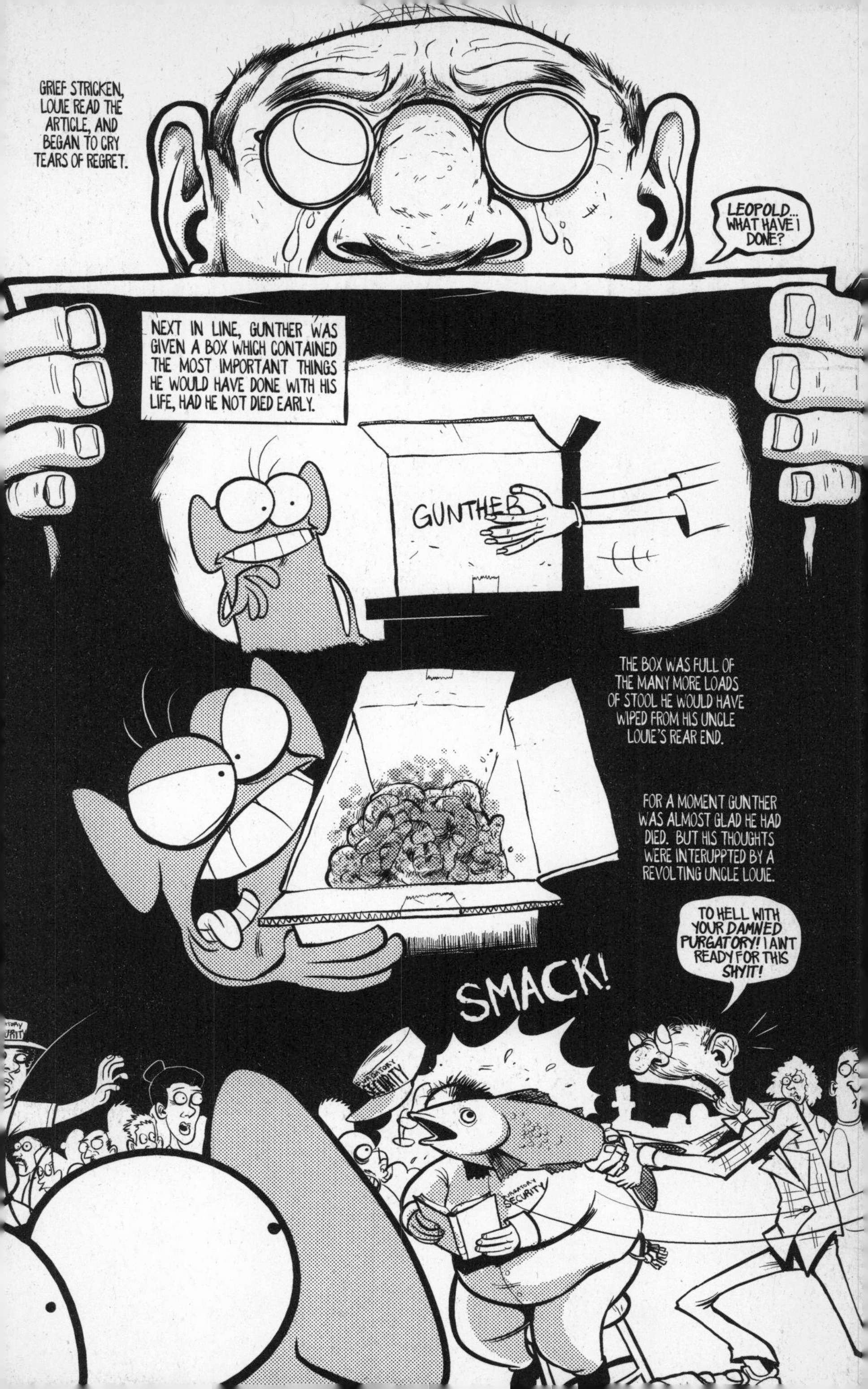
GRIEF STRICKEN, LOUIE READ THE ARTICLE, AND BEGAN TO CRY TEARS OF REGRET.
LEOPOLD... WHAT HAVE I DONE?
NEXT IN LINE, GUNTHER WAS GIVEN A BOX WHICH CONTAINED THE MOST IMPORTANT THINGS HE WOULD HAVE DONE WITH HIS LIFE, HAD HE NOT DIED EARLY.
GUNTHER
THE BOX WAS FULL OF THE MANY MORE LOADS OF STOOL HE WOULD HAVE WIPED FROM HIS UNCLE LOUIE'S REAR END.
FOR A MOMENT GUNTHER WAS ALMOST GLAD HE HAD DIED. BUT HIS THOUGHTS WERE INTERUPPTED BY A REVOLTING UNCLE LOUIE.
TO HELL WITH YOUR DAMNED PURGATORY! I AINT READY FOR THIS SHYIT!
SMACK!
PURGATORY SECURITY
PURGATORY SECURITY

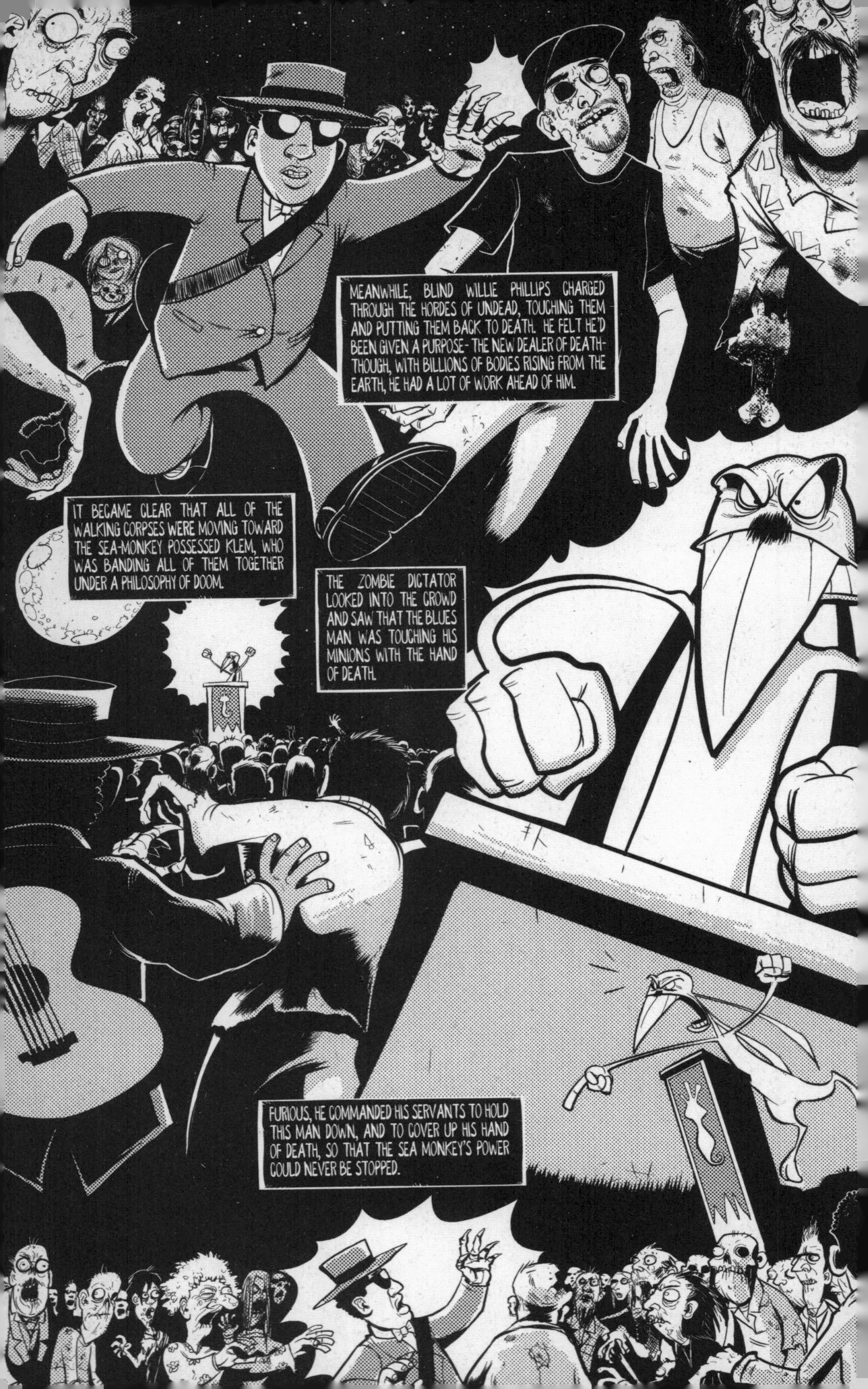

MEANWHILE, BLIND WILLIE PHILLIPS CHARGED THROUGH THE HORDES OF UNDEAD, TOUCHING THEM AND PUTTING THEM BACK TO DEATH. HE FELT HE'D BEEN GIVEN A PURPOSE- THE NEW DEALER OF DEATH- THOUGH, WITH BILLIONS OF BODIES RISING FROM THE EARTH, HE HAD A LOT OF WORK AHEAD OF HIM.
IT BECAME CLEAR THAT ALL OF THE WALKING CORPSES WERE MOVING TOWARD THE SEA-MONKEY POSSESSED KLEM, WHO WAS BANDING ALL OF THEM TOGETHER UNDER A PHILOSOPHY OF DOOM.
THE ZOMBIE DICTATOR LOOKED INTO THE CROWD AND SAW THAT THE BLUES MAN WAS TOUCHING HIS MINIONS WITH THE HAND OF DEATH.
FURIOUS, HE COMMANDED HIS SERVANTS TO HOLD THIS MAN DOWN, AND TO COVER UP HIS HAND OF DEATH, SO THAT THE SEA MONKEY'S POWER COULD NEVER BE STOPPED.

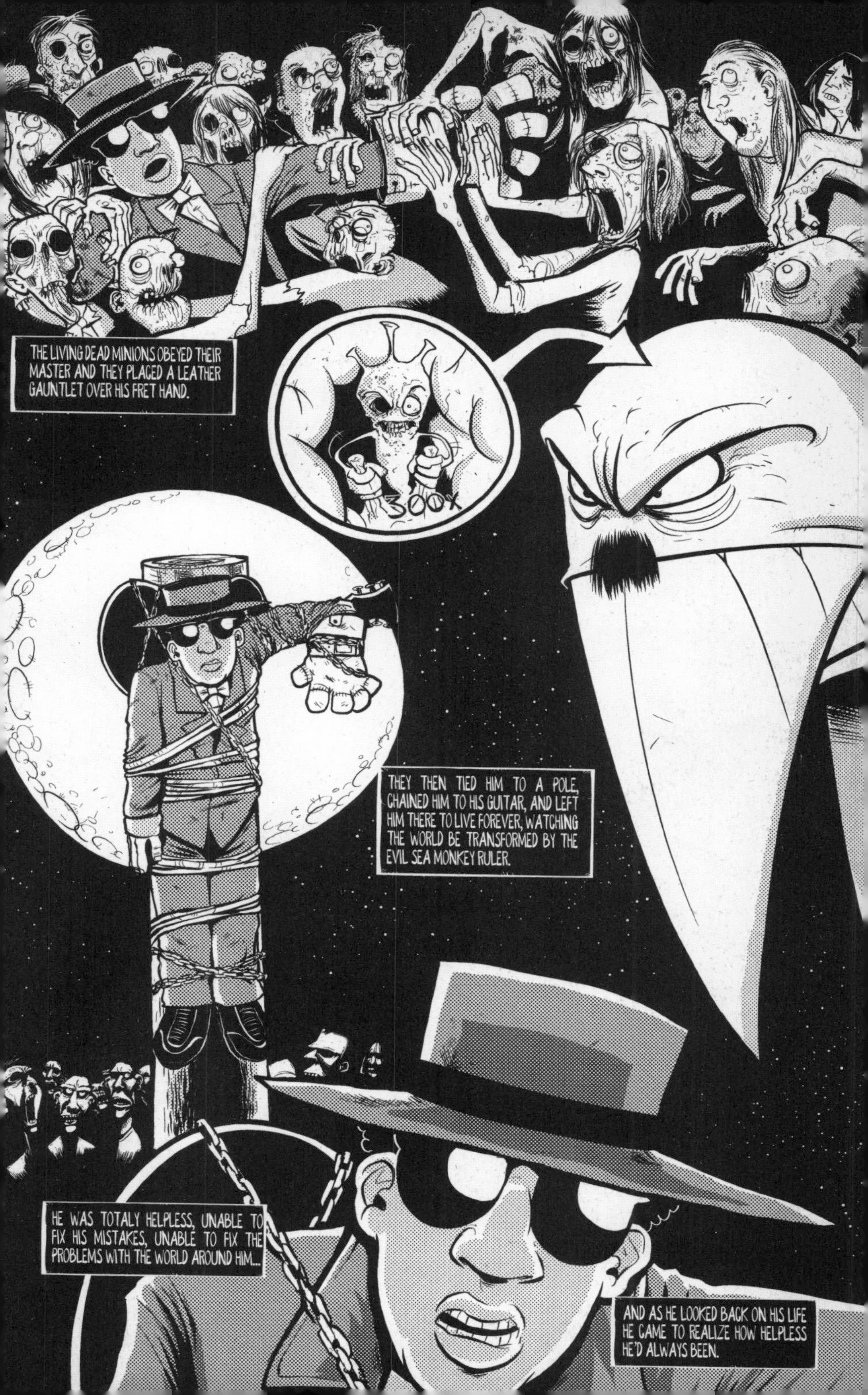
THE LIVING DEAD MINIONS OBEYED THEIR MASTER AND THEY PLACED A LEATHER GAUNTLET OVER HIS FRET HAND.
300X
THEY THEN TIED HIM TO A POLE, CHAINED HIM TO HIS GUITAR, AND LEFT HIM THERE TO LIVE FOREVER, WATCHING THE WORLD BE TRANSFORMED BY THE EVIL SEA MONKEY RULER.
HE WAS TOTALY HELPLESS, UNABLE TO FIX HIS MISTAKES, UNABLE TO FIX THE PROBLEMS WITH THE WORLD AROUND HIM...
AND AS HE LOOKED BACK ON HIS LIFE HE CAME TO REALIZE HOW HELPLESS HE'D ALWAYS BEEN.

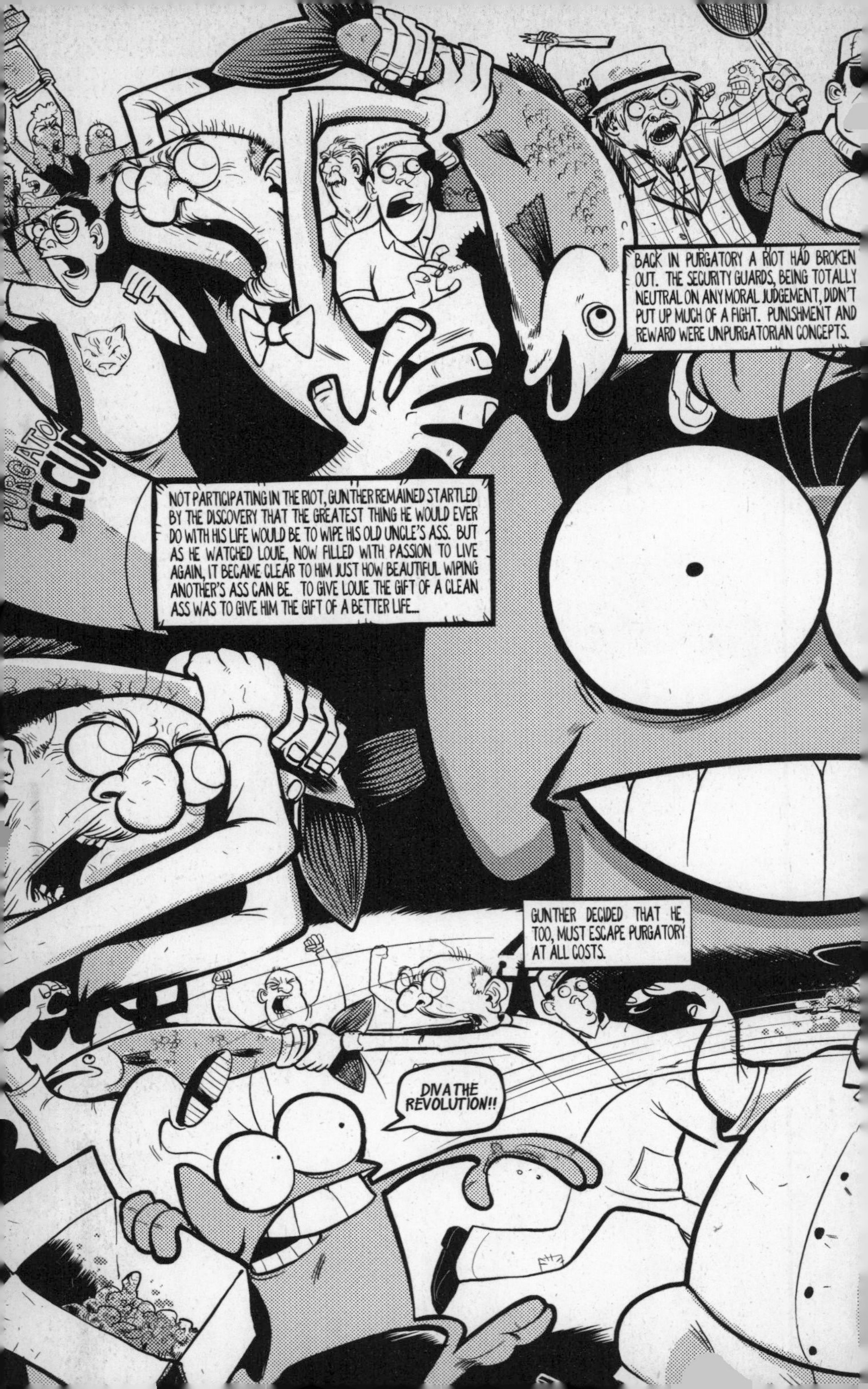
BACK IN PURGATORY A RIOT HAD BROKEN OUT. THE SECURITY GUARDS, BEING TOTALLY NEUTRAL ON ANY MORAL JUDGEMENT, DIDN'T PUT UP MUCH OF A FIGHT. PUNISHMENT AND REWARD WERE UNPURGATORIAN CONCEPTS.
PURGATO SECUR
NOT PARTICIPATING IN THE RIOT, GUNTHER REMAINED STARTLED BY THE DISCOVERY THAT THE GREATEST THING HE WOULD EVER DO WITH HIS LIFE WOULD BE TO WIPE HIS OLD UNCLE'S ASS. BUT AS HE WATCHED LOUIE, NOW FILLED WITH PASSION TO LIVE AGAIN, IT BECAME CLEAR TO HIM JUST HOW BEAUTIFUL WIPING ANOTHER'S ASS CAN BE. TO GIVE LOUIE THE GIFT OF A CLEAN ASS WAS TO GIVE HIM THE GIFT OF A BETTER LIFE...
GUNTHER DECIDED THAT HE, TOO, MUST ESCAPE PURGATORY AT ALL COSTS.
DIVA THE REVOLUTION!!

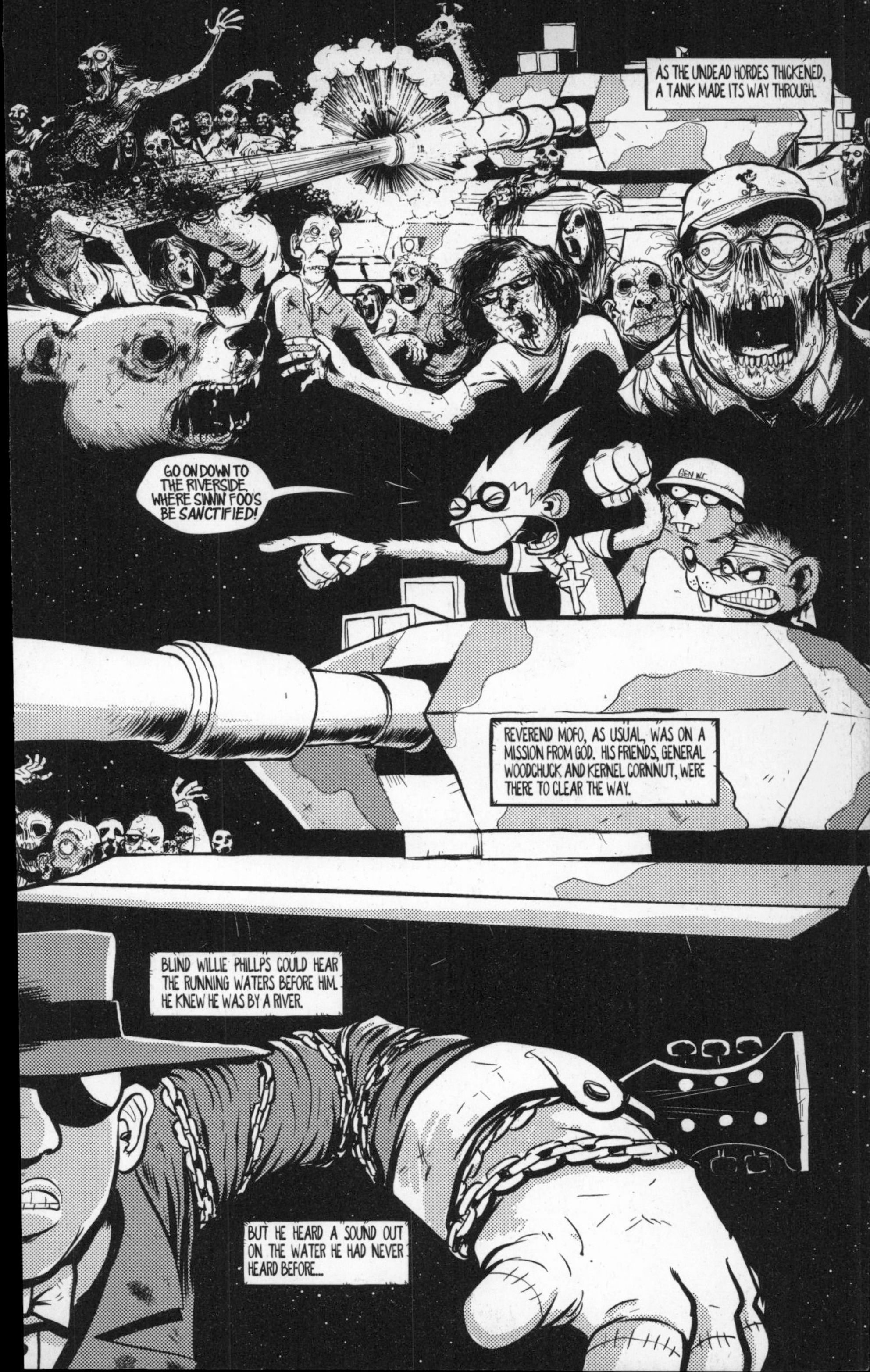

AS THE UNDEAD HORDES THICKENED, A TANK MADE ITS WAY THROUGH.
GO ON DOWN TO THE RIVERSIDE, WHERE SINNIN FOO'S BE SANCTIFIED!
GEN W.C.
REVEREND MOFO, AS USUAL, WAS ON A MISSION FROM GOD. HIS FRIENDS, GENERAL WOODCHUCK AND KERNEL CORNNUT, WERE THERE TO CLEAR THE WAY.
BLIND WILLIE PHILLPS COULD HEAR THE RUNNING WATERS BEFORE HIM. HE KNEW HE WAS BY A RIVER.
BUT HE HEARD A SOUND OUT ON THE WATER HE HAD NEVER HEARD BEFORE...

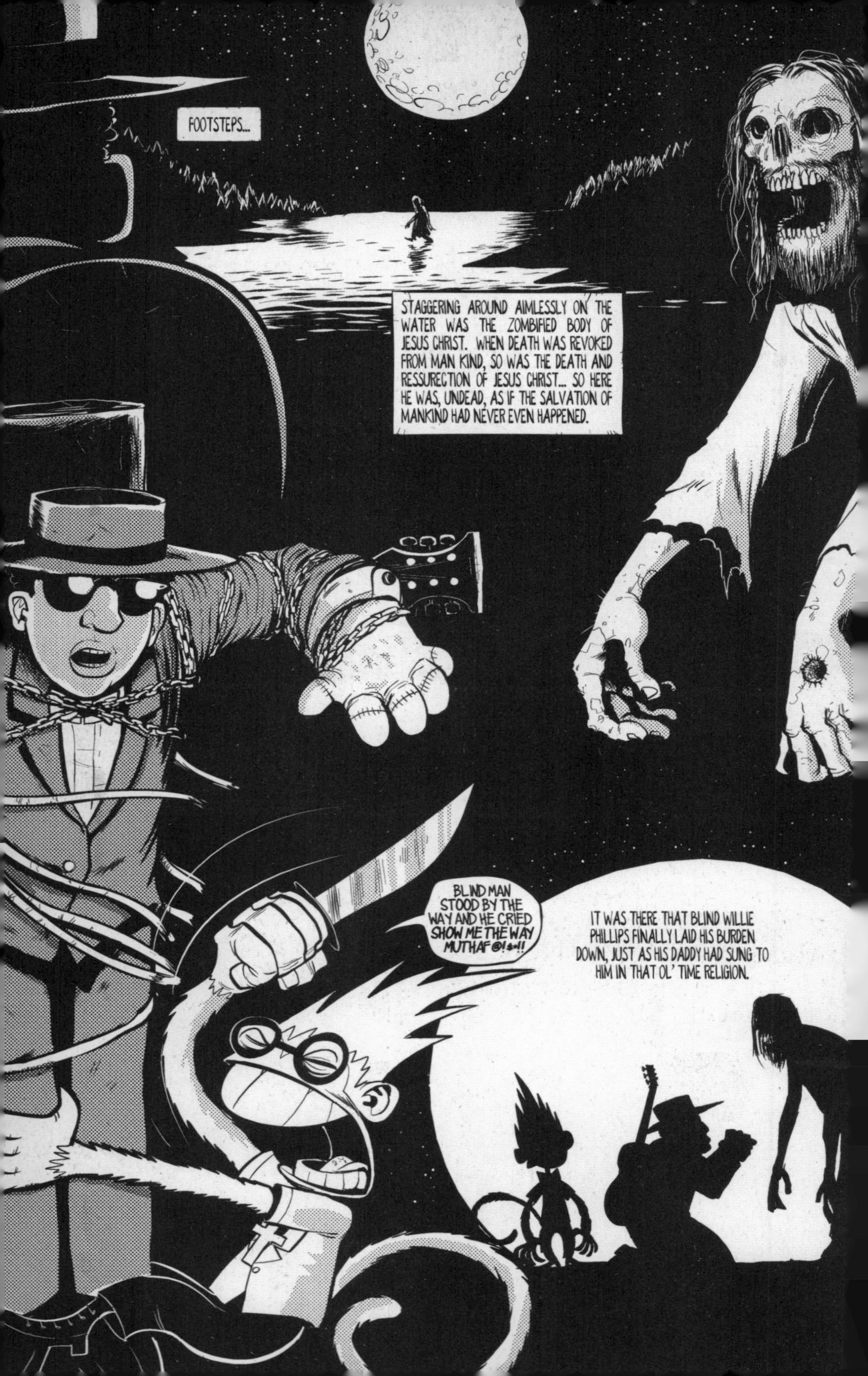
FOOTSTEPS...
STAGGERING AROUND AIMLESSLY ON THE WATER WAS THE ZOMBIFIED BODY OF JESUS CHRIST. WHEN DEATH WAS REVOKED FROM MAN KIND, SO WAS THE DEATH AND RESSURECTION OF JESUS CHRIST... SO HERE HE WAS, UNDEAD, AS IF THE SALVATION OF MANKIND HAD NEVER EVEN HAPPENED.
BLIND MAN STOOD BY THE WAY AND HE CRIED *SHOW ME THE WAY MUTHAF@!$•!!*
IT WAS THERE THAT BLIND WILLIE PHILLIPS FINALLY LAID HIS BURDEN DOWN, JUST AS HIS DADDY HAD SUNG TO HIM IN THAT OL' TIME RELIGION.

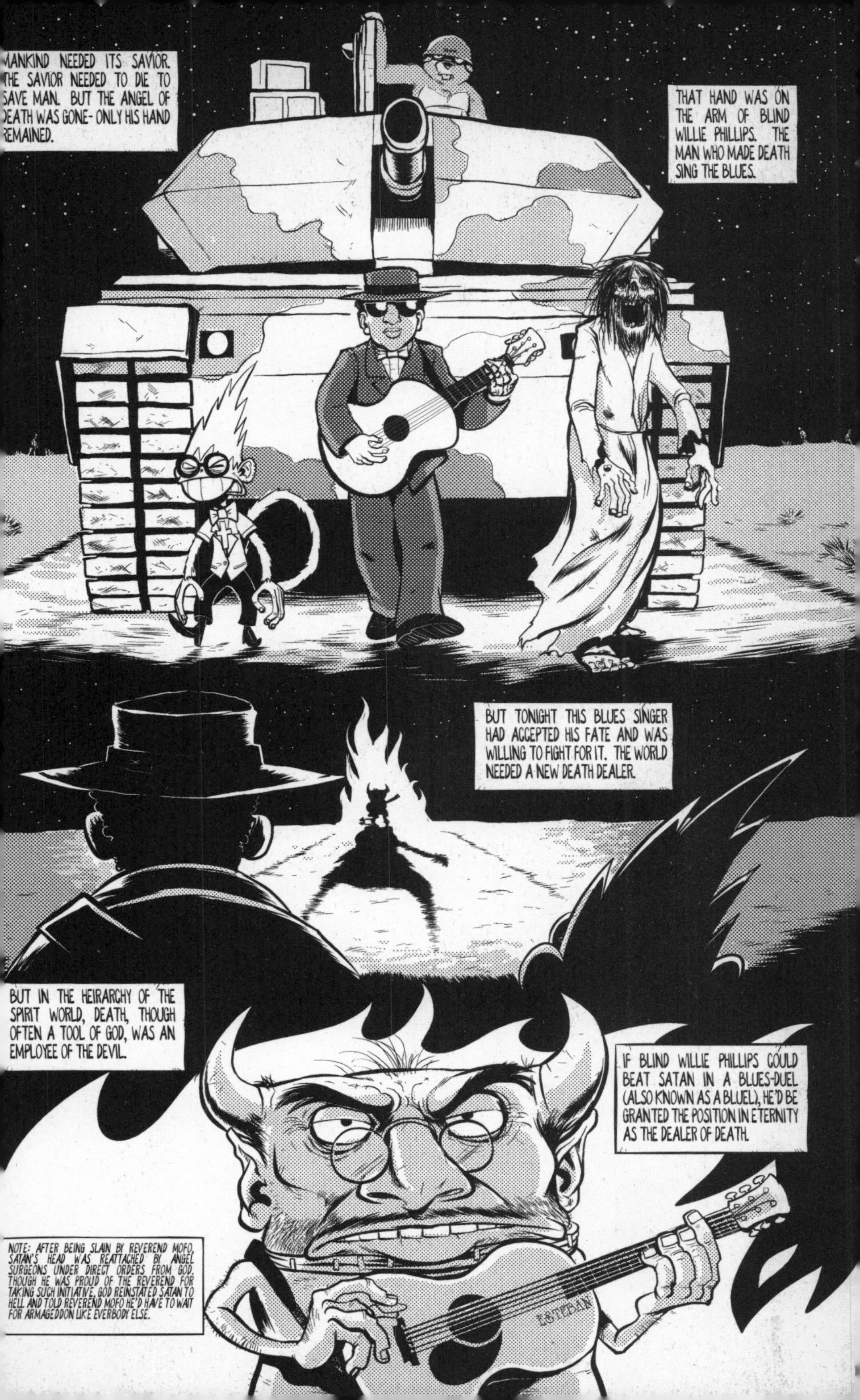
MANKIND NEEDED ITS SAVIOR. THE SAVIOR NEEDED TO DIE TO SAVE MAN. BUT THE ANGEL OF DEATH WAS GONE- ONLY HIS HAND REMAINED.
THAT HAND WAS ON THE ARM OF BLIND WILLIE PHILLIPS. THE MAN WHO MADE DEATH SING THE BLUES.
BUT TONIGHT THIS BLUES SINGER HAD ACCEPTED HIS FATE AND WAS WILLING TO FIGHT FOR IT. THE WORLD NEEDED A NEW DEATH DEALER.
BUT IN THE HEIRARCHY OF THE SPIRIT WORLD, DEATH, THOUGH OFTEN A TOOL OF GOD, WAS AN EMPLOYEE OF THE DEVIL.
IF BLIND WILLIE PHILLIPS COULD BEAT SATAN IN A BLUES-DUEL (ALSO KNOWN AS A BLUEL), HE'D BE GRANTED THE POSITION IN ETERNITY AS THE DEALER OF DEATH.
NOTE: AFTER BEING SLAIN BY REVEREND MOFO, SATAN'S HEAD WAS REATTACHED BY ANGEL SURGEONS UNDER DIRECT ORDERS FROM GOD. THOUGH HE WAS PROUD OF THE REVEREND FOR TAKING SUCH INITIATIVE, GOD REINSTATED SATAN TO HELL AND TOLD REVEREND MOFO HE'D HAVE TO WAIT FOR ARMAGEDDON LIKE EVERBODY ELSE.

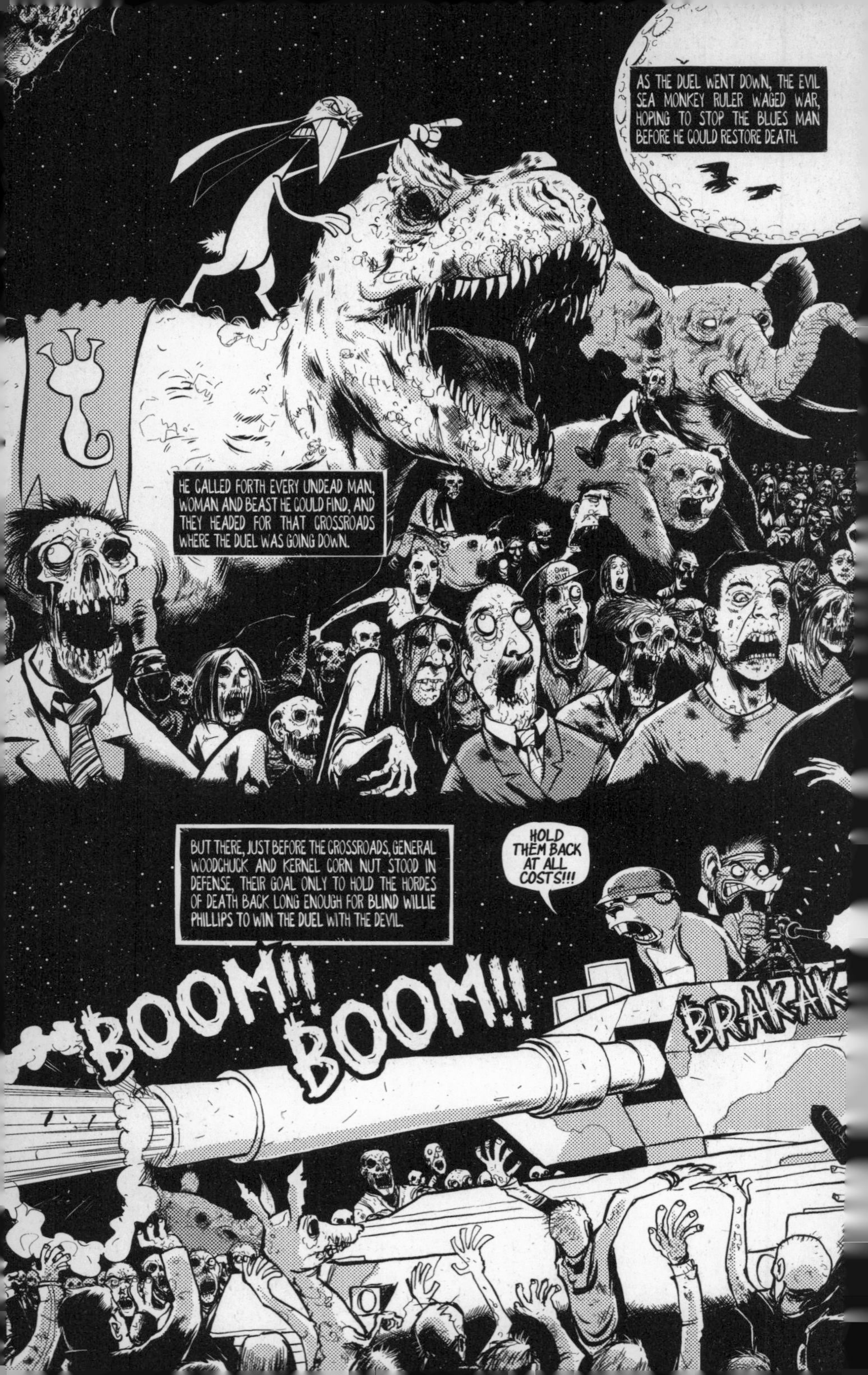

AS THE DUEL WENT DOWN, THE EVIL SEA MONKEY RULER WAGED WAR, HOPING TO STOP THE BLUES MAN BEFORE HE COULD RESTORE DEATH.
HE CALLED FORTH EVERY UNDEAD MAN, WOMAN AND BEAST HE COULD FIND, AND THEY HEADED FOR THAT CROSSROADS WHERE THE DUEL WAS GOING DOWN.
BUT THERE, JUST BEFORE THE CROSSROADS, GENERAL WOODCHUCK AND KERNEL CORN NUT STOOD IN DEFENSE, THEIR GOAL ONLY TO HOLD THE HORDES OF DEATH BACK LONG ENOUGH FOR BLIND WILLIE PHILLIPS TO WIN THE DUEL WITH THE DEVIL.
HOLD THEM BACK AT ALL COSTS!!!
BOOM!! BOOM!!
BRAKAK

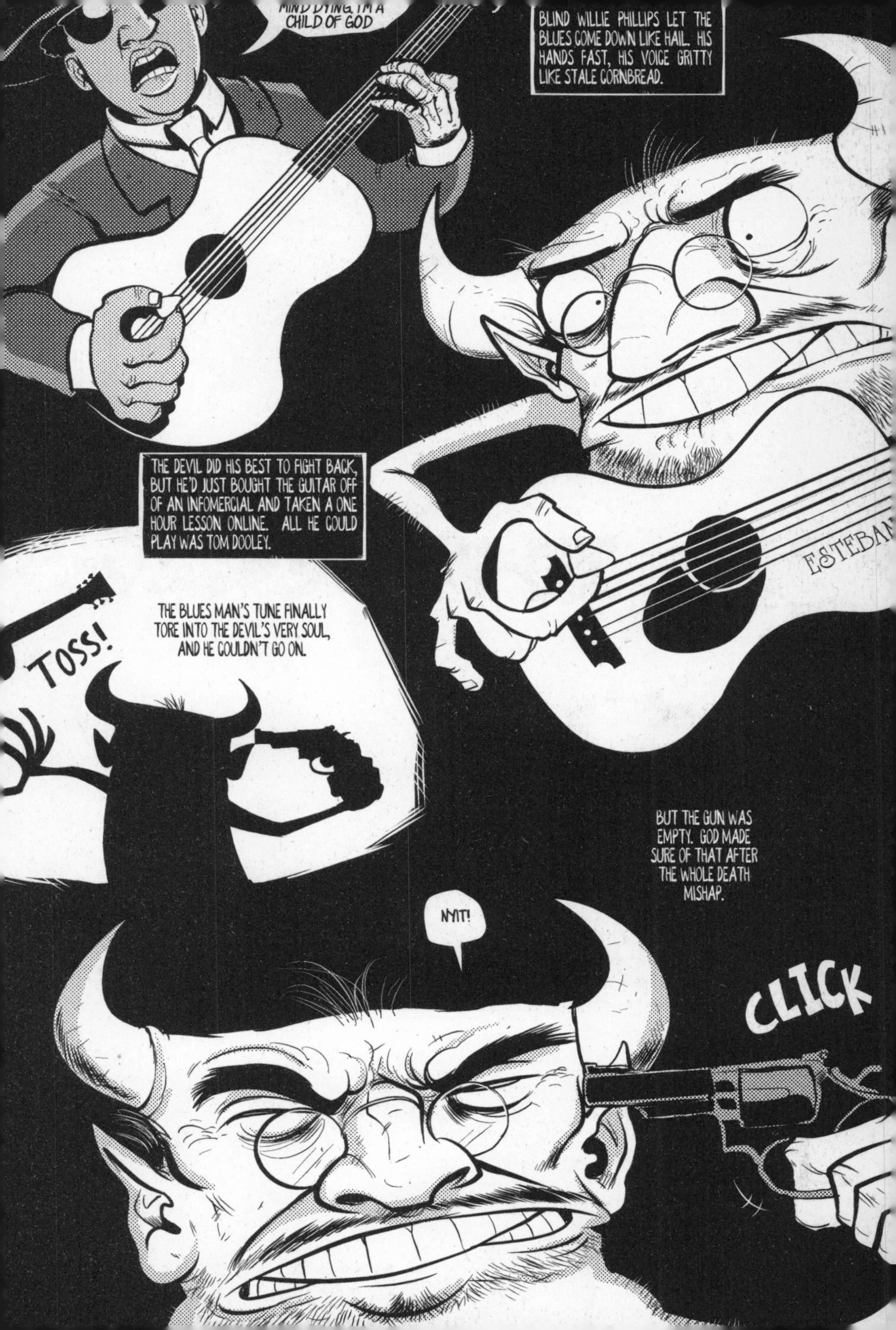
MIND DYING, I'M A CHILD OF GOD
BLIND WILLIE PHILLIPS LET THE BLUES COME DOWN LIKE HAIL. HIS HANDS FAST, HIS VOICE GRITTY LIKE STALE CORNBREAD.
THE DEVIL DID HIS BEST TO FIGHT BACK, BUT HE'D JUST BOUGHT THE GUITAR OFF OF AN INFOMERCIAL AND TAKEN A ONE HOUR LESSON ONLINE. ALL HE COULD PLAY WAS TOM DOOLEY.
THE BLUES MAN'S TUNE FINALLY TORE INTO THE DEVIL'S VERY SOUL, AND HE COULDN'T GO ON.
TOSS!
BUT THE GUN WAS EMPTY. GOD MADE SURE OF THAT AFTER THE WHOLE DEATH MISHAP.
NYIT!
CLICK

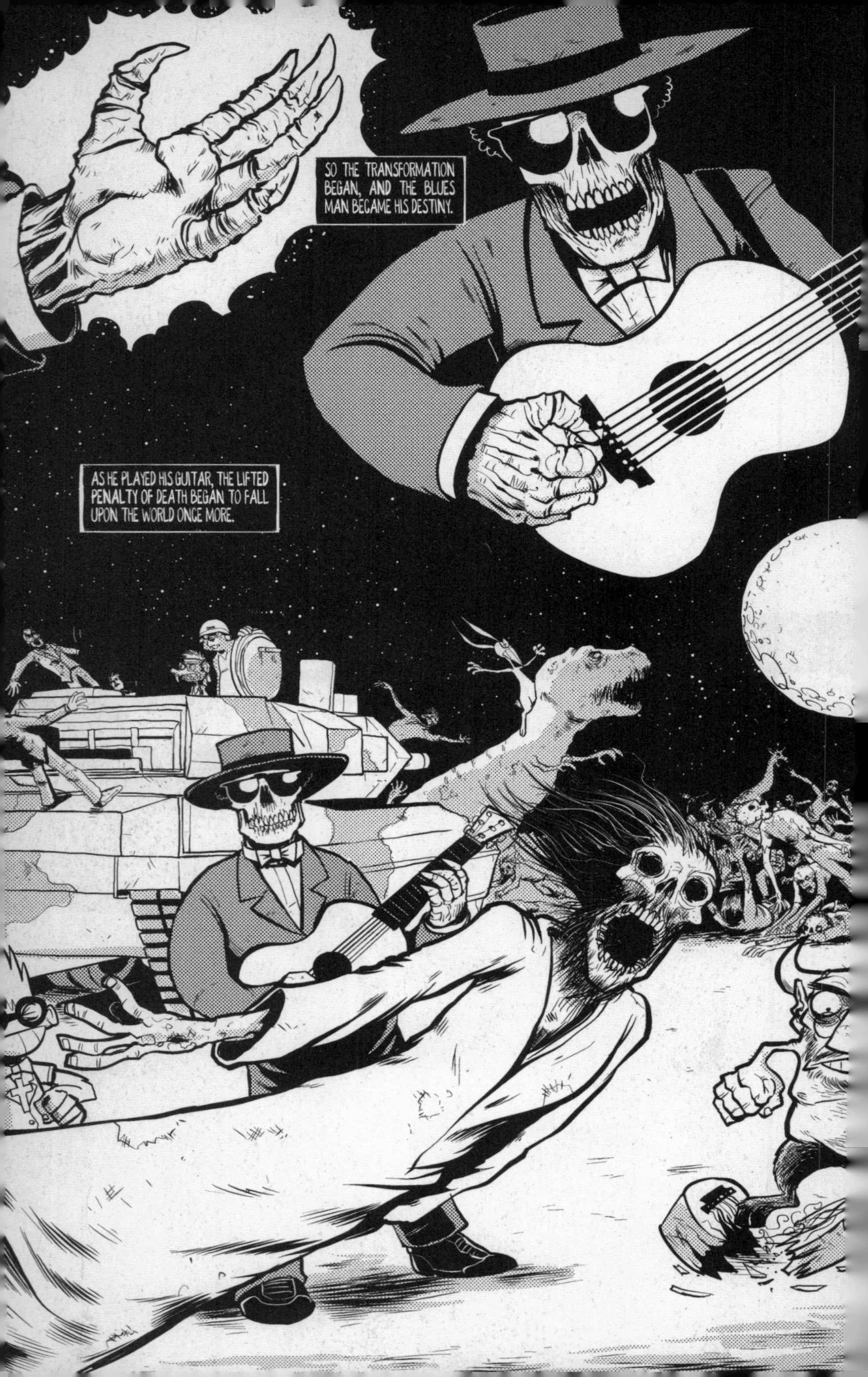
SO THE TRANSFORMATION BEGAN, AND THE BLUES MAN BECAME HIS DESTINY.
AS HE PLAYED HIS GUITAR, THE LIFTED PENALTY OF DEATH BEGAN TO FALL UPON THE WORLD ONCE MORE.

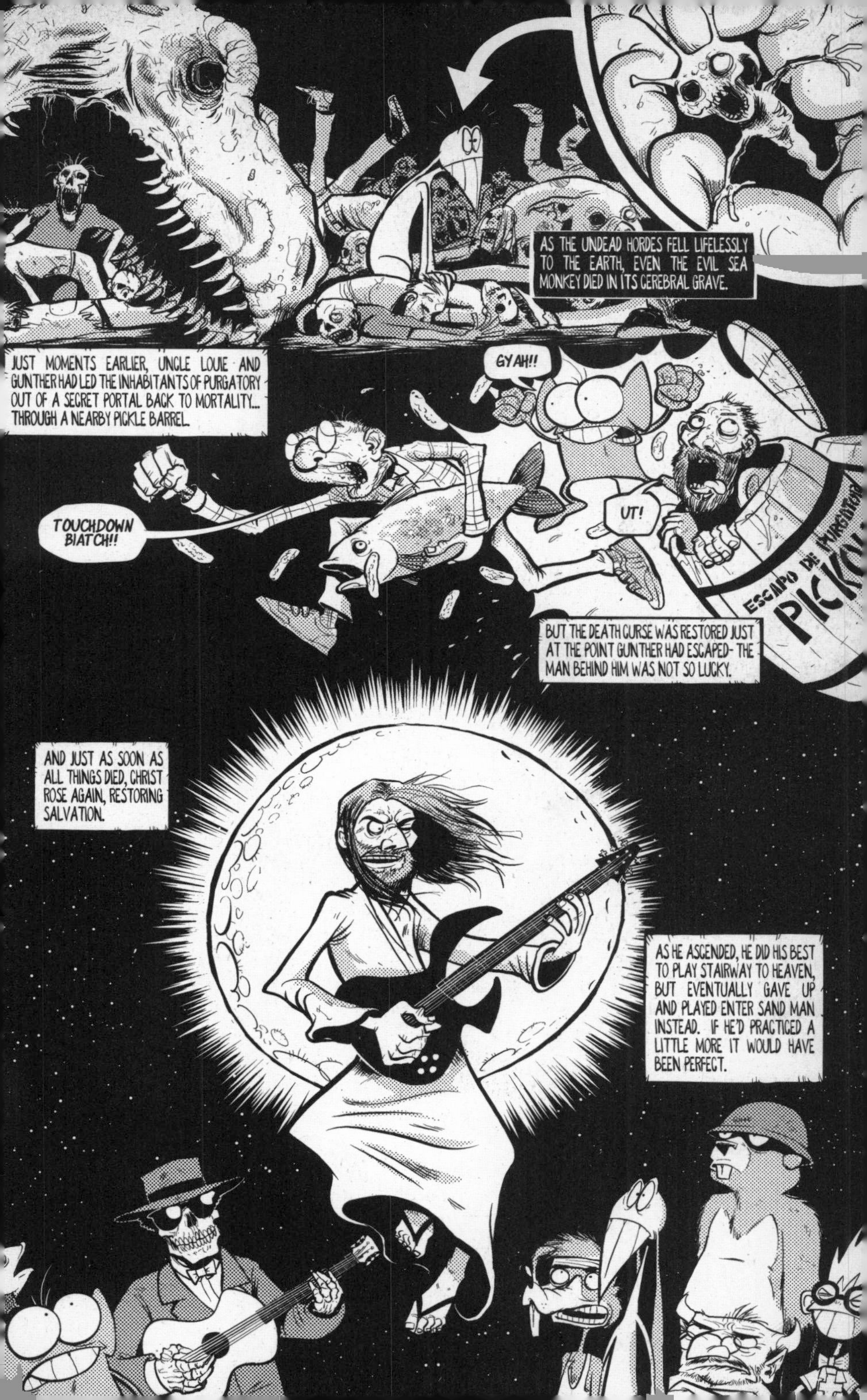
AS THE UNDEAD HORDES FELL LIFELESSLY TO THE EARTH, EVEN THE EVIL SEA MONKEY DIED IN ITS CEREBRAL GRAVE.
JUST MOMENTS EARLIER, UNCLE LOUIE AND GUNTHER HAD LED THE INHABITANTS OF PURGATORY OUT OF A SECRET PORTAL BACK TO MORTALITY... THROUGH A NEARBY PICKLE BARREL.
GYAH!!
TOUCHDOWN BIATCH!!
UT!
ESCAPO DE PURGATORIO
PICK
BUT THE DEATH CURSE WAS RESTORED JUST AT THE POINT GUNTHER HAD ESCAPED- THE MAN BEHIND HIM WAS NOT SO LUCKY.
AND JUST AS SOON AS ALL THINGS DIED, CHRIST ROSE AGAIN, RESTORING SALVATION.
AS HE ASCENDED, HE DID HIS BEST TO PLAY STAIRWAY TO HEAVEN, BUT EVENTUALLY GAVE UP AND PLAYED ENTER SAND MAN INSTEAD. IF HE'D PRACTICED A LITTLE MORE IT WOULD HAVE BEEN PERFECT.

...AND SO, FROM THAT DAY FORWARD, ANYTIME SOMEONE HEARD THE TUNE OF BLIND WILLIE PHILLIPS, IT MEANT DEATH WAS A KNOCKIN' AND IT WAS TIME TO GO HOME.

Lord, I just can't keep from crying sometimes
Lord, I just can't keep from crying sometimes
When my heart's full of sorrow and my eyes are filled with tears
Lord, I just can't keep from crying sometimes

My mother often told me, angels bonded your life away
She said I would accomplish, but trust in God and pray
I'm on the King's Highway, I'm travelin' everyday

'Cause I just can't keep from crying sometimes

My mother, she's in glory, thank God I'm on my way
Father, he's gone too, and sister she could not stay
I'm trusting Him everyday, to bear my burdens away

'Cause I just can't keep from crying sometimes

I thought when she first left me, I'd pray for a little while
Soon it all would be over, and I'd journey on with a smile
But the thought as I get older, I think of what I told her

And I just can't keep from crying sometimes
Well, I just can't keep from crying sometimes
When my heart's full of sorrow and my eyes are filled with tears
Lord, I just can't keep from crying sometimes

LORD, I JUST CAN'T KEEP FROM CRYING BY BLIND WILLIE JOHNSON

ORY OF
ON
USE
1902

MEMORY OF
OBERT
NSON

AUGUST 16, 1938

IN MEMORY OF
BIG BILL
ONZY

IN MEMORY OF
WASHINGTON
PHILLIPS

IN MEM
BLIN

IN MEMORY OF

BLIND WILLIE
JOHNSON

1897–1945

END

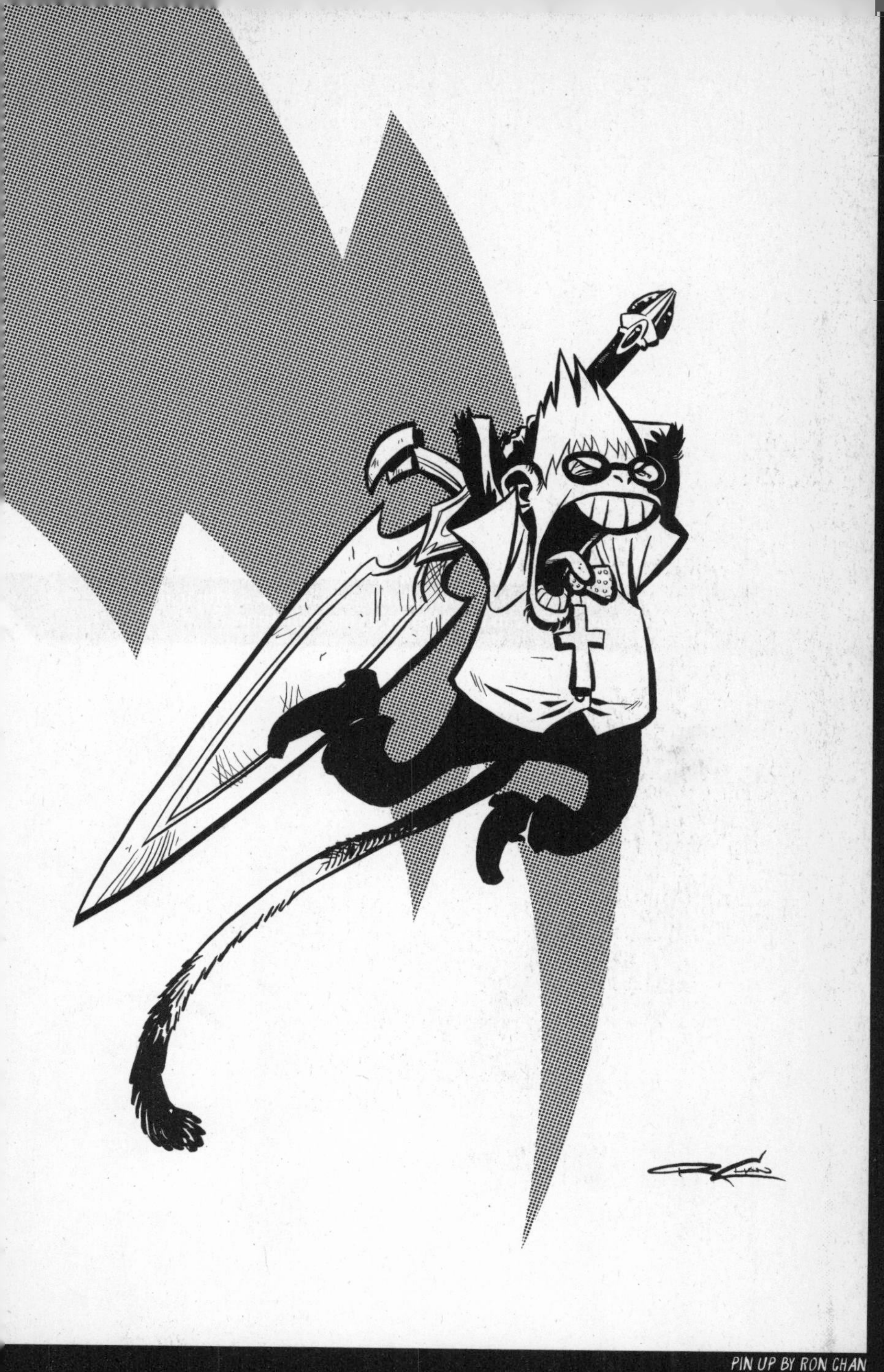

PIN UP BY RON CHAN

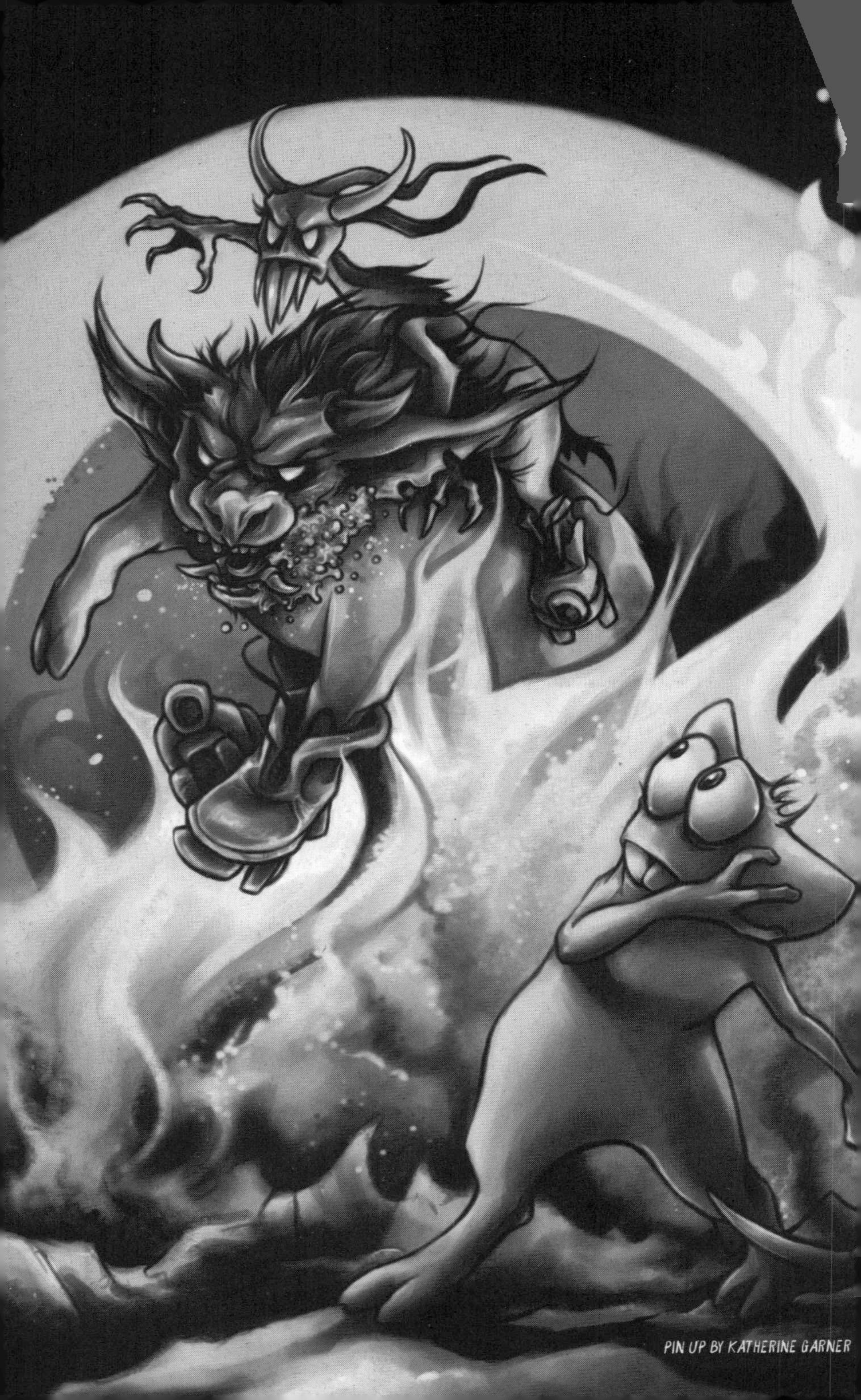

PIN UP BY KATHERINE GARNER

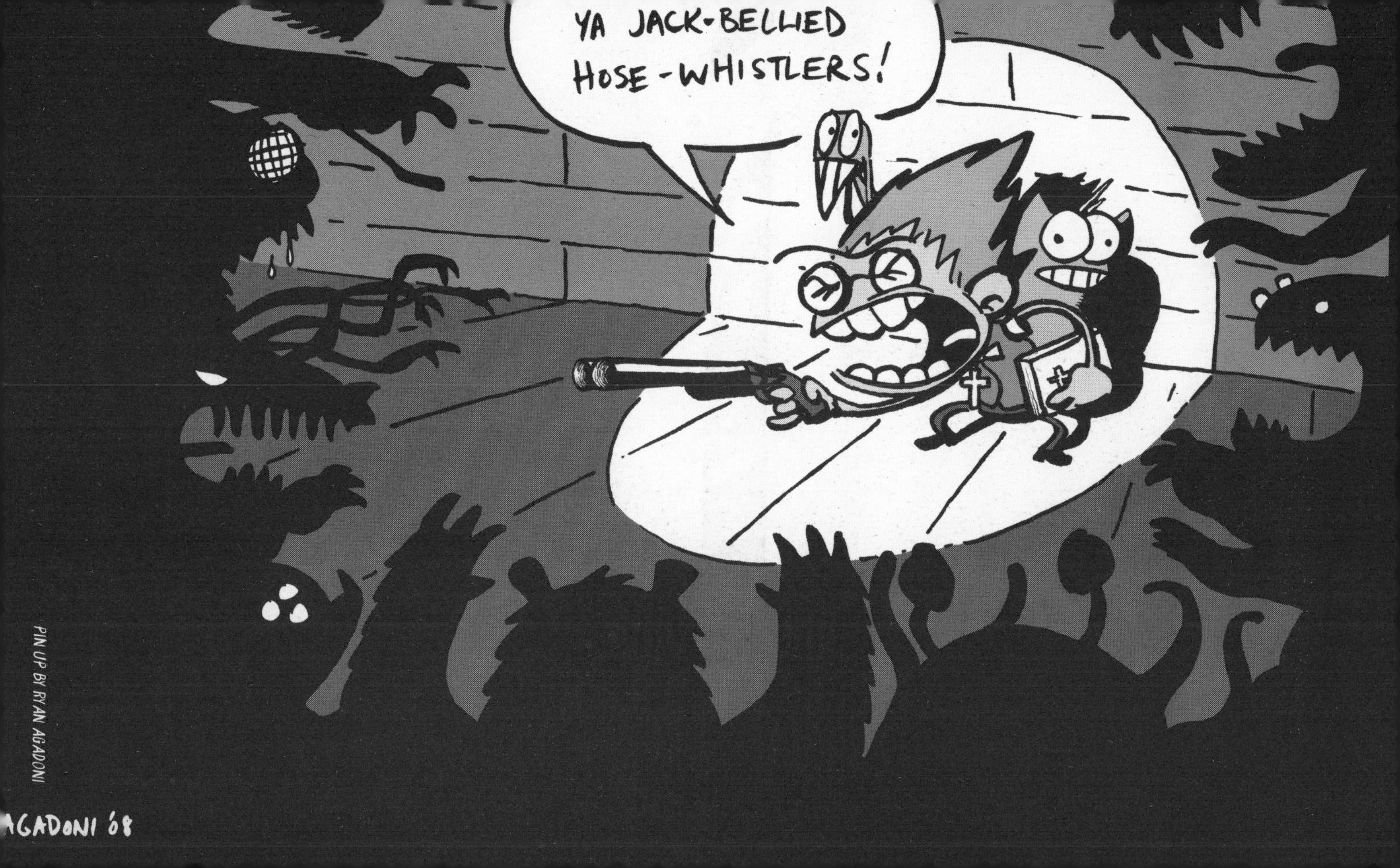
YA JACK-BELLIED HOSE-WHISTLERS!
AGADONI '08

PIN UP BY RYAN AGADONI

ABOUT THE AUTHORS

ETHAN NICOLLE IS A WHITE, OBESE, UNKEMPT AMERICAN MALE WHO LIVES IN AN ATTIC. HIS TENDENCY TO DRAW COMICS FOR LONG PERIODS OF TIME, WITHOUT SHOWERING, CAUSES HIM TO TAKE ON SMELLS SIMILAR, BUT NOT LIMITED TO, FRITOS CORN CHIPS. HE'S ONE OF THOSE "LITTLE HEAD, BIG BODY" GUYS. CURRENTLY SINGLE, HE HAS NOT FELT THE TOUCH OF A WOMAN FOR QUITE SOME TIME. HE LIKES SHORT DRIVES NEAR THE BEACH, AND ANYTHING WITH MEAT IN IT.

CURRENTLY LOCATED IN HIS PARENTS' GARAGE, **ISAIAH NICOLLE** RARELY SEES THE LIGHT OF DAY AS HE WAKES UP AT THE CRACK OF **4PM** DAILY TO DO HIS RITUALS OF VIDEO GAMES, FOOD, AND WRITING ABOUT FARTS, NINJAS, AND WOODCHUCKS. HE WEARS THE SAME SHIRT EVERY DAY, WITHOUT WASHING, TO PREVENT GLOBAL WARMING. CURRENTLY SINGLE, ISAIAH IS A MALE SEEKING A FEMALE WHO CAN COOK, CLEAN, AND CHANGE ADULT DIAPERS, AND IS WILLING TO WEAR A SHOCK COLLAR FOR DISOBEDIENCE.

ALSO AVAILABLE

CHUMBLE SPUZZ BOOK ONE:
KILL THE DEVIL.
RELEASED JANUARY 2008

NOW AVAILABLE FROM SLG PUBLISHING
AND PRETTY MUCH ANY BOOK SELLER
THAT'S NOT A STUPID DUMB FACE.